Enhancing Teaching in Higher Education

This book brings together a collection of thought-provoking and challenging accounts from higher education lecturers and practitioners who are using research and innovative techniques to improve student learning and teaching.

Providing accessible accounts of new developments, it outlines how to apply learning theory and best practice to everyday teaching, and provides advice on overcoming problems of implementation.

Evidence is drawn from both funded projects and innovative practitioners from a wide range of disciplines and backgrounds, and covers areas including approaches to learning, working with students, enhancing the progress and development of students and supporting and developing your own practice.

Enhancing Teaching in Higher Education addresses major issues for learning and teaching in higher education today and will be a reliable source of advice and ideas for new and experienced lecturers wanting to improve their students' learning.

Peter Hartley, Professor of Education Development and Head of the Teaching Quality Enhancement Group, School of Lifelong Educational and Development, University of Bradford, UK.

Amanda Woods, Senior Research Fellow, Division of Primary Care, School of Community Health Sciences, University of Nottingham, UK.

Martin Pill, Senior Lecturer in Environmental Health, and chair of the Faculty Teaching Learning and Assessment Committee, Faculty of Applied Sciences, University of the West of England, UK.

D0488983

Enhancing Teaching in Higher Education

New approaches for improving student learning

Edited by Peter Hartley, Amanda Woods and Martin Pill

Routledge
Taylor & Francis Group

LONDON AND NEW YORK

First published 2005 by Routledge
2 Park Square, Milton Park, Abingdon, Oxon OX14 4RN

Simultaneously published in the USA and Canada
by Routledge
270 Madison Ave, New York, NY 10016

Reprinted 2005

RoutledgeFalmer is an imprint of the Taylor & Francis Group

Typeset in Times by Florence Production Ltd, Stoodleigh, Devon
Printed and bound in Great Britain by TJ International Ltd, Padstow, Cornwall

British Library Cataloguing in Publication Data
A catalogue record for this book is available from the British Library

Library of Congress Cataloging in Publication Data
  Enhancing teaching in higher education: new approaches for improving
  student learning / edited by Peter Hartley, Amanda Woods, and Martin Pill.
       p. cm.
    Includes bibliographical references.
  1. College teaching. 2. Learning. I. Hartley, Peter, 1946–   II. Woods,
  Amanda, 1963–   III. Pill, Martin.
  LB2331.E66 2004
  378.1'2—dc22   2004011425

ISBN 0–415–34136–1 (hbk)
ISBN 0–415–33529–9 (pbk)

Contents

Illustrations

Figures

Boxes

Contributors

Colin Beard is a Senior Lecturer and University Teaching Fellow at Sheffield Hallam University, with main research interests in innovative learning environments and experiential learning. He is an International Environmental and Management Development consultant and lead author of *The Power of Experiential Learning*. A Chartered Fellow of the CIPD, he is a member of the Editorial Review Panel of the Journal of Adventure Education and Outdoor Learning for the Institute for Outdoor Learning. Colin delivers Master Classes on Innovative Experiential Learning in Singapore, China, India and Finland.

Glynis Cousin is a Senior Adviser at the Higher Education Academy. She supports educational development and research initiatives in UK universities and is a Fellow of the Staff and Educational Development Association.

Teena J. Clouston is a Senior Lecturer in the Department of Occupational Therapy, Cardiff University, Cardiff. Areas of research interest lie in education, particularly PBL and e-learning, occupational science and organisational culture. Publications include a co-edited book: *Health and Social Care: An Introduction for Allied Health Professionals* (Elsevier, 2005).

Jane Fox, formerly Head of Nursing and Midwifery at University College Worcester, is currently seconded to the Department of Health (Skills for Health), undertaking work related to the development of a Partnership Quality Assurance Framework for England. She has a particular interest in Accreditation of Prior Learning (L. Nyatanga, D. Forman and J. Fox, *Good Practice in the Accreditation of Prior Learning*, Cassell: London, 1998), interprofessional learning (Institute of Learning and Teaching small project award 2002/3) and concept mapping.

Jo Smedley is Assistant Director of Combined Honours at Aston University, Birmingham. She is also Visiting Senior Lecturer in Informatics at Halmstad University, Sweden. Her research interests lie in the area of e- and blended learning, human computer interaction and reflective learning. Details of publications are available at www.aston.ac.uk/comb hons/jo/.

Peter Hartley is Professor of Education Development and Head of the Teaching Quality Enhancement Group at the University of Bradford. One of the first group of National Teaching Fellows in 2000, he has produced educational multimedia (*The Interviewer*,

Gower, 2004) and a series of textbooks on human communication (e.g. *Business Communication*, with Clive Bruckman, Routledge, 2001).

Gwyneth Hughes is the e-Learning Co-ordinator at the University of East London. She is the leader of a short Masters-level course, Application of Learning Technologies, which has been accredited by both SEDA and the ILTHE and has national recognition. Her recent research and publications are in the area of e-learning and retention.

Annie Huntington is employed as a Principal Lecturer in the Department of Social Work at the University of Central Lancashire. She is a qualified social worker, nurse and psychotherapist with a particular interest in interactive approaches to learning and teaching.

Alan Hurst (Department of Education, University of Central Lancashire and trustee of Skill: National Bureau for Students with Disabilities) has published papers and books and presented keynote addresses and workshops on disability in higher education at many national and international conferences. Currently he is managing a project to compile a staff developer's handbook for use in connection with raising awareness about inclusive learning.

David Major is Director of the Centre for Work Related Studies at University College Chester. He has been involved in a number of national work-based learning (WBL) initiatives and has been working, with others, on the WBL curriculum at Chester since 1990.

Kathryn McFarlane is careers adviser and University Learning and Teaching Fellow in the Careers and Employability Service at Staffordshire University. As well as working as a careers adviser, she contributes to the curriculum through various modules, and has been Module Leader for a centrally-run Careers Module. She has been chair of the University's Student Employability Group, which seeks to promote the employability agenda in the University.

Peter Mangan is Lecturer in Education in the Department of Continuing Education, City University, London and Director of the department's Certificate in Continuing Studies. His main research is in the area of social reconstruction in societies emerging from civil conflict, with a particular research focus on possible roles for the web as an enabling tool in such reconstruction scenarios.

Jenny Moon is based at Exeter University and is involved in Educational Development. She has worked on various aspects of programme structure since involvement in credit developments in Wales in the mid-1990s. She has published widely on the issues of programme structure and also on the processes of learning and reflection in learning. Her chapter in this book brings these two areas of work together.

Dot Morrison is Senior Lecturer within the Institute of Health and Social Care at University College Worcester working mainly with pre- and post-registration nursing students. She has a particular interest in the nature of knowledge, which underpins professional practice, and developing learning and teaching strategies to enhance student engagement.

Uma Patel is Lecturer in e-Learning in the School of Arts, City University. She has respon-sibility for e-learning applications. Her research is the design of tools and conditions for adult learning and professional development. She is interested in the role of technology in constructions of professional identity, and the relationship between technology identity and empowerment.

Jenny Phillips has worked in educational development within Higher Education for several years, at both The Nottingham Trent University, and Birkbeck College, London. Her specialist interests include assessment, accessibility of learning, technology-enhanced learning and key skills.

Martin Pill is Senior Lecturer at the University of the West of England, Bristol where he chairs the Faculty Teaching Learning and Assessment Committee. He is Reviews Editor for the journal *Active Learning in Higher Education*, and has run workshops and seminars on teaching and learning in this country and abroad.

Julie-Anne Regan is a Senior Lecturer in the School of Health and Social Care at University College Chester. She is the progamme leader for the MSc in Health Promotion but also works with pre- and post-registration nursing students to develop their teaching and learning skills, with the aim of enhancing their experiences of Higher Education.

John Shaw is Principal Lecturer in Learning and Teaching for the Business Department, London Metropolitan University. He has been teaching in Higher Education since 1972 in a variety of settings – from access courses to postgraduate, from Croatia to Trinidad. He has a variety of papers published including two articles in the THES, and the chapter in the recent SEEC book on foundation degrees (*Making Foundation Degrees Work*, edited by Lyn Brennan and David Gosling (SEEC, 2004)).

Vivien Sieber is currently introducing learning technologies into the Medical Science Division, University of Oxford and is involved with a virtual learning environment and computer-aided assessment. She had university-wide responsibility for learning tech-nologies at London Metropolitan (former University of North London) and managed the Teaching and Learning Technology Centre which delivered staff training and multimedia development. Vivien gained extensive teaching experience in genetics and study skills whilst at The University of East London.

John P. Wilson is the Continuing Professional Development Manager at the University of Oxford. He has worked with many organisations and spent two years working in Sweden, and four years in Saudi Arabia. He has directed an MEd in Training and Development and has edited, *Human Resource Development: Learning and Training for Individuals and Organisations* (2nd edn, Kogan Page, 2005) and jointly authored *The Power of Experien-tial Learning: A Handbook for Trainers and Educators* (Kogan Page, 2001).

Amanda Woods is currently Senior Research Fellow at the Division of Primary Care, University of Nottingham on secondment from her post as Lecturer in Child Health at the School of Nursing. She is a social scientist and public health nurse and holder of a prestigious Department of Health Primary Care Researcher Development Award which has enabled her to pursue her research interests in public health and childhood safety promotion. Her recent publications have been related to the learning needs of health care professionals.

Preface

We hope that lecturers in higher education (HE) from every subject background will find this book both useful and challenging: useful because it contains a wide range of practical ideas which we can immediately apply to our own teaching; and challenging because the chapters invite us to reconsider and re-evaluate the ways we teach our students. We have tried to concentrate on issues and developments that are having an important impact on the ways that we all teach increasing numbers of undergraduate students.

These are interesting times as far as the development of teaching and learning in HE is concerned. On the one hand, there has been a stream of initiatives over the last decade, all designed to improve the quality of learning and teaching (and also the status of teaching) within universities. An important example in the UK is the HE Academy. This was established in 2004 with 'ambitious aims' and a 'focus on students and improving their experience', as described by its first chief executive, Paul Ramsden, in his first address to the annual funding body conference. The Academy's long-term ambition is to provide 'an authoritative national voice on teaching and learning issues, promoting the professional development of staff through a range of services and supporting the enhancement work of universities and colleges' (www.heacademy.ac.uk, April 2004). At institutional level, the new Centres for Excellence in Learning and Teaching aim both to reward excellence and to encourage innovation in teaching and learning. At individual level, the National Teaching Fellowship Scheme rewards institutional nominees who have been recognised for particular contributions to teaching and learning: this scheme expanded from 20 to 50 awards per annum in 2004.

These initiatives and others represent both an increasing recognition of the importance of university teaching at all levels – from institutional strategy to individual initiatives – and an increasingly interventionist stance by both funding bodies and the government. These trends now characterise higher education in many countries, although the specific combination of the schemes listed above has no or few direct counterparts in other parts of the world. But we cannot say that they have been universally accepted as appropriate models for educational change: all the initiatives have been debated in some detail and we can find strong arguments for both their value and their limitations.

The combination of increasing intervention and rapid expansion has led to some sharp contradictions and tensions. To illustrate the tensions and pressures, Paul Ramsden describes higher education as facing 'an almost certain future of relentless variation in a more austere environment' (Ramsden, 1998: 3). But he also argues that 'teaching is one of the most delightful and exciting of all human activities when it is done well' (Ramsden, 2003: 5). The form of such teaching has also become a focus of lively and often heated debate, and this is now regularly represented in both academic and press coverage. For example, consider a typical selection of articles taken from a few weeks' issues of the *Times Higher Education Supplement*. One, with the deliberately provocative title of 'Audit models "kill teaching"', contrasted comments from Sally Brown's professorial lecture, defining excellence in teaching to include 'passion for the subject' and 'commitment to students' learning', with concerns from Ben Knights about the 'shift away from academic disciplines and expert knowledge in favour of generic teaching' (Utley, 2004). A personal article from Peter Abbs described 'the current educational reality' as a 'blank pragmatism' and asked: 'can the personal and liberating elements of education survive?' (Abbs, 2004). In the same issue, Ken Bain described his research study of a sample of 'outstanding teachers' in various universities. Common features across different subject areas included attempts to 'create natural critical learning environments' and 'challenge students to rethink their assumptions' (Bain, 2004). There is no doubt that the quality and form of university teaching continues to arouse strong feelings and commitment.

So we have powerful forces urging (and funding) educational change, serious debate (and some profound concerns) about the likely outcomes of this change, and some considerable operational problems evident in the expansion of HE. In the middle of this lively turmoil we have the daily task of teaching and the approaches and perceptions of university staff. A recent UK survey found that a majority of university academics felt that modern students are less prepared than their predecessors for university life and that this has potentially damaging implications for the curriculum. This same survey found that most academics also felt that students were primarily motivated by concern over job prospects. Only a small percentage felt that students were mainly pursuing knowledge for its own sake. Such perceptions may have negative outcomes if they colour our approaches to teaching, especially when research on student attitudes paints a more complex (and also more encouraging) picture of students as 'conscientious consumers' (Higgins *et al.*, 2002).

The focus of this book is on this operational level – what we do as teachers and lecturers to influence student learning – although many of our chapters make some comments on the organisational and political contexts that affect what we do. All of our contributors are actively involved in the enhancement of student learning and most have a significant teaching load. So this book is primarily written by university lecturers for university lecturers. But it is not intended as a comprehensive primer or guidebook on teaching practice, as these already exist (e.g. Fry *et al.*, 1999; Light and Cox, 2002; Ramsden, 2003). Rather, it is a collection of chapters on important current (and future) issues in undergraduate higher education – important issues that have been identified by the practitioners 'at the sharp end' – and it is also a source of ideas (and hopefully inspiration) on how practitioners can influence the shape and processes of student learning. Also, unlike some handbooks on university teaching, we have operated a 'light-touch' editorial policy and so you will find some tensions and contradictions between chapters. As with all good teaching, our fundamental aim is to encourage debate and dialogue.

All the chapters discuss issues that the authors feel strongly about and we hope you can sense the commitment and enthusiasm that underpin each contribution. If this level of commitment is as widespread as we believe it is then the future of teaching and learning in HE is assured.

The structure of the book

The book is organised into four main sections, but this is not intended to be a watertight or exclusive categorisation. Many of our chapters tackle overlapping themes and so the fit of chapters into sections is sometimes a bit arbitrary. The individual chapters are briefly summarised below under the four part headings.

Approaches to learning

Our first section invites you to consider and evaluate your overall approach and perspectives on learning and teaching in HE. The first chapter offers an approach that can be applied to any curriculum and any/every subject area. Colin Beard and John Wilson argue that educational theories in the past have not tried to cover all the possible components or variables that underpin the learning process. Their Learning Combination Lock is a systematic process that enables the educator to consider (and select from) a vast range of ingredients available in the development of learning processes. The lock may also be used as a diagnostic tool to examine existing programmes, helping us to determine whether these programmes cover the main elements of the learning process.

Beard and Wilson give examples and illustrations to show how the model can be used. They emphasise that it should not be used mechanistically but, rather, as a diagnostic aide memoire. It can also be added to and developed according to the considerations of the programme and the needs of the learner.

Moving from an over-arching tool to more specific interventions, David Major argues the case for work-based learning, comparing evidence from the well-established Alverno institution in the US with data from his own students at University College Chester. Using evidence from student interviews and course outcomes, he argues that this form of learning can provide insights and learning that we cannot expect from conventional instruction.

Annie Huntington explores approaches to interactive learning by reflecting upon her own very substantial teaching experience. She looks at both opportunities and issues for lecturers who wish to move along the spectrum towards interactive teaching. Of course, in one sense all teaching is interactive and this is why we need to consider a spectrum that ranges from the inclusion of interactive exercises within an otherwise tutor-controlled lecture to frameworks and strategies where students have to confront their personal responses to the material and engage in reflective practice. One of her strategies is to share theories with students. And this is a practice that crops up in several of our chapters, where students are encouraged to test and apply theories to their own personal experience rather than simply accepting them as truths that cannot be challenged in any context. She also raises problems of ethical practice and the difficulties of dealing with students' emotional responses, another theme that crops up in subsequent chapters.

Working with students

Jane Fox and Dot Morrison provide both a step-by-step model to introduce concept mapping to your students and a thorough analysis of their students' reactions to this method. They conclude that the planned use of concept maps can make an important contribution to student learning. Their experience is not only that it helps students understand particular topics/concepts but it also provides a strategy to foster higher-order learning and cognition, encouraging students to be analytical rather than simply descriptive. Some students continue to incorporate concept mapping as an important ingredient in their own learning repertoire.

If we are encouraging students to take more responsibility for their own learning (and adopting techniques such as problem-based learning) then we need to consider how we operate as members of staff to support students working in this way. Tina Clouston offers the view from the student perspective, using the experiences of student participants whose views were collected through questionnaires, focus groups and narratives over a two-year period. And it is important to recognise that students do not necessarily view excellent teaching in the same way as academic staff do.

There are a number of important lessons for all of us in this chapter. For example, the 'good news' is that you do not have to adopt a particular personal style, which may not suit you, in order to achieve effective outcomes. The 'bad news' is of course that self-awareness is a very important skill that is not simply acquired overnight. It requires constant review and is also extremely hard work.

Peter Hartley notes the increased application of group methods in HE teaching and asks what (and how) students learn from these group activities and projects. He argues that much of our current knowledge about group dynamics has been derived from particular non-educational contexts and that this has worrying implications for our interactions with student groups. In other words, we have fairly limited evidence about how student project groups really 'work'. After offering examples that show how prescriptions about group behaviour based on business or organisational evidence may not apply to student groups in quite the same way, he shows how we can turn this situation to our advantage. We need to involve students in inquiry into their own group processes and use this as a vehicle to develop their critical and reflective skills.

Gwyneth Hughes' chapter focuses on the process of learning online and the resources available to help online learners, such as tutorials on web searching. She responds to two key questions: how can we embed learning-to-learn online skills into the curriculum?; and how are learners best encouraged to use learning-to-learn resources? Using models such as Salmon's stages for successful e-moderating and relating this to her own research on different student attitudes to online learning, she demonstrates a number of ways of getting students involved. The chapter concludes with a useful checklist for including learning-to-learn online skills in your curriculum.

Jo Smedley investigates 'blended learning', where the use of human and technological components can overcome the respective limitations of face-to-face and e-learning. The roles and responsibilities of learners and tutors in a blended learning experience are highlighted, with particular emphasis on the design issues inherent in a successful blended learning course. Finally, a set of case studies demonstrate blended learning in action and provide evidence of the diversity of the student experience that can be achieved via the creative use of this style of learning.

Self-directed learning has become one of the new slogans. But what do students make of it? Julie-Anne Regan's chapter summarises the main results from a year-long study of students' perspectives of self-directed learning (SDL). She concludes that facilitating students to become self-directed learners needs to be as carefully planned as the subject content of the curriculum. This means an incremental approach to developing independent learners, offering more direction at the start of the programme until students are better equipped to assess their own learning needs. Failing to facilitate SDL in this way can create barriers to becoming an independent learner and cause the student unnecessary anxiety and distress. One intriguing outcome of this study is the strong link between SDL and tutor-centred approaches such as lectures. This link appears stronger than has previously been highlighted in the literature on SDL.

Enhancing student progression and development

The next group of chapters deals with various aspects of student progression and development. We start by looking at issues associated with the move to describe the curriculum in terms of specified outcomes at different levels, which has now become the dominant model of curriculum development in the UK.

Jenny Moon investigates the notion of progression in learning as described in the level descriptors. Starting from the analysis of the content of the level descriptors (i.e. the concepts of learning that are written into the descriptors), she manages to reveal some of the issues and consequences that result from this way of describing HE learning and teaching.

Jenny Phillips explains the development of the Keynote Guide to Personal Development Planning (PDP). PDP is now an obligatory component of UK HE, although it has been implemented in very different ways. After outlining the national context that made a PDP guide a priority for the Keynote project, she covers the development, evaluation and redesign of the Guide, focusing on choice of technology, content and usability issues. Finally, she looks at approaches to integrating PDP within different subject areas, and discusses some key issues arising from the alternative models. The evaluation of all these approaches highlights some common themes, including the need to brief students fully on the concept of PDP and what is expected of them, and the very difficult issue of tying PDP in with assessment.

Kathryn McFarlane starts her chapter with a definition of employability and an outline of why it is important to undergraduates and graduates. She continues to set two challenges – initially, to consider what opportunities your students have to develop their employability skills and, later, to explore how you might build on these opportunities. Using her own advice as a starting point, she outlines the existing employability-related programmes at her own university and explains their plans for the future.

Supporting and developing staff

The final chapters raise issues of staff support and development, ranging from the use of the web to support staff development through to the impact of recent disability legislation. Common themes are the importance of staff development and the variety of mechanisms that can be used to help staff develop new approaches to teaching and learning. Especially important is the professional approach that academic staff employ. We all have a responsibility not simply to enhance our own subject expertise but also to develop our understanding of issues related to student learning.

John Shaw considers how teaching staff learn about learning. His case study, working with colleagues on a franchised course, shows how the practice of education research (and in his case, action research) had a very powerful impact. Research findings were used to make improvements to the curriculum which made a very significant difference – for example, student retention improved by 30 per cent. This improvement can partly be attributed to the special attention that the student sample received, but the structural changes to the course had longer-term effects. And, of course, action research can be ongoing and maintain impetus. Perhaps more important in the long run, especially given the limited financial resources, was the positive impact on staff – he describes the process as 'the key to a major block to staff development'.

Vivien Sieber explores the main barriers to using ICT and Learning Technology encountered by academic staff and, to a lesser extent, by institutions, and describes a range of initiatives designed to overcome them. She discusses barriers under three main categories: technical and skill issues; issues relating to learning and teaching; and issues arising from lack of appreciation of opportunities or fear. She concludes that progress depends on two related and complementary processes: teaching staff must overcome the barriers of fear of technology and appreciate the opportunities offered to enhance their teaching; and institutions must recognise the investment in infrastructure, support and staff needed to develop the necessary materials.

Peter Mangan and Uma Patel focus upon an increasingly important group of staff – those on part-time hourly contracts, often referred to as visiting lecturers (VLs). Their case study is an online staff development facility, AMBIENT, which has been developed to address VLs' learning requirements, using information from self-assessment of their learning needs. They explore the issues that can act as barriers to VLs' online learning success, and expose as problematic the relationship between the availability of web-based staff development and evidence of successful learning. These issues include predictable ones, for example access to the web and ICT skills, but also the unexpected, for example where working out professional identity in the context of the 'new managerialism' in higher education has assumed a new urgency. They conclude by reflecting upon the paradoxes inherent within online staff development.

Alan Hurst argues that none of us can ignore the implications of changes to legislation covering discrimination that have applied to the UK HE sector from September 2002. We may all share the values of encouraging access to higher education but the recent legislation does give us additional responsibilities. We can no longer simply respond to students' difficulties *after* they arrive in our classrooms. The legislation obliges us to anticipate that students with particular disabilities will wish to attend our courses and we need to make 'reasonable adjustments' to make sure that those students are not discriminated against. In other words, we need to plan in advance to make our courses accessible and inclusive rather than solving problems after they emerge. He advocates the 'four As': awareness of disabilities, audit current practices, anticipate future needs, and action to implement inclusive learning. Perhaps the most powerful message in this chapter is the conclusion that if we make these adjustments to our provision then we are actually more likely to benefit *all* students.

In our final chapter, Glynis Cousin argues that many of our attempts to encourage equal opportunities are based upon mistaken or misleading notions of human identity. She argues very powerfully that we must resist attempts to classify individuals in over-restrictive categories or boxes. Given that one of the main themes running through this book is the search for ways of encouraging student autonomy and self-confidence, then this argument is an appropriate place for us to wind up this volume.

We hope that you do find at least some of the content is useful and you should certainly find some, if not many, of the ideas challenging. We also hope that this will stimulate further dialogue, again echoing the spirit of our last chapter.

Peter Hartley, Amanda Woods
and Martin Pill

Acknowledgements

This book started as an ILT initiative – members were invited to propose chapters which discussed important concerns and innovations in HE teaching. It would not have happened without the enthusiasm and commitment of Sally Brown and we are also indebted to Stephen Jones for his considerable patience and unflagging support.

References

Abbs, P. (2004) Why I . . . believe the higher education bill will increase alienation from learning, *Times Higher Education Supplement*, 7 May, 14.

Bain, K. (2004) Art of old masters in moulding minds, *Times Higher Education Supplement*, 7 May, 23.

Fry, H., Ketteridge, S. and Marshall, S. (1999) *A Handbook for Teaching and Learning in Higher Education: Enhancing Academic Practice*, London: Kogan Page.

Higgins, R., Hartley, P. and Skelton, A. (2002) The conscientious consumer: reconsidering the role of assessment feedback in student learning, *Studies in Higher Education*, 27, 1, 53–64.

Light, G. and Cox, R. (2001) *Learning and Teaching in Higher Education: The Reflective Professional*, London, Sage Publications.

Ramsden, P. (1998) *Learning to Lead in Higher Education*, London: Routledge.

Ramsden, P. (2003) *Learning to Teach in Higher Education*, 2nd edition, London: RoutledgeFalmer.

Utley, A. (2004) Audit models 'kill teaching', *Times Higher Education Supplement*, 23 April, 2.

Part one

Approaches to learning

Ingredients for effective learning: the Learning Combination Lock

Colin Beard and John P. Wilson

Introduction

Do all your first year students still arrive bright and keen at 9.00 a.m. on a Monday morning in the last week of the semester? How do we design their learning experience to sustain interest, motivation and enthusiasm? Do we go with our instincts and encourage learning through applying methods that have worked in the past, or do we base our teaching on theories of learning and, if so, which ones from the vast range that exists?

Our answer to this dilemma is a model that offers a systematic process for the educator to consider and select from a vast range of ingredients available in the development of learning processes: the Learning Combination Lock (LCL). The LCL can also be used as a diagnostic tool to examine existing programmes and determine whether they cover the main elements of the learning process.

The LCL is not intended to be used mechanistically but rather as a diagnostic aide-memoire that may also be added to and developed according to the considerations of the programme and the needs of the learner. This chapter describes the LCL and offers a range of clues and practical applications that may be used to enhance your students' learning environment and link theory and practice.

Introducing the LCL

Theories of learning, education, training and development are frequently developed in isolation from one another. As a result, even educational specialists find it difficult to construct a coherent and integrated overview of their subject. And the vast majority of people involved with individual and work-based learning only appear to use a restricted number of theories (Brant, 1998). Many have neither the breadth of knowledge to select from a wider range of possibilities and options, nor do they possess a meta-model with which to contextualise and make sense of other theories with which they come into contact. The LCL provides such a meta-model. It is underpinned by models of experiential learning and theories of perception and information-processing (for a full explanation, see Beard and Wilson, 2002 – this chapter concentrates on the applications and implications).

The LCL brings together (for the first time, to our knowledge) *all* the main ingredients of the learning equation (Figure 1.1). In the past these ingredients have often been discussed in isolation, thus giving only a partial picture of the learning environment. We need to identify all the core components to help practitioners in Higher Education diagnose and design activities that create high-quality learning experiences for students. For example, Light and Cox (2001: 109) note that:

> The design of this relationship between lecture structures and activities provides the key location for creativity and innovation in lecturing. Even given the usual academic constraints of what is 'permissible' as well as those of space, time, resources and so forth, the permutations and possibilities available to the lecturer are limited primarily by their imagination and confidence.

As lecturers we need to experiment and sometimes take risks in our own learning journeys. The LCL can support the creative exploration of activity design, although we cannot ignore the institutional difficulties of generating effective approaches:

> The cultural environment of higher education does little to foster active learning to strengthen critical thinking and creativity skills in its students. . . . Faculty are given little time, budget, encouragement or support to develop 'active learning' tools that assist in developing these skills. Incorporating 'active learning' pedagogic techniques, for example, developing and running exercises, group projects, or simulations, is risky for a faculty and there is no guarantee that these techniques will work or that students see the benefits of this form of pedagogic method. Fortunately, but slowly, the cultural environment that places barriers to moving toward more innovative pedagogical tools is eroding away.
>
> (Snyder, 2003: 159)

We are not presenting fixed choices in the LCL but offering many more possibilities to experiment with and reflect upon. Starting on the left, the *learning environment* tumbler identifies various components found in the physical external environment that may be used as part of the learning process. Adjacent is the tumbler that examines the core components of *learning activities*. The third tumbler represents the *senses* as the mediator that connects the external environment with the internal cognitive environment. Our senses alert us to the presence of the stimuli that begin the process of perceiving and interpreting.

The *emotions* tumbler presents some of the vast range of emotional responses we can make and is a very powerful aspect of the learning equation. In designing a learning programme we may wish to instil certain emotions to enhance the learning situation as well as manage and recognise the emotional agenda of the broader student experience.

The fifth tumbler explores various *forms of intelligence* whose development may be the objective of the learning process.

The final tumbler represents various *theories of learning*. There is still so much that we do not know about learning, so it is important to be aware of the various learning

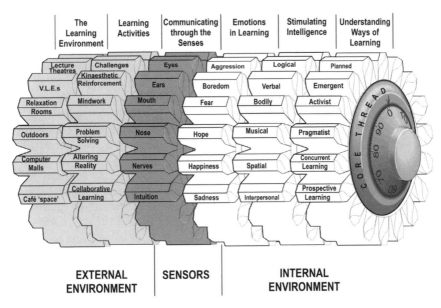

Figure 1.1 The Learning Combination Lock by Colin Beard

theories and also our own underlying theories of how learning may best be facilitated. By making these explicit we may better understand our own thinking and the behaviour and motives of learners.

The tumblers explained

Tumbler 1: the learning environment

The external learning environment provides opportunities to encourage learning. For example, outdoor environments increasingly provide very real opportunities for the individual to learn in a deep way about themselves and their interactions with others. And, it isn't only the external environment that can provide valuable opportunities to learn. The design and use of the indoor student learning environment is beginning to metamorphose. Whereas in the past it was strongly associated with the lecture theatre and textbooks, nowadays it includes: distance education sites; common areas such as halls; social group work space with sofas; outdoor green spaces; amphitheatres; video clips; and virtual discussion groups. An illustration of the transition in thinking is the definition of the learning environment by Indiana University, and their support for active learning:

> A physical, intellectual, psychological environment which facilitates learning through connectivity and community.
>
> (www-lib.iupui.edu/itt/planlearn/part1.html,
> accessed 27 November, 2004)

Well-established research shows that students learn best when they are actively engaged rather than being passive observers . . . there are three avenues an institution can promote to foster active student learning. First, certain teaching methodologies, such as problem-based learning, promote active student involvement. Second, the classroom furnishings can either enhance or hinder active student learning. Thus, tables and moveable chairs enhance while fixed-row seating hinders active learning. Finally technologies which require student initiative, such as interactive video-discs, promote active learning.

> (www-lib.iupui.edu/itt/planlearn/execsumm.html,
> accessed 27 November, 2004)

Of course, 'furnishings' represent a small fraction of the many physical elements that can be managed in the learners' environment. Informal learning environments are increasingly being recognised and used for more formal learning. While students traditionally spent many hundreds of hours learning in lecture theatres and seminar rooms, learning space is increasingly spilling over into, and being used alongside: informal learning spaces; drama studios; stage; laboratory; virtual learning environments; lecture theatres; seminar rooms; café learning spaces; group spaces; stand-up corridor computer malls; and even innovation rooms and relaxation lecture theatres, including the use of hammocks in lecture theatres in Finland, specifically designed to enhance the creation of certain mental states, such as relaxed alertness (see also Beard and Wilson, 2002). There is growing evidence elsewhere too that new learning spaces are evolving:

> [Arizona State University has a] special Kaleidoscope room [which] holds 120 students; however, the faculty is never more than five rows away from any student. The instructor relates to a few *groups* of students rather than a *mass* of 120 students . . . the atmosphere is one of work, action, involvement. . . . Stanford University has designed highly flexible technology-rich class-lab learning environments using bean bags for much the same purpose as tables. . . . We recommend that the entire planning process for design and renovation of classrooms includes faculty and staff with expertise in learning methodologies.
>
> (www-lib.iupui.edu/itt/planlearn/part1.html,
> accessed 27 November, 2004)

Unfortunately, the lack of knowledge about the relationship between buildings and learning, and the lack of dialogue between academics and facilities managers is still constraining developments (Beard and Matzdorf, 2004) and so academics are often left to merely adapt to *given* space. Furthermore, the replacement of old learning spaces with new facilities is expensive and is a long-term investment.

Smith (1998) argues that: 'We are not designed to sit slumped behind a piece of wood for an hour and ten minutes at a time, nor are we designed to sit for three hours in front of a television screen or a computer terminal.' Similarly, Jensen (1995) refers to the work of Dunn and Dunn (1978) who found that 'at least 20% of learners are significantly affected, positively or negatively, by seating options or lack of them'. So perhaps we do need to explore more innovative use of existing space until such time that the design of learning space sits more at ease alongside pedagogical requirements. Floor space and wall space can be used for creative, more active engagement of learners (see case study 3 below).

Technological tools are also influencing learning space, with items such as interactive whiteboards, which can enable the instant capturing of fresh, 'live' and indigenous intellectual property. As pedagogy interacts with the operational facilities and media technology, the learning environment will undergo rapid change. This will change the future layout of walls and learning space and enable active movement of people and information. This is important, for we believe that good learning environments will increasingly provide areas that maximise the *flexibility and mobility* of information, people and space, enabling the physical viewing of information and concepts from different perspectives.

Tumbler 2: the learning activities

This second tumbler explores principles of designing *learning activities*. Creating a real sense of engagement in an active *learning journey*, to bridge the gap between where a student starts and the desired learning outcomes, over periods of time such as a semester or a year or the duration of a degree, can be a transformative experience for students. Journeying, with its sense of setting off, building, constructing, changing and arriving, includes all the important conceptual ingredients to generate powerful experiential learning.

The American Association for Higher Education (AAHE) states that an important principle for good practice in undergraduate education should be the development of an environment in which 'active learning' is encouraged (Snyder, 2003: 159). Snyder also refers to a number of studies comparing active learning with those using passive learning, showing that active learning methods generally result in greater retention of material at the end of a class, superior problem solving skills, more positive attitudes and higher motivation for future learning.

By 'active' learning methods we mean intellectually, physically and emotionally more active as well as more active in the design and selection of learning activities. Active learning can offer a greater depth of information-processing, greater comprehension and better retention, in contrast with the passive learning techniques that characterise the typical classroom, in which lecturer wisdom is offered for students to dutifully record notes. Active learning involves students doing something and taking a participatory role in thinking and learning. The milieu of activities can include elements such as: kinaesthetic activity; mental challenges; experiencing a learning journey; overcoming obstacles; following or changing rules; and altering reality (see Beard and Wilson (2002) for a full explanation of altering reality). Although much more research is needed into learning activities used in Higher Education, a basic typology of activity might for example include:

1   Creating a sense of a learning *journey* for students, with a clear vision of the bigger picture, with a clear destination, and route maps to guide the way.
2   Creating and sequencing an array of *intellectually, physically and emotionally* stimulating 'waves' of activities.
3   Adjusting or suspending elements of *simulation* and *reality* to create learning steps.
4   Creating activities to stimulate and regularly alter moods . . . acknowledge the student experience, create relaxed alertness, *understand peak or flow learning*.
5   Using the notion of *constructing* or *deconstructing* activities, such as physical objects, or non-physical items, e.g. the gradual construction of a model, a concept, historical maps, key ingredients, typologies, a phrase or poem.
6   Creating and managing the *learning community* through a mixture of collaborative, competitive or co-operative strategies.

7   Creating and *acknowledging feelings*, values, targets, ground-rules, restrictions, obstacles and allowing students to address identity, change, success and failure.

8   Considering *multi-sensory teaching* – see the next cog – experiment with building in a holistic 'sense' of the material covered . . . consider the sensory enhancement of material, e.g. touch, smell, colour . . .

9   Providing elements of real or perceived *challenge* or risk . . . and allow students to address risk and the stretching of personal boundaries.

10 Introducing complex design, sorting and/or *organisational* skills.

11 Developing generic *functional* student skills alongside specific course content work – such as literature searching, writing introductions, conclusions, researching skills, etc.

12 Designing *quiet time* for reflection – using the notion of physical and mental 'space'.

13 Allowing the *story* of the learning experience (including emotions) to be told by the learners (student progress files, learning logs, reflective exercises, group reflective dialogue).

Tumbler 3: the senses

The third tumbler considers the role of the senses. Neuro-linguistic programming (O'Connor and Seymour, 1995) tells us that good educators use communication that conveys visual, auditory and touch messages to engage a broader range of learners in a more effective way. Learners may have preferred ways of receiving and handling sensory data in order to construct their own 'map' of reality whereas lecturers may rely exclusively on their own preferred representational systems when communicating. Auditory dominant students might like audio tapes, talks, rhythms and sounds while kinaesthetically dominant students like physical activity, which might include physical challenge or active drama and role-play. With large groups of students, sample products can be passed around the lecture theatre to enable students to feel, see, move, explore and try out. Environmental awareness in product-design students is heightened when I wind up a clockwork radio and allow music to play quietly in the background at the same time as discussing principles of sustainable product design and distributing items, e.g. fleeces made of plastic; pencils made from waste vending machine cups; balls that generate light; kinetic watches; plastic bricks; solar panels – they all make the experience more alive and memorable.

Enhancing and awakening the senses and linking them to the learning activities can create more powerful learning. Sensory stimulation alters moods and emotions and can increase learning. The more senses we stimulate in an activity the more memorable the learning experience will become because it increases and reinforces the neural connections in our brains. The greater the involvement of the participants in the learning activity the deeper will be their learning and therefore the greater the effect on future thought and behaviour. This is highlighted, for example, in the work of Thayer (1996) on the role of everyday moods.

Tumbler 4: the emotions

Our education institutions are predominantly concerned with rational and scientific approaches to intellectual enquiry, whereas 'emotions and feelings are . . . most neglected in our society: there is almost a taboo about them intruding into our education institutions,

Case study 1: a journey through degrees of reality to develop practical negotiating skills

The course: negotiating skills for public rights of way officers – public access to the UK countryside

Negotiating is a 'broad skill', involving the building of the many composite narrow skills such as listening, questioning, diplomacy and so on. On this course we identified the many narrow sub-skills such as influencing, persuasion, listening, tactics, entry, developing rapport, closing and so on. The sessions use 'narrow skills' practice. The latter part of the course then used broad skills practice: but with varying levels of reality or simulation as follows:

From: low content reality

Exercise A: redecorating the office
This is a paper exercise from a standard package on negotiating. It concerns a contract price to decorate an office suite. People are asked to identify opening gambits and write their answers on paper.

Exercise B: driving a bargain
This is a written exercise about cars – people are told that this is a warm-up for a real car exercise when people can pit their wits against real negotiators.

Exercise C: buying a new car
Real cars and log books are used. Cars can be inspected and faults found, both inside and outside, as they are located in the car park. The participants negotiate with trained negotiators who are located in an office where the deals will take place. Final agreements are written in sealed envelopes so that the winners can be decided later.

To: high content reality

Exercise D: negotiating access to UK land on behalf of the public
Real negotiators are again present. Real job information is provided, e.g. complex facts and figures on sheep headage payments, ranger support offered, etc. For participants, the incentive is to try to do a good job in front of their peers; put all the skills and knowledge acquired on the course into practice; and meet their own pre-set prices and subsidy targets decided in their negotiating plans. They argue their case with real negotiators and are debriefed afterwards. Videos are replayed with self and peer assessment.

(adapted from Beard and McPherson, 1999)

Case study 2: using different senses

The course: teaching taxonomy and classification to botany students

Popular objects, and popular media can act as physical and visual metaphors for learning. Here, the teaching of the classification of animals uses a bag of assorted nuts, bolts and screws for students to create a classification system or an identification key . . .

Students are divided into teams and receive a bag of various nails, staples, screws, nuts and bolts, etc. They are told they are renowned taxonomists, and that they have to develop a classification scheme that meets the established rules of the Linnaean system. They also have to be prepared to defend their classification scheme orally.

The students have to make a phylogenetic chart of their classification scheme using the poster paper, tape and objects, including all of the categories from phylum to species.

They are asked to consider a range of probing questions, such as the rationale that was used for each category and the criteria they used to differentiate among categories? Did they rely more on 'form' or 'function'? Or derived and ancestral traits? They also have to consider the difficulties and issues associated with the difficulties and differences between classifying inanimate objects and living organisms.

This activity is taken from the web site: www.jrscience.wcp.muohio.edu/lab/taxonomylab.html, accessed 1 May, 2004.

particularly at higher levels' (Boud et al., 1993: 14). Fineman (1997: 13) makes a similar observation: 'Learning is inextricably emotional and of emotions. The traditional cognitive approach to management learning has obscured the presence and role of emotion.' Similarly Light and Cox explain that:

Students regard knowledge and learning as something external and objective, right or wrong. This sort of epistemological perspective is extremely difficult to give up if it is held with any conviction, a conviction that quite often goes back to early childhood and may be strongly invested in emotion. Teachers and the learning environment may be vested with many of the qualities of parental or childhood authority figures. The difficult transitions from the security of dualism into the security of relativism is not simply a matter of absorbing new ideas or information, but is very much a **restructuring at an emotional level as well as a cognitive level**, and may be accompanied by extreme anxiety.

(Light and Cox, 2001: 57, emphasis added)

During the past few years this failure to consider emotional awareness has decreased as a result of writings on emotion and emotional intelligence. Goleman (1995) championed the subject and drew on the work of Salovey and Mayer (1990) who classified emotional intelligence into five main domains: knowing one's emotions, managing emotions, motivating oneself, recognising emotions in others, and handling relationships.

Our view is that the emotional tumbler represents the crucial 'gatekeeper' to deep learning. Managing the emotional climate, accessing emotion, mapping or encouraging change in the basic emotional make-up of students is a difficult yet necessary skill for lecturers. Mortiboys (2002) looks at the potential for using emotional intelligence to make HE lecturing more satisfying and effective. He scrutinises the case for the development of emotionally intelligent lecturers and refers to research into areas such as classroom climate and lecturer qualities. Students responded to questions about their favourite session using words such as 'enthusiastic', 'fascination', 'being valued', 'confident', 'curious' and 'excited'.

> It can be inferred that a number of these responses, both positive and negative, are reactions to the lecturer. In the same way that a lecturer influences, but is not wholly responsible for, the performance of their students, so it is with the feelings aroused by students. Whether you refer to your role as a facilitator, lecturer, tutor or educator, there are times when you interact with individual students and/or groups of students and the way you are affects the way they feel, which in turn influences their predisposition to learning.
>
> (Mortiboys, 2002: 10)

Being able to acknowledge and sense underpinning emotions and, where appropriate, steer the emotional bases of student behaviour, is a key skill requiring an understanding of factors affecting student motivation, such as identity, sociality, meaning and orientation. This needs emotional maturity, responsibility and personal understanding by tutors. Students are increasingly being encouraged to undertake personal and professional development portfolios and progress files which, through reflective exercises, help them to examine their emotional states in the learning journey.

Learning is enhanced when people discover things for themselves through their own emotional engagement. This requires a commitment to discovery, experimentation and reviewing of personal emotional goals and visions. Emotional intelligence underpins learning as a basic building block. In order for any experience to be interpreted in a constructive manner it is essential that learners possess abilities such as:

- confidence – in their abilities;
- self-esteem – in order to recognise the validity of their own views and those of others;
- support – from others with whom they work and bounce off ideas; from lecturers when they get grades, marks or feedback;
- trust – they must have confidence in the validity of the views of others and be able to incorporate them with their own where necessary.

By combining the 'adventure waves' of Mortlock (1984) with the 'flow learning' from Cornell (1989) and the work of Dainty and Lucas (1992) it is possible to create a six step *emotional wave*. For example, lecturers might map and plan the emotional journey of waves that the student experiences throughout a semester. For example, is it realistic to try to convey complex information to freshers on their first morning when they may be disorientated? Surely, we should consider and tap into their emotions to enhance the learning process. Preparation might be done through the use of twelve cards identifying the types of emotions during each week of the semester, which is a different approach to the planning process. In programme design we might consider the six steps thus:

1   Create conditions for pre-contemplation – reading, thinking, imagining the bigger picture and the journey.
2   Awaken participant enthusiasm – intellectual ice breakers and energisers.
3   Start to focus attention and concentration – medium-sized activities, narrow key skills.
4   Direct and challenge the personal experience – larger, broader skills.
5   Share participant enthusiasm – using quality reflective/reviewing activities.
6   Encourage quiet personal reflection.

Emotions and the concept of emotional intelligence could have been incorporated in the next tumbler, i.e. *forms of intelligence*. However, we believe that emotion is a critical component of learning and should be considered *independently* of the other forms of intelligence thus meriting a separate tumbler.

Case study 3: using flow learning

Course: developing critical reading in postgraduate students

We used the mood-setting frame of *lounging about reading the Sunday newspapers* – but instead of newspapers we used academic journal articles from a range of well-known sources. The participants soon had their shoes off, sitting or lying on comfortable sofas, sometimes with cats sleeping next to them, and with soft rainforest music playing. Coffee percolators bubble away, Earl Grey tea is on offer and lemon scents the air. The articles are from *People Management*, and *Management Learning, Management Education and Development, People and Organisations, Training and Development, Industrial and Commercial Training, Sloan Management Review, Harvard Business Review*, and many others. Hardly Sunday morning reading!

Subtly included in the reading material were articles that encouraged students to be aware of themselves; to be critical of these articles. We were encouraging students to become more relaxed about the 'literature' associated with their subject, to encourage them to share, become fascinated, get copies of lots of material because they wanted to take it home, and to learn to communicate and explore their findings with each other.

Following the reading the tutor acted as a scribe and facilitator. The subsequent evaluation of the session showed that students wanted more time in future to repeat these explorations of the literature and to *play with concepts and ideas in this relaxed way*. One student said: 'During these sessions, differing views concerning the same articles were discussed and new insights developed based on individual experience outside the articles. This led to a spin of ideas that spurred more new ideas, and re-shaped some of my initial thoughts of the article.'

(adapted from Beard and McPherson, 1999)

Tumbler 5: forms of intelligence

The fifth tumbler addresses the nature of intelligence. In addition to emotional intelligence there are also other forms of intelligence that need to be considered and addressed in learning design. Before Gardner's (1983) book, *Frames of Mind*, much emphasis was placed on IQ. Gardner drew attention to the notion, and importance, of other forms of intelligence and proposed seven types: linguistic; logical/mathematical/scientific; visual/spatial; musical; bodily/physical/kinaesthetic; interpersonal; and intrapersonal. Stimulating these many forms of intelligence is key to inclusive pedagogy. Verbal/linguistic learning activities might include: reading books, journal logs, debate, storytelling, verbal humour, poetry, creative writing. Bodily/kinaesthetic learning activities might include: role play, moving laminated cards, things to touch/feel, using physical metaphors, encouraging movement, stick-it labels that can be rearranged. Mathematical logical activities might use mind maps, systems processing, force field analysis, assigning numbers to things. Visual/spatial learning activities might use wall charts, spatial anchors, gestures by lecturers, guided visualisation or imagery, visual aids, sketches and diagrammatic representations. More examples can be found in Beard and Wilson (2002).

Tumbler 6: ways of learning

The sixth and final tumbler in the LCL focuses upon the various types of learning theory which, on the one hand, may be widely recognised and applied, e.g. cognitive learning theory (Bruner, 1990); or, on the other hand, may be personal ones that remind us that we think and learn most effectively in the mornings after a cup of tea! The main message is that in order to enhance learning there should be some explicit recognition and understanding

---

Case study 4: using space to walk the talk
Course: mapping history

Students research the history first in groups. The following week they map the environmental history on the floor using laminated coloured cards that represent different contents . . . blue for laws such as the National Parks Act, yellow for NGOs, grey for QUANGOS such as the Countryside Agency or English Nature, orange for key events in history such as the Wars or the Mass Trespass (1932). In addition, there are other cards with dates on and blank cards to fill in. All the essential kit is presented in a plastic video case. The picture-map layout on the floor or table demonstrates their knowledge of the subject and when finished students walk the talk presenting the historical picture as they proceed. This kinaesthetically reinforces the learning and tests understanding in a visual-oral way.

The same can be done with a literature review and key texts. The texts are spread out in a large space and debated and discussed as people move around them – the spatial re-organisation and debate is key. Explore similarities and differences. Use newspaper stories first to explore these skills with less experienced people.

of the advantages and limitations of our espoused and tacit theories (Polanyi, 1967) on knowledge and learning. This awareness and examination of our approaches to learning, whether as a learner or enabler of learning in others, should lead to more considered and appropriate learning opportunities rather than instinctive or random methods to the selection of learning approaches.

The theories of learning are too numerous to mention here although a number of categories have been detailed by Beard and Wilson (2002: 194–5). The LCL is sufficiently accommodating to incorporate, to some degree, these categories and theories of learning. While no model can fully represent the learning process, the LCL does attempt to provide a meta-perspective and act as an aide-memoire.

Summary of the advantages of the LCL

- It provides a broad perspective of the learning process and its various elements and theories.
- It is sufficiently flexible to incorporate the main behavioural, cognitive and humanist schools of learning without placing them in opposition to each other.
- It provides a systematic approach to the support of learning.
- The checklist of elements for each tumbler provides an aide-memoire for the educator, trainer and developer.
- The metaphor of the combination lock should not limit the use of only one ingredient from each tumbler. In practice learning events may incorporate several elements from a tumbler.

But also remember:

- The metal rod running through the core of the LCL represents the needs of the learner. These should be central to any consideration of the various options available in each of the tumblers.
- It should not be used as a one-armed-bandit approach to selecting the ingredients for experiential learning activities. The learning needs and objectives should be carefully considered before addressing each tumbler in turn and selecting those combinations that are likely to be effective.
- The LCL is not an exclusive list of the tumblers and elements that might be considered in the design of the learning event. It allows trainers, educators and developers to add to the lock and build their own personalised set of learning permutations that respond to learning needs, thus adding to the millions of combinations. We encourage you, the reader, to customise the model for your own particular requirements.
- The LCL should not be applied in a mechanical fashion without an understanding of the tumblers and the principles of learning. Rather, it should be considered a form of reference source to guide the design and delivery of programmes.

Conclusion

The LCL identifies the main components of the learning process. Detailing these elements in the six tumblers enables systematic consideration of the potential ingredients and provides the opportunity to select from an almost infinite number of learning permutations.

The value of the LCL lies in the extent to which it is considered, applied and further developed. Please feel free to use and adapt this model for your own purposes. As Kurt Lewin stated: 'There is nothing so practical as a good theory.'

References

Beard, C. and McPherson, M. (1999) 'Design of Group-Based Training Methods', in Wilson, J.P. (ed.), *Human Resource Development*, Kogan Page, London.

Beard, C. and Wilson, J. P. (2002) *The Power of Experiential Learning: A Handbook for Trainers and Educators*, Kogan Page, London.

Beard, C. and Matzdorf, F. (2004) *Space to Learn? Unwrapping Conversations about Physical Learning Environments*, Sheffield Hallam University.

Boud, D., Cohen, R. and Walker, D. (1993) *Using Experience For Learning*, Open University Press, Buckingham.

Brant, L. (1998) '"Not Maslow again!" A study of the theories and models that trainers choose as content on training courses', MEd dissertation, University of Sheffield.

Bruner, J. S. (1990) *Acts of Meaning*, Harvard University Press, Cambridge, MA.

Cornell, J. (1989) *Sharing the Joy of Nature*, Dawn Publications, Nevada City, CA.

Dainty, P. and Lucas, D. (1992) 'Clarifying the confusion: A practical framework for evaluating outdoor development programmes for managers', *Management Education and Development*, Vol. 23 No. 2, pp. 106–22.

Dunn, R. and Dunn, K. (1978) *Teaching Students Through their Individual Learning Styles: A Practical Approach*, Reston Publishing Co., Reston, VA.

Fineman, S. 'Emotion and management learning', *Management Learning*, Vol. 28 No. 1, pp. 13–25.

Gardner, H. (1983) *Frames of Mind: The Theory of Multiple Intelligences*, Basic Books Inc., New York.

Goleman, D. (1995) *Emotional Intelligence: Why it can Matter More than IQ*, Bantam, New York.

Jensen, E. (1995) *Brain Based Learning – the New Science of Teaching and Training*, The Brains Store Publishing, San Diego, CA.

Light, G. and Cox, R. (2001) *Learning and Teaching in Higher Education: The Reflective Professional*, Sage, London.

Mortiboys, A. (2002) *The Emotionally Intelligent Lecturer*, Staff and Educational Development Association, SEDA Special 12, Birmingham.

Mortlock, C. (1984) *The Adventure Alternative*, Cicerone Press, Cumbria.

O'Connor, Joseph and Seymour, John (1995) *Introducing Neuro-linguistic Programming: Psychological Skills for Understanding and Influencing People*, Thorsons, London.

Polanyi, M. (1967) *The Tacit Dimension*, Doubleday, New York.

Salovey, Peter and Mayer, John D. (1990) 'Emotional Intelligence', *Imagination, Cognition and Personality*, No. 9, pp. 185–211.

Smith, A. (1998) *Accelerated Learning in Practice*, Network Educational Press Ltd, Stafford.

Snyder, K. (2003) 'Ropes, poles, and space – active learning in business education', *Active Learning in Higher Education*, Vol. 4 No. 2 (July), pp. 159–67.

Thayer, R. (1996) *The Origin of Everyday Moods*, Oxford University Press, Oxford.

2

Learning through work-based learning

David Major

Introduction

In this chapter, I argue that, through work-based learning (WBL), learners appear to have a much better understanding of the learning process than is gained through conventional teaching methods. I will concentrate on the impact of the WBL experience, which is offered by an increasing number of HE Colleges and Universities, defining WBL as fully accredited negotiated units or programmes of learning through work, either for students in full-time higher education or for full-time employees who are also part-time higher education students.

The evidence that underpins my argument comes from two main sources: empirical research findings from studies carried out at University College Chester, and the findings of a longitudinal study into student learning undertaken by Alverno College, Milwaukee. I shall discuss how learning occurs through WBL, what is distinctive about it, and what the conditions are under which learning through work comes about. Close attention will be given to the notions of critical reflection and critical self-awareness as key features of learning through work.

My main contention is that WBL requires learners to assume a greater degree of responsibility for their own learning than do conventional learning methods. This greater responsibility, together with critical reflection as a key ability in WBL, leads to learners developing a greater understanding about how learning occurs. This ability to understand more about the learning process while, at the same time, developing knowledge and understanding, is one that is transferable to other, more conventional, learning contexts, if learners are made more responsible for their own learning and if they learn how to critically self-reflect.

The key questions to be asked in this chapter concern *how* people learn through work and what, if anything, is *distinctive* about WBL, and the *conditions* under which WBL occurs. Anything of real merit that can be said in these contexts must, of course, be grounded in empirical evidence and relatively little is available at the present time. Exceptions are Boud and Solomon (2001) who include some WBL case studies, and

Garrick's (1998) enquiry into informal learning in the workplace which is based on an empirical investigation. More recently, articles such as Wrennal and Forbes (2002), and Dreuth and Dreuth-Fewell (2002) have appeared. However, Tennant's words still ring true: 'research in understanding learning in the workplace is still in its infancy' (Boud and Garrick, 1999: 177).

Empirical research findings from Alverno College (US)

An important longitudinal study undertaken by staff of Alverno College, Milwaukee, US on 'learning that lasts' includes evidence gathered from their off-campus experiential learning (OCEL) programme of the importance of OCEL for the reinforcement of learning (Mentkowski et al., 2000). OCEL is very similar in concept to the definition used in this chapter for WBL for UK full-time undergraduates. Alverno is famous for its abilities-based curriculum – a distinctive approach to curriculum design whereby students, irrespective of their academic discipline, and alongside that discipline, develop competence in eight abilities: communication, analysis, problem solving, valuing in decision making, social interaction, developing a global perspective, effective citizenship, and aesthetic engagement. The College has undertaken research over a 25-year period into the lasting nature of an abilities-based education and their study shows how this education is retained and reinforced through work. A key Alverno educational assumption is that 'education goes beyond knowing to being able to do what one knows' (Mentkowski et al., 2000: 57) and, therefore, all Alverno students have to complete an OCEL requirement as an integral part of their degree studies. The understanding that learning is a holistic process and one best achieved through collaboration is also key to the Alverno philosophy.

In the Alverno view, learning is best understood as integrative and experiential, characterised by self-awareness, as being active and interactive, developmental and transferable with learning processes built around these assumptions (ibid.: 61). This would appear to go some way towards explaining the 'how' of WBL from the Alverno perspective, in that it is part of a broader educational process that combines College-based study with off-campus experiential learning. However, the distinctive Alverno philosophy is clear that experiential learning is as relevant to on-campus as to off-campus learning in that it is 'a concept and practice that must permeate a college curriculum in a systematic and developmental manner' (ibid.: 8). Again to quote Mentkowski et al.: 'learning involves the whole student: knowing and doing work together in a dialectic whereby each is constantly redefining the other' (ibid.: 8).

The 'how' also points to the significance of collaboration in learning that opens up the opportunity for a 'diversity of voices' (ibid.: 46) and leads to individuals becoming participant researchers through the development of a culture of inquiry. The Alverno researchers discovered that evidence pointed to students not truly understanding the curriculum abilities until in the workplace (ibid.: 103). They also found that the abilities continued to develop after graduation, provided that the graduates were persistent in referring back to the conceptual models that they had learned in College (ibid.: 103).

While evidence from the Alverno empirical research is not conclusive so far as WBL is concerned, there are some important pointers to 'how' people learn, and that 'how' includes the experience of taking knowledge into the workplace and integrating it with the further experience of 'doing' for new learning and new knowledge to occur. This suggests that a distinctive feature of WBL is the integration of knowledge and action as part of the learning process, with new or enhanced knowledge emerging as the product of learning. This, in turn, suggests that, among the conditions under which learning through work occurs, the learner must have access to relevant knowledge to integrate into the learning through work process. A further condition appears to be that the learner must have developed a spirit of inquiry such that the intention to learn from experience is foregrounded.

Empirical research findings from University College Chester (UK)

The Alverno research identifies, among others, the following key features of the learning process:

- knowledge is retained and reinforced through practical application;
- learning is a holistic process, crucially involving the self-awareness of the learner;
- learning is best achieved through collaboration with others.

These findings are corroborated by recent research carried out by the Centre for Work Related Studies at University College Chester into the student experience of WBL. This involved a structured questionnaire survey of full-time undergraduate students on non-vocational degree programmes on completion of a six-week placement, and semi-structured interviews involving 31 students, the majority of whom were in full-time employment, undertaking WBL at either undergraduate or postgraduate levels.

The importance for learning of the theory/ practice interplay

The idea that knowledge is retained and reinforced through practical application was confirmed by some of the Chester learners when they identified the theory/practice inter-face as an important place for learning. A number of respondents indicated that theory really only made sense to them when informing a practical purpose. A female student on a six-week placement commented:

> I find theories really difficult to remember if I don't see their practical application. On the placement we mixed it in at the same time, the theory behind what we were doing, and they both fitted together; they helped each other. They went hand in hand. You know, 'We are doing this because . . . and you need to do this because . . .'

Thus, effective learning may be best facilitated by a curriculum that presents learners with the opportunity to become involved in the relationship between theory and practice, and not where the two are regarded as being in some way separate from one another. A female postgraduate in full-time employment noted:

I mean sometimes it is just by looking at the whole situation at work, seeing what's going on and then in your mind's eye you've got all this theory and you can see people behaving exactly as you have read about someone's theory or personality or different traits and you can see it exactly coming through in the workplace or outside the workplace. So, it's all a mixture really. It goes across the board. It's more of an unconventional learning in that sense, it's not learning as in a school or college environment, it's more a learning in society such that you feed in one with another and it doesn't necessarily go from the book to the workplace, it could go from the workplace back to the book.

Thus, the model of WBL employed at University College Chester introduces students to theoretical concepts (for example, concepts associated with learning styles, team roles, project management, self management and development, and so on) which they are then asked to reflect on in the light of the practical experience of the workplace. In addition, theories and concepts drawn from academic subject knowledge (full-time undergraduates) and professional knowledge (part-time undergraduates and postgraduates in employment) are similarly reflected on in the context of their application in the workplace. Such engagement of theory and practice almost inevitably results in new knowledge gains for the student, leading to the development and enhancement of their knowledge in their academic or professional areas.

The strength of WBL, and a distinctive feature of it, may then be in its ability to accommodate both theory and practice and, therefore, it may be an effective vehicle for a higher education curriculum that recognises the importance for learning of the theory/practice interplay. The Alverno research, as indicated above, shows that there is something about the integration of knowledge and action that leads to effective learning. Barnett (Boud and Garrick, 1999), from a theoretical perspective, would also appear to support the idea that learning is a complex process and is not complete unless knowing and doing are combined and, in turn, combined with reflective processes.

Learning as an holistic process, engaging both the cognitive and affective domains

More than half of those interviewed as part of the Chester study claimed either that WBL had brought about growth in self-knowledge, or that it had changed their view of themselves, or that it had brought about self-examination. A full-time undergraduate, on completion of her six-week placement, commented: 'One thing I realised during WBL was that you are sort of forced to look at yourself and I've never really done anything like that before.'

Much of this increase in self-awareness is undoubtedly connected with the process of critical reflection, which is a key higher-order critical skill associated with WBL and one which has the power to assist individuals with the process of meaning-making. Others spoke of various ways in which WBL had influenced their lives or impacted on them as human beings. For example, a female student in full-time employment, for whom HE was a new experience, said:

I've grown as a person which I wouldn't have done unless I'd done this course because I've been involved in so many multi-disciplinary groups working together with a

common aim really so it certainly has changed me. . . . Like it's been a huge struggle
I can't deny that but, from a personal point of view, it's been great. In the year
I've learnt so much and, as I said before, I believe in myself and I'm much more
confident now.

If this is the case, then it suggests that WBL is a powerful way of learning that engages
the affective domain as well as the cognitive and has the potential to bring about more
holistic ways of being and knowing than, arguably, is the case through more conventional forms of higher education study. The place of emotions in the learning process is
commented on by Garrick who claims that, according to adult learning theory, 'learning
can be most effective if one's emotions are engaged in the learning process'(Boud and
Garrick, 1999: 220). He points to the role of emotion in learning found in the human-
istic tradition and among those interested in emotional intelligence. If WBL does, indeed,
impact on the affective domain, as claimed by the respondents, then this provides reinforcement to the idea that it is a much more holistic approach to learning and, therefore,
one could argue, better equips people to live and work in the real world.

A note of caution, however, needs to be struck in that some, at least, of the subjects
could be considered to be highly impressionable. Full-time undergraduate students, new
to a form of experiential learning conducted in the workplace, frequently undergo a steep
learning curve during the course of the six weeks of the placement which makes quite
an impression on them. Usually, learning in this way is an entirely new experience for
them and the experience of change (from the lecture room to the workplace) can be
stimulating, exciting and invigorating. My past experience of talking with students during
and shortly after their placements is that, typically, they:

- are full of enthusiasm for what they have been doing;
- have had, in many cases, an entirely new experience (even those students who have
  worked throughout their degree studies express their excitement at being able to
  experience work in a profession of their choosing, as do mature students with a
  record of employment);
- have often had the opportunity to apply their learning to a task for an employer.

All of this can have quite an impact and create the impression of having had a unique
experience.

Another group of students, on whom WBL appeared to make a considerable impression, consisted of a number of people in full-time employment who had not expected to
ever engage in HE level study (from the university perspective, this is a reminder of the
potential of WBL as an agent of widening participation). For them, an unanticipated
opportunity had opened up. Their discovery, that not only were they able to cope with
this level of study but that some of their professional competences were actually recognised as equating with higher education level learning, proved to be highly motivational.
Therefore, it is, perhaps, not surprising that a typical response was that WBL had impacted
on them hugely and in a very positive way in that they now valued themselves more
highly and recognised their capabilities and their contribution in the workplace.

For both of these groups, what I shall refer to as the 'novel factor' of WBL should
not be underestimated or ignored. However, the evidence of the interviews also suggests

that even some of those not falling into either of the above categories recognised something of the impact of WBL on them in terms of changed self-understanding and improved motivation. It may, therefore, be the case that, while the novel factor may play a part in the impact on the individual of the experience of WBL, it does not explain it in its entirety and there are other factors involved. It is my contention that these other factors are concerned with the distinctive features of WBL that cause the learner to engage in a wide variety of ways of learning within the context of a community of practice.

The importance of collaboration for effective learning

As a result of changes to the work structures and patterns of many businesses and organisations, with a tendency towards flatter hierarchies, team approaches, group tasks and the emergent notion of the learning organisation, work almost inevitably involves people in various forms of collaboration and engages them in interpersonal relationships in a variety of ways. The evidence from the Chester research seems to suggest that most students recognise this and the opportunities it presents for learning in community and not in isolation. Thus, they acknowledge that learning through work involves an awareness of interdependency, mutuality and collaboration, giving WBL a strong relational dimension. This raises issues for higher education, not least in terms of the way in which assessment of learning is undertaken. It also contrasts quite starkly with the conventional culture of learning in higher education with its emphasis on individualism and personal achievement.

The significance of the evidence, however, should not be over-stated, nor should the differences between WBL and conventional higher education be polarised. There is no reason, for example, why much learning on the university campus cannot be undertaken using more collaborative methods (many university departments now like to refer to themselves as learning communities) and sometimes learning in the workplace may be best achieved through lone activity, such as reading a book or writing an article. However, it remains the case that a distinctive feature of WBL is that, typically, it occurs within a community of practice, which itself facilitates much of the learning that occurs and, therefore, places emphasis on the notion of relational learning. Any form of collaborative learning implies that there are two principal forms of learning occurring simultaneously: that is, (1) learning about the topic or subject under consideration, and (2) learning about the others who are engaged in learning with you which, in turn, almost inevitably leads to more self-learning.

Critical reflection as a key capability in WBL

Reference has already been made to the key role of critical reflection in WBL and so it seems appropriate to comment on the evidence of the Chester qualitative research in this regard. The evidence suggests that, through critical reflection, change has been brought about for individuals in respect of their views and attitudes towards themselves, their work and their worlds. A female student in full-time employment, and studying at postgraduate level comments:

I think I can see clearer. I think I saw things before but I tend to see the whole picture of what's going on, of the whole organisation, and not just from my one perspective.

And a female in full-time employment studying at undergraduate level notes:

I also try to see things from other perspectives and I don't just believe what is reported in the newspapers or on the television. I try to sit back and think and reflect and I try to consider other people's beliefs and consider what drives them to do the things that they do.

Whereas critical thinking has always been highly prized in higher education, critical reflection has been less so. Critical thinking implies a degree of detachment and objectivity in relation to the object of (conceptual) thought, whereas critical reflection has a strong subjective element that, of course, may account for its more cautious treatment in the academic world. Critical reflection seems to me to carry with it the weight of critical thinking but brings the self into the equation. Thus, in critical reflection there is an attempt to examine the implications for the self (and, therefore, to make (construct) or to remake (reconstruct) meaning for oneself) in relation to whatever it is that is under critical scrutiny. Critically reflective capabilities are shown to be crucial to Barnett's (1997) view of higher education when he identifies three key features of the 'critical being' which, he argues, is the responsibility of higher education to produce: namely, critical reasoning, critical self-reflection and critical action. Barnett's argument is that a university education should enable an undergraduate to go beyond the capability of critical reasoning (which a conventional university education has provided for and should continue to provide for), to engage in critical self-reflection (leading to a reappraisal of beliefs and values), and to promote engagement in critical action in the world (such as might be expected from a responsible citizen). I have attempted to make the case elsewhere (Major, 2002) for WBL as a form of higher education that has the capability to produce the 'critical being' that Barnett argues should be synonymous with the concept of graduateness.

Critical reflection is the key capability of the reflective practitioner, is at the heart of the model of praxis espoused in liberation thinking, and is considered by some to be a key aspect of WBL methodology. However, critical reflection is not necessarily an intuitive process. It is one that people have to learn, especially if they are to achieve a depth of reflection acceptable to higher education. Thus, those responsible for delivering programmes of WBL must also be charged with the responsibility for facilitating the development of students' critically reflective capabilities. That critical reflection is a capability that develops through learning and experience is implied by one of the Chester postgraduate respondents who noticed that her peers, who had undertaken WBL previously, possessed a greater understanding and insight than she did concerning learning in the workplace. Similarly, two other postgraduate students, who had undertaken WBL as part of their undergraduate studies, noted their own development in their ability to critically reflect, suggesting that, to some extent, it is a learned process.

Understanding the learning process/learning to learn through WBL

Learning how to learn requires an understanding of the learning process and the evidence from the Chester research suggests that students, through WBL, gain a better understanding of how they learn than they may do through more conventional forms of learning. In WBL, students are required to accept a considerable degree of responsibility for their own learning and this gives them greater freedom to determine how they are going to learn. The research confirms that there is a wide variety of ways in which people may learn through work. In interview some students tended, if anything, to emphasise practical learning over theoretical, though respondents generally took a balanced view, recognising that different learning needs required different approaches. In analysing student responses to a question concerned to elicit something of the various ways in which people learn, six categories emerge:

- experiential learning
- conventional learning
- instructional learning
- reflective learning
- relational learning
- other ways of learning.

The question was not in any sense meant to be about the physiological workings of the brain or to engage in any form of psychological study but simply an attempt to find out about people's learning preferences and how, when free from the constraints of a more controlled learning environment (such as the university or college), they went about their learning. It was more to do with methods of learning and the idea that, through WBL, people probably engaged in a wider variety of ways of learning than they would in a more conventional form of higher education.

It seems reasonable to assume from the information given by the respondents that, when free to do so, the way in which individuals go about learning is inclined to match their preferred learning style. It also seems reasonable to assume, though the survey did not attempt to deal with this, that access to a broad range of learning styles has the potential to lead to more holistic ways of understanding learning and, thus, has the potential to lead to the capability of learning to learn. The evidence does support the view that, whatever else students learn through WBL, they also learn about themselves. This inevitably means that at least an element of emotional learning is brought into the equation. Arguably, it is self-learning that gives rise to an understanding of how one learns which, in turn, leads to a greater awareness and understanding of the process of learning itself or of learning to learn.

If this is the case, then WBL is consistent with Carl Rogers' (1983) holistic philosophy of learning with its emphasis on people's understanding of how they learn rather than what they learn. This is a sophisticated process and one that many learners, I suspect, may never contemplate. It is a process that a conventional university education may not require one to consider. The difficulty some of the respondents had initially in engaging with a question that asked them 'how' they learn suggests they may never have been asked that question before. The fact that most were able to engage with it to some degree, having thought about it in the context of WBL, suggests to me that having greater responsibility for their own learning, together with experiencing a broader range of ways of learning, better equips people to understand something of the learning process

Summary

In this chapter I have attempted to show that effective learning, in my view, is essentially a holistic process that integrates knowing and doing in a critically reflective way and, moreover, that WBL is a sound facilitator of learning of this quality. I have tried to say something about *how* people learn through WBL (emphasising the theory/ practice interplay, the role of critical reflection, and the importance of collaborative learning), pointing to what I consider to be its *distinctive features* (including the integration of knowledge and action as part of the learning process, the foregrounding of learning about the self, the importance of accepting responsibility for one's own learning, and the experience of learning in more holistic ways) and the *conditions* under which such learning occurs (including being part of a community of practice, being exposed to a wide variety of ways of learning, and being prepared to regard work as the curriculum). Through conversations with those engaged in WBL, it has become clear to me that they appear to be more conscious of, and have a much better understanding of, the learning process than might be brought about through more conventional forms of learning. They appear to learn more about learning and develop the capacity of learning to learn. I have argued that this comes about, partly at least, as a result of the greater responsibility for their own learning that WBL places on the learners and that this, together with critical reflection as a key capability, leads to them developing a greater understanding as to how learning occurs. Boud and Symes may well be right when they say that, where work is the curriculum, as it is in programmes of WBL, this provides 'a radically new approach to what constitutes university study' (Symes and McIntyre, 2000: 14). Radical though it may be, I hope to have shown that there are sound educational reasons why the university should fully embrace WBL and accept it as a legitimate contributor to the higher education curriculum.

References

Barnett, R. (1997) *Higher Education: A Critical Business*, Society for Research into Higher Education/Open University Press, Buckingham.
Barnett, R. (1999) 'Learning to Work and Working to Learn', in Boud, D. and Garrick, J. (eds) *Understanding Learning at Work*, Routledge, London.
Boud, D. and Garrick, J. (eds) (1999) *Understanding Learning at Work*, Routledge, London.
Boud, D. and Symes, D. (2000) 'Learning for Real: Work Based Education in Universities', in Symes, D. and McIntyre, J. (eds) *Working Knowledge: The New Vocationalism and Higher Education*, Society for Research into Higher Education/ Open University Press, Buckingham.

Boud, D. and Solomon, N. (eds) (2001) *Work-Based Learning: A New Higher Education?*, Society for Research into Higher Education/Open University Press, Buckingham.

Dreuth, L. and Dreuth-Fewell, M. (2002) 'A Model of Student Learning in Community Service Field Placements: Voices from the Field', *Active Learning in Higher Education*, 3, 3, 251–264.

Garrick, J. (1998) *Informal Learning in the Workplace*, Routledge, London.

Garrick, J. (1999) 'The Dominant Discourses of Learning at Work', in Boud, D. and Garrick, J. (eds) *Understanding Learning at Work*, Routledge, London.

Major, D. (2002) 'A More Holistic Form of Higher Education: the Real Potential of Work-Based Learning', in *Widening Participation and Lifelong Learning, the Journal of the Institute for Access Studies and the European Access Network*, 4, 3, 26–34.

Mentkowski, M. and Associates (2000) *Learning that Lasts*, Jossey-Bass, San Francisco.

Rogers, C. (1983) *Freedom to Learn*, Charles E. Merrill, New York.

Symes, D. and McIntyre, J. (eds) (2000) *Working Knowledge: The New Vocationalism and Higher Education*, Society for Research into Higher Education/Open University Press, Buckingham.

Tennant, M. (1999) 'Is Learning Transferable?', in Boud, D. and Garrick, J. (eds) *Understanding Learning at Work*, Routledge, London.

Wrennall, M. and Forbes, D. (2002) 'I Have Learned that Psychology is Linked to Almost Everything We Do', *Psychology Teaching Review*, 10, 1, 90–101.

3

Interactive teaching and learning: exploring and reflecting on practice

Annie Huntington

Introduction

This chapter focuses on interactive approaches to learning and teaching by exploring general issues for practice. I include reference to theory and explore examples from my own practice – I have worked (full time and part time) in diverse educational settings (including Further Education, Higher Education, Adult Education and Prison Education) with many different student groups. These examples will hopefully engage you, the reader, in an encounter with me, the writer, as I present and consider issues in a transparent and, hopefully, non-prescriptive way. Focusing on the how (methods) as well as the what (subject-specific content) has been integral to my development since I first began providing learning opportunities in 1989. Since then I have tried to rise to the challenge of working with colleagues and students in ways that enhance learning, sometimes despite the impact of wider national or organisational agendas that shape the terrain for educational practice. Finally, the chapter contains tasks and practice examples, which I hope you will find useful as you explore the material presented.

Task A: warming up to the topic

Before reading further please consider the following questions:

- How would you define interactive approaches to learning and teaching?
- What beliefs shape your understanding of the educator's role?
- How do your beliefs impact on your use, or not, of interactive approaches?

Introducing interactive approaches

Interactive approaches are not just about the delivery of discrete units of learning – for example, modules or lectures. Interactive approaches to education can be used at any point in a learner's journey from admissions to graduation – for example, group interviews rather than individual interviews for applicants or 'informal' graduations where staff and students generate an event to mark the completion of a course. Further, learning opportunities that might be labelled as interactive fall on a spectrum, which includes:

- techniques – for example, uncompleted handouts which have gaps that students fill in during a lecture, using a quiz in a seminar or asking a supervisee for feedback as to how you are getting on as their supervisor (Gibbs and Habeshaw, 1988);
- methods that are highly interactive and can be used to supplement or replace more traditional learning opportunities such as lectures and seminars – for example, problem-based learning (PBL);
- frameworks for learning that are more or less likely to lead the individual to consider their interactions with material presented, work undertaken, people encountered and their responses to their experiences – for example, reflective practice.

Attempts to generate and integrate interactive experiences within institutions are, for me, reflective of my politics (feminist and socialist), personal experiences (as a white working-class woman of origin undertaking a first degree in the 1980s) and professional socialisation (as a social worker and psychotherapist). These guide my educational practice, which is based on the belief that education should be:

- student-centred (people first);
- strengths-based (focuses and builds on what students already know/can do) and cumulative;
- participatory (involves students as active participants not passive recipients);
- holistic (acknowledge that students, like staff, are thinking *and* feeling social actors);
- respectful of diversity and difference (inclusive).

Interactive approaches provide opportunities for innovative, creative and potentially liberating educational encounters (for learners and educators) but they may also generate fear and resistance – for example, if power shifts or when staff and students need to re-think their roles and relationships. Further, there may be local institutional blocks to integrating interactive approaches (e.g. colleagues' scepticism or negativity) or wider institutional hurdles to negotiate (e.g. accessing rooms that can be used for group work rather than lectures). Interactive approaches are not a panacea and staff, as well as students, may have negative as well as positive experiences in practice. Planning, preparation and peer support are likely to minimise the potential for the latter but there are no insurance policies. Part of the power and beauty of interactive approaches is the endless kaleidoscope of possibilities in practice. Yet, the inevitable uncertainty generated when we move away from more traditional approaches (e.g. the lecture where you talk and students listen until the last few minutes when they might ask questions) can also block individual or collective attempts to change delivery of learning opportunities.

Using interactive approaches: some concerns about practice

There are many agendas that may impact on the extent to which we can integrate inter-active approaches in practice. The following is neither definitive nor exhaustive but, rather, offers an exploration of issues I have engaged with, and continue to explore, in my practice. These echo and reflect research and theorising for practice (e.g. see Gibbs, 1994) while recognising the importance of both material and cultural concerns when considering the use of interactive approaches in education.

National and organisational priorities

Change in education is inevitable as institutions invent and reinvent themselves over time and space (Ketteridge *et al.*, 2002). However, the pace, scope and impact of change is likely to vary – for example, within different types of educational institution. International factors (e.g. globalisation) shape national priorities (Middlehurst, 2002) and national priorities (for example widening participation) shape local practice (Cuthbert, 2002). Knowledge-based economies lead to changing expectations as evidenced by the rela-tively recent focus on the importance of 'learning to learn' so that people are equipped with the capacity to be 'lifelong learners' (Middlehurst, 2002). Although it is possible to argue that academics have implicitly been involved in lifelong learning (i.e. they under-take research and produce accounts of projects that consolidate or challenge established thinking), the need to be explicit about this, including with regard to the teaching agenda, is relatively new.

Employability is a key issue for students (Ketteridge *et al.*, 2002b) and, I would argue, for the majority of staff. Therefore, people need to be able to articulate and explicitly demonstrate that they have embraced (complied with) particular agendas. This is as true for educationalists (at least in some institutions) as it is many other occupational groups. For example, staff need to consider the impact of continuing professional development to ensure 'career long competence' (Pennington and Smith, 2002) and may be encouraged (in some instances required) to gain teaching qualifications. As academic staff (to vary-ing degrees) have been encouraged (directed) to improve the quality of teaching they have also had to absorb the impact of other changes (e.g. increasing workloads, changed terms and conditions of service, changing demands from students who have increasingly diverse needs and expectations).

The creation of the HE Academy in the UK and other initiatives like the Centres for Excellence in Teaching and Learning suggest a focus on method rather than content (academics should already be subject specialists). Innovation in learning and teaching is driven by different and what seem, at times, like competing and contradictory agendas. In the process new 'liberty' as well as new 'discipline' (Cuthbert, 2002) has been created. However, for many the capacity to see the opportunities offered may be limited by the anxiety, fear and even anger generated by recent changes to their working environments and lives. Alternatively some staff or some departments may see such agendas as irrele-vant since research is the dominant interest and marker of success within their institution. Engaging with debates about methods, then, may hold little or no interest for some.

Academic identities vary significantly (Ketteridge *et al.*, 2002) and the extent to which individuals, members of particular disciplines or institutions consider the how (rather than the 'what' of education) will vary markedly, as will the rewards (intrinsic and extrinsic) for doing so.

Sharing theory for interactive practice

Students, like staff, don't belong to a homogeneous group with shared histories, expectations or abilities. Approaches to learning and the extent to which any particular student or group of students positively responds to particular educational experiences and opportunities will vary (it is inevitable). Sharing theories and models with students, as part of the introduction of interactive approaches, can be very useful as it facilitates the development of a shared sense of meaning and purpose. Otherwise students, particularly but not exclusively those who are used to more didactic approaches, may not understand why they are being asked to engage in activities that are alien to them. There is a range of material that can be usefully interrogated with students to inform our use, and their experience, of interactive approaches. For example, Honey and Mumford's (1992) manual of learning styles delineates four types: activist, reflector, theorist and pragmatist. Although criticisms can be made (e.g. it is restricted typology of human experience and/or people may draw on different learning styles to match circumstances), it is useful to share the typology with students. For example, it can act as a stimulus to discussion focused on their previous learning experiences and identification (for themselves) of preferred approaches to learning, which may then inform their responses to the integration of interactive approaches.

Practice example 1

The course: teaching a 40 credit module (focused on working with children and their families) to a 2nd year group of 55 social work students in 2002 (including those following DipHE/BA/MA programmes as it was an integrated award).

This incorporated workshops (using material prepared by each workshop facilitator), self-directed study groups and whole group study seminars (both using material prepared by the module leader). Developing the capacity to work well with others (teamwork) is central to good social work practice. Integrating self-directed study groups into the module offered students an opportunity to work together with their peers without a member of staff.

It began with an interactive first day, which included exploration of a range of theories for practice that students might find useful as they engaged with the module team, the material presented and each other. The rationale for the module structure and format was presented (focusing on 'learning to learn', 'working together' and 'affective and cognitive competence') then a range of interactive techniques was used to enable students to 'get to know each other' (particularly important as they had limited opportunities to do so in the first year as the cohort included in excess of 200 students) followed by the exploration of theory for practice (e.g. transactional analysis, as a model of interpersonal communication). Students then spent time in their self-directed study groups negotiating their ground rules and undertaking their first self-directed tasks before concluding the day with a question and answer session, which focused on their experiences and the theories presented.

In subsequent sessions students might refer to, or be referred to, theories explored on the first day when discussing process issues (e.g. problems in their self-directed study groups). Further, they were exploring (in action) theories that are integral to social work practice (e.g. with regard to interpersonal communication and group functioning).

Student evaluation, both formative (midway through the module) and summative (at the end of the module) was mixed (probably unsurprisingly) with some students identifying aspects that indicated deep learning had occurred and others identifying problems (e.g. linked to self-directed groupwork) that they believed had negatively impacted on their learning experience and module outcomes.

This module embodied principles and values associated with interactive approaches to learning, which informed the sharing of theory for practice with students. However, this alone was clearly not sufficient to ensure a positive experience for students who were asked to engage in self-directed group work. Although social work students often understand the importance of 'working together' at a cognitive level (particularly after they have completed a practice placement as these students had) they may struggle to put their understanding into practice when engaged in 'real world' encounters with their peers.

Ethical concerns

Exploring the ethics of educational practice is of increasing interest as writers (e.g. MacFarlane, 2002) identify ethical dilemmas and, at least in some nation states, educators attempt to articulate ethical principles for university teaching (e.g. Canadian Society for Teaching and Learning in Higher Education). As MacFarlane highlights, discussion of ethics within the academy has largely focused on concerns about academic freedom, tenure decisions in US universities, interpersonal abuse (e.g. sexual harassment), organisational abuse (e.g. equipment theft) and research related matters (e.g. misuse of research funds), while ethical issues associated with the 'day to day dilemmas associated with managing student learning' (MacFarlane, 2002: 169) have largely been ignored. The notion of 'pedagogical competence' is important when considering ethical aspects of the use of interactive approaches as identified in the Canadian code of ethics: 'A pedagogically competent teacher . . . is aware of alternative instructional methods or strategies, and selects methods of instruction that, according to research evidence (including personal and self-reflective research), are effective in helping students to achieve course objectives' (Society for Teaching and Learning in Higher Education, 1996).

The use of interactive approaches needs to enhance student learning. Understanding the operation of power and the effects of power is necessary if staff are to ensure their interventions are likely to lead to more, not less, empowering educational experiences for students (and arguably themselves). Knowledge and understanding, like insight, don't necessarily shape, or change, behaviour. Those who hold 'power-saturated' roles, as academics do, need to routinely and critically reflect on their own performance (paying particular attention to ethical aspects) if they are committed to the creation of positive learning environments and optimal learning outcomes for students: 'Peter Drucker famously differentiated efficiency – doing things right – from effectiveness – doing the right thing. When in doubt, the effective academic needs to do the right thing' (Cuthbert, 2002: 47).

Interactive approaches, particularly but not exclusively specific methods (e.g. problem-based learning), can be perceived and received in many different ways by staff and students alike. Just as psychologists need to consider the ethics of particular experiments (particularly in the light of trenchant critics of research that treated people as passive objects rather than active subjects) so, too, educators need to consider the ethics of using particular techniques or exercises with individuals or groups. For example, exercises that result in the generation of conflict in groups (e.g. as part of management training) may be used to focus participants' attention on important processes but can be damaging to self esteem or people's perceptions of themselves or others. Scapegoats are easily created in groups as they hold the 'shadow dimensions which are unacceptable to its image of itself' (White, 2002: 120). Educators need to be cognisant of this and ensure that inter-active experiences are respectful, life affirming encounters that are unlikely to result in harm to participants (physical, emotional or psychological).

Embedding a focus on ethical issues is important as changes are made, implemented and evaluated into courses or, in some instances, departments. Although there is limited material that addresses ethical issues for educators there is a wealth of material that can be adopted and adapted from other professional domains. For example, Bond's 6-step model for ethical problem solving (for counsellors and psychotherapists) could be explored and applied (Bond, 2000).

Technical matters: the importance of process and task

Managing the self when in contact with 'another', or 'others', is interesting, rewarding and challenging work. Managing interactions in groups is more complex as there are many different layers to communication, interaction and action. Those with responsibility for facilitating the work of educational groups will need to be technically competent and emotionally robust. Using interactive approaches in education often brings us into more direct and immediate contact with learners, albeit to varying degrees (e.g. depending on the setting or subject). Whatever style a facilitator adopts (e.g. democratic or autocratic) they have two main tasks: ensuring group cohesion is developed and maintained and ensuring the group successfully completes their task(s) (Jaques, 2000). Consequently, group facilitators must focus on 'what' (task) and 'how' (process).

Emotions and emotional labour

Using interactive approaches inevitably engages educators and learners alike as thinking and, importantly, feeling subjects in relationship with other thinking, feeling subjects. Within the academy the focus is usually on cognition not affect as students, and staff, are expected to think, argue and judge between competing claims. However, using inter-active approaches often generates emotional heat as they offer greater opportunities (to

---

Task B: an example

What factors might you need to consider if you were thinking about integrating small group work (defined as focused activity with clearly identified learning outcomes using a range of stimulus material and group tasks, and not traditional seminars) into a module?

Having thought about the question, you might have identified:

● Resource issues – for example, room size or seating arrangements.
● Course material – what will be used? How will this enable student learning to achieve module outcomes?
● Group composition – how will groups be organised (e.g. if you are splitting a large group into a number of smaller ones)?
● Group facilitation – what role(s) will you have? What facilitation style do you adopt?
● Group norms – how will the group set and manage 'ground rules'?
● Module assessment – how will work associated with the module be assessed?
● Module evaluation – when and how will students assess their learning experiences?

As before, the early explicit exploration of theory for practice with students can be useful as it creates analytic distance and grounds their experiences (see Chapter 6 for another perspective on this).

---

varying degrees) for debate, discussion and interaction. Increasing use of interactive approaches often results in more immediate and, at times, emotionally charged, encounters, which staff need the skills and confidence to manage. This is unsurprising if we, for example, consider:

● the emotional nature of some subject matter (e.g. child abuse);
● the emotional nature of being a learner (often linked to previous experiences);
● the traps or games (e.g. 'ain't it awful', where people sit round reinforcing each others' sense of powerlessness) that groups can fall into as Hawkins and Shohet (1989) identify when exploring peer supervision in the helping professions;
● the roles that students may take or be given particularly, but not exclusively, in small groups (e.g. the 'joker', the 'know it all' or the 'scapegoat');
● the roles staff may take or be given (e.g. the 'father' or 'mother').

Managing the self while using interactive approaches can be hard work. Using interactive approaches requires emotional intelligence (Mortiboys, 2002). This term has come into popular usage since Daniel Goleman's book in 1995 (and it is mentioned in several other chapters in this book). Further, there is overlap with the more established term 'emotional literacy' as defined by Claude Steiner. Debate about definitions abounds as do texts to facilitate the development of emotional intelligence in learners of all ages. For the purposes of this chapter I am adopting Mortiboys' definition, which relates the

Practice example 2: small group work

Providing an experiential group-based certificate course for staff employed to work with people who misuse substances included exploration of Belbin's (1993) work on team roles. People have different strengths and learners, like workers, usefully identified dominant roles in their repertoire before exploring the range of roles represented in the learning group. Exploration of differing aspects of roles and possible 'missing roles' led to useful consideration of group dynamics every time we offered this course. As an example, one group realised they had no 'completer/ finishers' in their midst. Consideration of the potential implications for group functioning usefully led into a discussion of team functioning in their work settings and the explicit use of theory to try to understand their experiences in the learning group.

Focusing on process issues might also lead to identification of particular concerns, which may need more active management when using interactive approaches. For example, an explicit focus on conflict in groups can help participants understand that this is a normal aspect of human interaction (Fewell and Wolfe, 1991), which needs to be managed not ignored if people are to work together productively. One place to start is Tuckman's (1965) original 4-stage model (forming, norming, storming, performing) of group functioning, which has been subsequently amended to incorporate two additional stages (adjourning and mourning). This offers a general model of group development that can be usefully explored with group members. For another example, Nelson Jones (1990) articulates a useful 5-step systematic approach to managing conflict in groups that might be shared and used by students and staff. The model (CUDSA) focuses on: confronting the issue; understanding each person's position; defining the problem; seeking a solution and taking action.

Effective management of process issues is important as it will have an impact on the extent to which any group achieves the tasks set. Drawing on established theories for practice can provide the new and the experienced group facilitator with:

- models to inform the planning and delivery of interactive learning experiences;
- routes to normalise student and staff experiences.

See Chapter 6 for further discussion of group work with students.

term emotional intelligence to the capacity to recognise and manage emotions in oneself and in others.

The development of such emotional intelligence involves more than just exploration of theory. Considering the emotional labour involved when using interactive approaches is important if staff are to feel competent in their role and students are to have positive educational experiences. Although this may be more apparent in some subjects than others, the potential is apparent in any subject area as the focus is on process as well as content. However, the extent to which a focus on emotions is legitimated is likely to vary between institutions, departments and individuals.

Staff support

This leads me to consider the need for staff support when people engage with the learning and teaching agenda and begin to explore and develop their use of interactive approaches. Developing and sustaining staff 'confidence and competence' (Pennington and Smith, 2002: 264) needs to be an institutional priority as staff are any organisation's most valuable resource. This means institutions must invest resources into formal and informal internal support systems for staff (e.g. mentoring or peer discussion groups). This is true (at least as far as this writer is concerned) generally but is very important if (when) staff begin to experiment and hopefully extend their use of interactive approaches. The form, content and availability of staff support may vary (as may individual staff needs) but the availability of such should be a constant.

What do learners want?

Shorrock (2002: 61) asked students what they believed to be the characteristics of an effective academic. He compiled a list that included a number of variables (e.g. the lecturer listens). Having thought about his list it seems to me that students want academics to be reliable, constructive, responsive'and creative people. Positive communication and the capacity to take other people's perspectives and experiences into account are also important. Emotionally competent, subject specialists who understand the theoretical foundations of differing approaches to learning, who can draw on a range of teaching methods and use techniques in creative ways, would seem more likely to be judged as 'effective' by students than not. Educators interested in providing student centred education need to focus on process (how) as well.as product (what), which clearly includes consideration of interactive approaches.

Concluding comments

Educators, like managers, mediate between the needs of the individual, the task and the organisation. Individual learners have diverse needs and expectations. The changing educational landscape fundamentally affects the nature of the task as staff are encouraged to respond to diverse agendas (e.g. widening participation and enhancing retention rates) while managing the complex demands of the educator's role in the 'greedy university' (Gold, 2002: 95). Organisations have differing priorities and place the emphasis in different places but all, in recent history and to varying extents, expect staff to be research-active, efficient academic administrators, competent (in some instances gifted) educators and, in a number of institutions, active academic entrepreneurs. However, the rewards for focusing on teaching are, in many institutions, limited. As Ketteridge et al. identify, career progression for academic staff often 'relates more to research output than educational or pedagogic knowledge' (2002a: 277). This is despite the increasing emphasis on learning and teaching, the investment of significant resources at the national and local level, and changing institutional expectations within diverse educational establishments.

Ultimately, education needs to enable students to gain knowledge, skills and (where appropriate) values (to ensure they are fit for practice) associated with their discipline.

While not wishing to create new experts, with a monopoly on knowledge for education practice, I think careful consideration of one's own capacity and competence is required if we are to be assured that use of interactive approaches are appropriate, ethical and likely to enhance student outcomes. As educators seek to engage students in their own learning journeys, they inevitably experiment with new, or re-discovered, ways to work with students while exploring subject-specific material. However, many members of staff have neither training in, nor experience of, new approaches and methods prior to experimenting with them in practice. Further, many have limited support as they do so. This raises interesting issues that need to be identified and explored if staff are to feel confident in their adoption of interactive approaches and students are to receive positive educational experiences.

Experts are, unsurprisingly, plentiful in the academy and writing about aspects of practice usually implies we are some sort of expert. Although I, no more than you, cannot avoid these agendas I hope that this exploration has offered an open account of some of the issues I think it important to explore if we are interested in developing and embedding interactive approaches in education.

Task C

Finally, you might want to take time to reflect on the material presented in this chapter through exploration of the following questions. I acknowledge there may be others you have generated for yourself but hope these may be useful to you.

If you have not used interactive approaches but are interested in beginning to experiment think about:

- what support you need to do so;
- potential blocks to use;
- possible routes to overcome any blocks identified.

If you are a regular/well-established user think about:

- how you review your use (if you do);
- positive aspects of your use;
- areas of practice that have been difficult and/or you want to develop further.

Then (if appropriate for you) consider whether there is any action you want to take to introduce or improve your use of interactive approaches. Make notes for yourself and set a date to review these.

References

Belbin, M. (1993) *Team Roles at Work*. Heinemann, London.
Bond, T. (2000) Codes of Ethics and Practice, in Feltham, C. and Horton, I. (eds) *Handbook of Counselling and Psychotherapy*. Sage, London.

Cuthbert, R. (2002) The Impact of National Developments on Institutional Practice, in Ketteridge, S., Marshall, S. and Fry, H. (eds) *The Effective Academic: A Handbook for Enhanced Academic Practice*. Kogan Page, London.

Fewell, J. and Wolfe, R. (1991) *Groupwork Skills. An Introduction.* Health Education Board, Scotland.

Gibbs, G. (1994) *Improving Student Learning. Theory and Practice.* The Oxford Centre for Staff Development, Oxford.

Gibbs, G. and Habeshaw, T. (1988) *253 Ideas For Your Teaching.* Technical and Educational Services Limited, Bristol.

Gold, A. (2002) The Ethical Manager: Working With and Through Colleagues, in Ketteridge, S., Marshall, S. and Fry, H. (eds) *The Effective Academic: A Handbook for Enhanced Academic Practice*. Kogan Page, London.

Hawkins, P. and Shohet, R. (1989) *Supervision in the Helping Professions*. Open University Press, Milton Keynes.

Honey, P. and Mumford, A. (1992) *The Manual of Learning Styles*, 3rd edn. Peter Honey Publications, Maidenhead.

Jaques, D. (2000) *Learning in Groups*, 3rd edn. Kogan Page, London.

Ketteridge, S., Marshall, S. and Fry, H. (2002a) Making Choices: Routes to Success, in Ketteridge, S. Marshall, S. and Fry, H. (eds) *The Effective Academic: A Handbook for Enhanced Academic Practice*. Kogan Page, London.

Ketteridge, S., Marshall, S., Fry, H. with Watson, D. (2002b) Introduction to the Turbulent Environment, in Ketteridge, S., Marshall, S. and Fry, H. (eds) *The Effective Academic: A Handbook for Enhanced Academic Practice*. Kogan Page, London.

MacFarlane, B. (2002) Dealing with Dave's Dilemmas: Exploring the Ethics of Pedagogic Practice. *Teaching in Higher Education*, 7(2), pp. 167–178.

Middlehurst, R. (2002) The International Context for UK Higher Education, in Ketteridge, S., Marshall, S. and Fry, H. (eds) *The Effective Academic: A Handbook for Enhanced Academic Practice*. Kogan Page, London.

Mortiboys, A. (2002) *The Emotionally Intelligent Lecturer*. Staff Educational Development Association, Birmingham.

Nelson Jones, R. (1990) *Human Relationship Skills*. Cassell Education, London.

Pennington, G. and Smith, B. (2002) Career-Long Competence: Unattainable Ideal or Professional Requirement?, in Ketteridge, S., Marshall, S. and Fry, H. (eds) *The Effective Academic: A Handbook for Enhanced Academic Practice*. Kogan Page, London.

Shorrock, R. (2002) The Student Experience, in Ketteridge, S., Marshall, S. and Fry, H. (eds) *The Effective Academic: A Handbook for Enhanced Academic Practice*. Kogan Page, London.

Society for Teaching and Learning in Higher Education (1996) *Ethical Principles in University Teaching*. Online. Available at: www.umanitoba.ca/academic_support/uts/stlhe/Ethical.htm. Accessed 20 November 2002.

Tuckman, B. (1965) Developmental Sequence in Small Groups. *Psychological Bulletin*, 63, pp. 384–399.

White, L. (2002) *The Action Manual. Techniques for Enlivening Group Process and Individual Counselling*. Published by the author L. White, Toronto, Ontario, Canada. Online. Available at: http://www.lizwhiteinaction.com/manual/index.html. Accessed 11 December 2004.

Part two

Working with students

4

Using concept maps in learning and teaching

Jane Fox and Dot Morrison

Introduction

This chapter explores the potential value and issues associated with the use of concept maps to support learning and teaching, including the use of such maps within an assessment strategy, based on a case study where concept maps were introduced into a pre-registration nursing curriculum. We highlight issues and approaches/action points associated with the use of maps that have generic relevance to a range of subject disciplines. A concept map of the ideas presented within this chapter is provided as a summary and illustration of our approach.

Our interest in the use of concept maps arose initially from ad hoc use of maps within a range of curricula, particularly within Masters and undergraduate Degree level programmes. There was a need to explore complex and multi-faceted ideas and relate these to students' prior learning and work-based practices. The use of concept maps at this time was undertaken in recognition of the emerging literature, which valued this approach in assisting learning. Subsequently, however, we had the opportunity to become involved in the development of a new curriculum at Diploma level. This meant that we could reconsider learning and teaching approaches that could be systematically incorporated into the curriculum as a basis for the development of the students' repertoire of learning styles and tools. A small team was formed with this purpose in mind.

Concept mapping: basic principles

Novak (2001) describes concept maps 'as tools for organising and representing knowledge'. Of course, we can find other examples of 'spatial learning strategies' (All and Havens, 1997), including graphic representational forms such as flow charts, organisational charts (Novak and Gowin, 1984) and mind maps (Buzan, 1995).

Novak and Gowin (1984) distinguish their approach from other graphic representational techniques on the grounds that concept mapping is based on research done to test key ideas in Ausubel's (1968) cognitive learning theory. They identify the following main principles:

- Key ideas are presented in a hierarchy, which moves from the most general idea to the more specific.
- Key ideas are additionally arranged in domains or clusters, which visually define their association and related boundaries.
- The nature of interrelationships between the key ideas are identified through the use of 'relationship lines'. These lines are annotated to clearly indicate the nature of this relationship within discrete sections of the map and between the different domains.
- The lowest point of the hierarchical representation of ideas is illustrated by the use of relevant examples, sometimes known as 'end examples'.

In our work with students, we also suggest the addition of:

- the use of colour and/or symbols, including directional arrows, to further delineate key ideas, their boundaries and relationships/interrelationships;
- the inclusion of essential academic references if necessary;
- the use of a range of shapes to enclose key ideas;
- the use of a 'key' or 'legend' that clearly conveys the meaning of the elements/symbols used.

Reasons for using concept maps

Concept mapping was introduced into our curriculum as a teaching and learning strategy on the basis that it can:

- Facilitate the development of self-directed learning within which conceptual and propositional relationships can be reflectively and critically explored (Novak and Gowin, 1984). The ability to engage in such self-directed learning can arguably serve as a foundation for individuals' engagement in lifelong learning.
- Enhance problem-solving, particularly in the context of the acquisition and sequencing of new information through reflective thinking (All and Havens, 1997; Roth and Roychoudhury, 1992; and Deshler, 1990).
- Facilitate the integration of theory and practice and have value for inclusion within learning/professional portfolios (All and Havens, 1997).
- Aid the development of deep and meaningful learning, moving towards critical thinking rather than more surface approaches (Novak and Gowin, 1984; Daley et al., 1999). Thus, students are helped to 'learn how to learn' rather than simply acquiring role-based knowledge through observing another's practice (All and Havens, 1997). This is a particularly important dimension in the context of vocational or work-based learning.
- Have potential value in assessment during a student's learning journey (Caelli, 1998).

Concept maps have been used in the past in a range of contexts, for example to facilitate the analysis of qualitative data (Northcott, 1996). More commonly, however, concept maps have been discussed in the literature in the context of linking theory to practice, including the practice of nursing and midwifery (Baugh and Mellott, 1998; Beitz, 1998; All and Havens, 1997; Daley, 1996; and Irvine, 1995). Caelli (1998) and Wilkes *et al.* (1999) have explored the use of concept maps for understanding theoretical topics within health science and there is a small emerging body of literature that considers the use of concept maps in the development of transferable learning skills including reflection (Kuit *et al.*, 2001) and that of evaluation or planning (Novak and Gowin, 1984). There is growing interest in their application across a wide range of subject areas and this cross-disciplinary interest was reflected in the first international conference on concept mapping in 2004.

Using concept maps: defining good practice

The case study and evaluations have provided the opportunity for us to reflect upon the principles and emerging good practice in relation to the use of concept maps.

Fostering a shared understanding

While the literature does offer a number of perspectives in relation to concept mapping, it is important in the first instance for both the teaching team and the students to agree a shared definition, possibly as a handout that outlines the principles and subsequent teaching/group approaches.

Guiding the student

Initially it is important to help the student to relate the idea of concept maps to his/her existing understanding of maps used in the general sense (i.e. road or geographic maps). This can be achieved by asking the student to draw a map from an 'x to y location' of their choice. A review of the drawing will inevitably reveal the use of common symbols and directional arrows for example. This can then be compared to published geograph-ical maps, such as atlases and town/street maps. This exercise emphasises the importance of the use of a common or shared language or symbolism in order for the map to have meaning to others and be readily understood and shared. Consequently, the significance of using agreed approaches and symbols in concept mapping in order to aid transparency of meaning become evident.

A second but important step is to agree with the student a concept or question to be explored, which is generic in nature and is therefore a topic that everyone already has some knowledge or understanding of, for example holidays, the weather, etc. We believe it is helpful at this first stage to use a concept that is not part of the student study discipline, as this allows the guiding principles of concept maps to be explored in a neutral way.

The third step is to facilitate early thinking and development of the map through initial 'thought-storming'. In this context, thought-storming refers to the identification of

Case study

Concept mapping was introduced into a Department of Nursing and Midwifery in a Higher Education Institution when a new pre-registration Diploma in Higher Education Nursing course commenced in September 2000 (following the publication of 'Making a Difference', Department of Health, 1999).

Concept maps were introduced in several stages:

Stage 1: introductory session

During the first semester the principles of concept mapping were introduced in a classroom-based session with the opportunity to develop a map by working in small groups supported by the identification of additional resources and reading. Table 4.1 provides an example of a lesson plan to introduce concept maps which illustrates the steps we tend to use.

Table 4.1 Example lesson plan – introduction to concept mapping

Development 1	Introduce session and associated learning outcomes	5 mins Teacher-led
Development 2	Ask students to hand-draw a map showing a friend how to travel from A to B (e.g. home to shops) and to compare map with another student and identify common characteristics	10 mins Group activity
Development 3	Comparison of identified characteristics common to road maps: show published example, e.g. O.S. maps; identify use of symbols, colour, scale, directional arrows, key	10 mins Teacher-led
Development 4	Negotiate topic of map with group, e.g. holiday	2 mins Teacher-led
Development 5	Each student generates a thought-storm relating to chosen topic and compares result with peer	10 mins Student activity
Development 6	Review and discuss Novak's (2001) principles of concept mapping exploring the issue of cluster of ideas and the development of a hierarchy	10 mins Teacher-led
Development 7	Students review their thought-storms to identify clusters and hierarchy of ideas	20 mins Student activity
Development 8	Students work together in groups (no more than 6 per group) to develop a draft concept map, i.e. arrange ideas to show	40 mins Student activity

	clusters and hierarchy. Use of coloured pens, self adhesive notelets and A1 flip chart paper. N.B. Remind to incorporate key, linkages, cross-linkages and annotations along the linkage lines	
Development 9	Display resulting maps to enable students and staff to review	10 mins Student and teacher activity
	Discussion of how principles of mapping have/have not been used	8 mins Teacher-led
Conclusion	Review learning outcomes. Confirm provision of written teacher feedback/ comments. Make link to future assessment. Answer any remaining queries	10 mins Teacher-led

Stage 2: further development

This was followed by a further class-based developmental exercise in which the students worked in small groups to develop a concept map. These were displayed and peer reviewed. The unit teaching team provided written feedback and guidance on each map.

Stage 3: assessment

Then students had to complete an individual formal summative assessment which consisted of a concept map (20%) and supportive discussion paper (1,000 words, worth 80%). The rationale for this was that the construction of the concept map provided a tool to enable the student to develop not just the content of the essay, but to explore interrelationships within the material and encourage the development of critical thinking rather than simply the recall of facts. Attainment across the four groups to date has resulted in few fail grades.

Stage 4: reinforcement through further assessment

During the second semester a concept map and supportive discussion paper again formed the summative assessment.

Stage 5: revisiting the technique

During the third semester concept mapping was revisited in an interactive session to explore its relevance in identifying the theory underpinning practice. It is also a possible strategy for charting the student's professional development and growing appreciation of the richness and complexity of the knowledge underpinning nursing activity, which can be included in their personal professional learning portfolio.

Evaluation

Our evaluations indicate that while students find maps challenging they recognise their value and potential to aid learning. Additionally, following structured input, students are readily able to understand and apply the principles of cognitive maps.

A number of students continue to use concept maps to assist their individual learning, preparation for written assessments and general personal development including presentations, or as a part of a job interview. Students highlight the learning gained in terms of intellectual skills through the use of concept maps.

Our evaluation of the use of concept maps took place through individual written student evaluation by questionnaire (n = 188) and focus groups. A summary of the findings of the questionnaires is given below. For brevity, only data that demonstrates a trend derived from three cohorts at the end of their first semester is presented here.

- A small minority of students had used concept mapping in a formal way before, although some stated that they had used such strategies as 'thought-storming' and 'spidergrams' to aid thinking and learning.
- The majority of students identified concept mapping as challenging.
- The majority of students identified that concept mapping had helped them to identify and explain relevant points considerably or to some extent.
- Only 2 per cent of students stated that they would not consider using concept maps to aid learning in the future and three per cent stated that they had not felt that concept mapping had been helpful in developing their critical thinking skills.

Two focus group discussions were conducted involving 12 students from all years. The discussion generally reaffirmed the positive findings from the questionnaire. The following themes emerged:

- students understood the attributes of a map;
- there was some recognition of the value of maps as an aid to learning;
- there was a perception that particular personal attributes/cognitive styles were needed to use maps;
- students felt the need for periodic reinforcement and review on the principles of mapping;
- students saw value in organizing thought as a basis for group discussion or essay planning;
- concept maps were seen to support critical thinking;
- mapping helped to make links between theory and practice;
- clinical mentors/assessors were acknowledged as a helpful support in the development of concept maps;
- use of IT in the development of concept maps was mentioned as being important.

words/phrases associated with the given concept. This can be done either on an individual or small group basis. These are then recorded on paper in the shape of a 'spider diagram' where the key concept is placed at the centre and all other words/phrases radiate from the centre. Alternatively, the identified words or phrases can be placed on individual self-adhesive notelets (this is a preferred approach as it facilitates the next step more readily) and then arranged as a spider diagram. We would then encourage the students to thought-storm all the associated ideas, issues or aspects of the agreed concept and arrange them into a spider diagram. The spider diagram is then reviewed in order to identify perceived clusters that can be grouped, and redrawing these. This is the first of many redrafting activities that can, in themselves, prove to be a little laborious and perhaps dispiriting, hence use of self adhesive notelets as suggested above helps to minimise this process.

The next stage involves a further review(s) of the diagram(s) produced in order to begin to identify relevant hierarchical relationships and configurations together with the nature of such relationships as a basis for the development of annotated links being drawn on the map.

Clusters are identified and arranged in a meaningful configuration (e.g. horizontally or vertically). The map is redrawn showing the re-ordered hierarchy and the students consider what sort of relationship exists. These relationships are drawn and annotated.

Relevant academic references may be added and the students consider how the hierarchies and relationships can be optimally conveyed to the reader through the use of colour and symbols. These can then be reflected within a key or legend.

It is useful to review the map so far against the relevant literature. Does this alter the clustering, hierarchy or relationships? If it does the students will need to adjust the map accordingly. How can symbols and colour clarify and convey the intended meaning to the reader of the map?

A final map then incorporates all the guiding principles, including the use of end examples (Novak, 2001), and fully reflects the students' thinking about the concept, particularly the way in which elements of the concept are interrelated. Accordingly, the concept is presented in a multi-faceted and complex manner. For example, Figure 4.1 is the concept map we used to prepare this chapter. It also includes references to 'handy hints' that are available on the website.

In a work-based or practice learning setting, the map can be reviewed against at least two significant incidents from the student's work or practice. The student can then consider whether the map presented is fully applicable to the selected incidents or whether further modification is needed. The map and the students' reflections may produce learning that can be incorporated into a work-based/practice learning log or portfolio if appropriate. Finally, students can be invited to reflect upon the process of producing the map.

Conclusion

We believe that, while challenging, the use of concept maps can make an important contribution, not only to students' understanding of a particular topic or concept but, additionally, to providing the student with a strategy by which higher-order learning and cognition can be fostered and incorporated into their learning repertoire. Finally, there

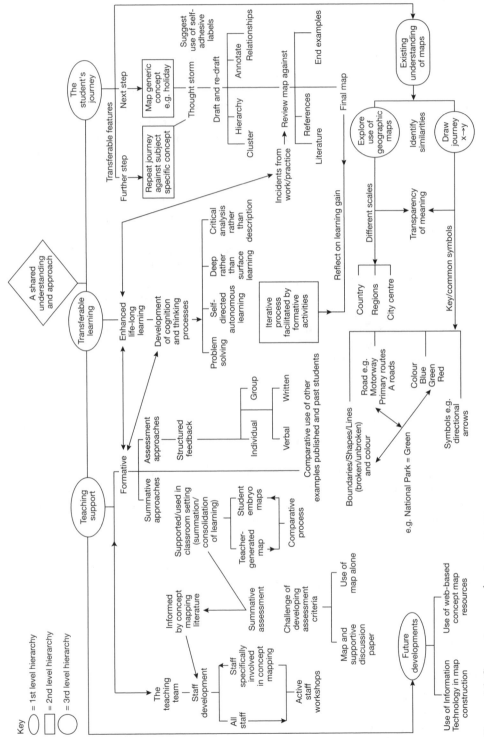

Figure 4.1 Concept map – chapter summary

Key

⬭ = 1st level hierarchy

▭ = 2nd level hierarchy

◯ = 3rd level hierarchy

are, of course, many and diverse opportunities to develop and use concept maps, which include the development of web-based resources and the use of information technology in the construction of maps themselves.

References

All, A. C. and Havens, R. L. (1997) Cognitive/Concept Mapping – A Teaching Strategy for Nursing, *Journal of Advanced Nursing*, 25, 6, 1210–1219.

Ausubel, D. P. (1968) *Educational Psychology: A Cognitive View*. Holt, Rinehart and Winston, New York.

Baugh, N. G. and Mellott, K. G. (1998) Clinical Concept Mapping as Preparation for Student Nurses' Clinical Experiences, *Journal of Nursing Education*, 37, 6, 253–256.

Beitz, J. M. (1998) Concept Mapping: Navigating the Learning Process, *Nurse Educator*, 23, 5, 35–41.

Buzan, T. (1995) *Use Your Head*, BBC Books, London.

Caelli, K. (1998) Shared Understanding: Negotiating the Meanings of Health Via Concept Mapping, *Nurse Education Today*, 18, 317–321.

Daley, B. J. (1996) Concept Mapping: Linking Nursing Theory to Clinical Nursing Practice, *The Journal of Continuing Education in Nursing*, 27, 1, 17–27.

Daley, B. J., Shaw, C. R., Balistrieri, T., Glasenapp, K. and Piacentine, L. (1999) Concept Maps: A Strategy to Teach and Evaluate Critical Thinking, *Journal of Nursing Education*, 38, 1, 42–47.

Department of Health (1999) *Making a Difference*, Department of Health, London.

Deshler, D. (1990) Conceptual Mapping; Drawing Charts of the Mind, in Mezirow, J. and Associates (eds) *Fostering Critical Reflection in Adulthood: A Guide to Transformative and Emancipatory Learning*, Jossey Bass, San Francisco.

Irvine, L. M. C. (1995) Can Concept Mapping Be Used to Promote Meaningful Learning in Nurse Education?, *Journal of Advanced Nursing*, 21, 1175–1179.

Kuit, J. A., Reay, G. and Freeman, R. (2001) Experiences of Reflective Teaching, *Active Learning in Higher Education*, 2, 2, 128–142.

Northcott, N. (1996) Cognitive Mapping: An Approach to Qualitative Data Analysis, *NT Research*, 1, 6, 456–463.

Novak, J. and Gowin, B. (1984) *Learning How to Learn*, Cambridge University Press, New York.

Novak, J. D. (2001) *The Theory Underlying Concept Maps and How to Construct Them*, online, available at: www.cmap.coginst.uwf.edu/info/ (accessed 6 April 2004).

Roth, W. and Roychoudhury, A. (1992) The Social Construction of Scientific Concepts or the Concept Map as Conscription Device and Tool for Social Thinking in High School Science, *Science Education*, 76, 5, 531–557.

Wilkes, L., Cooper, K., Lewin, J. and Batts, J. (1999) Concept Mapping; Promoting Science Learning in BN Learners in Australia, *The Journal of Continuing Education in Nursing*, 30, 1, 37–44.

5

Facilitating tutorials in problem-based learning: students' perspectives

Teena J. Clouston

Introduction

> I know I cannot teach anyone anything, I can only provide an environment in which he can learn.
>
> (Carl Rogers, 1983)

Present drivers for change in the government's agenda for higher education include widening participation, and increasing quality, flexibility and diversity. To enable this, the Dearing Report (NCIHE, 1997) suggested providing an inspiring environment by setting out clear learning outcomes to enable more active, participative students and by encouraging the development of skills necessary for lifelong learning and critical analysis. Although by no means exclusively so, these terms sit well within a problem-based, student-centred approach to learning as both methods are linked philosophically by their shared focus on self-directed study and student empowerment.

This chapter sets out to offer you the opportunity to explore some of the principles and thinking underpinning problem-based and student-centred learning. It also offers you the opportunity to consider facilitation skills and how you might use them, based on the experiences of student participants whose views were collected through questionnaires, focus groups and narratives over a two-year period. I have aimed to represent their views and their voices as credibly as possible, while recognising that my role and my experiences as a problem-based learning facilitator have provided the framework not only for this chapter but for how their voices were heard.

Throughout the chapter the terms tutor or facilitator are used to denote the 'teacher' role while student and learner are used interchangeably.

What is problem-based learning?

Problem-based learning (PBL) has a variety of meanings depending on the individual perspective (Barrows, 1986). For the purpose of this chapter it is defined as a dynamic, integrative concept that engenders a critical, explorative approach and encapsulates a self-directed, active process of learning. It differs from the traditional teaching structure by utilising key 'real-life' problems which are used both as the initial trigger for learning and to create a point at which new learning or critical thinking can be applied and re-applied until understanding is achieved. In this way information is built up over time and understanding is gained in small chunks that eventually form a larger whole. Barrows and Tamblyn (1980: 71) suggest a 'closed loop' or 'reiterative' model as follows:

- identify the objectives for the session;
- interaction with the problem;
- identify the self-study questions raised by the work with the problem;
- self-directed study;
- application of acquired knowledge back to the problem;
- review and synthesise what has been learned;
- evaluation.

This suggests a cyclical or, perhaps more correctly, a spiral, multi-dimensional structure to PBL with an emphasis on developing problem-solving skills and an opportunity to develop self-directed learning. Through this process the student is empowered to make choices about their own learning needs (Haith-Cooper, 2000; Barrows and Tamblyn, 1980). Moreover, by working through the problem-solving process in an integrated and reiterative way, students not only develop critical reasoning skills, but learn how to generalise these to everyday situations they may encounter. As a consequence, the PBL process, in theory, engenders lifelong learning by providing a platform for learning the basic skills necessary to critically reason, problem-solve and learn from future experiences. Therefore, PBL has two main educational objectives as it creates not only a need to explore the knowledge related to the problem, but also the development and application of critical reasoning and problem-solving skills. As such, PBL is a form of learning that expounds learning for understanding rather than recall of content. As students' problem-solving skills develop throughout the PBL process, a more atomistic, superficial approach to learning is generally replaced by a more in-depth one (Cust, 1996). Finally, as PBL tends to take place in small groups, students have to work cooperatively to achieve their collective learning outcomes and, thus, their level of independence is measured by their ability to work cooperatively with others. Consequently, communication skills, collaborative skills and reflective/self evaluation skills can also be developed. In this way, the trigger in PBL can serve as an organising structure for students from various disciplines or professions to develop an understanding of each others' concerns and skills, thus enabling the opportunities to work together and to develop as a team (Barrows and Tamblyn, 1980).

As a result of the structure of the PBL tutorial, both the group dynamics and the individual group members can impact on how the group functions. Thus, the emphasis of both the individual and group cannot be understated. This personal aspect of learning differs substantially from more traditional methods and requires an element of engagement for the learners that may not be necessitated in traditional classroom settings. As a result, students must evidence motivation to learn in this way. Their engagement in the process is integral to a positive and effective learning opportunity and intrinsic motivational factors impact on the learning process in a more profound way than extrinsic methods (Cust, 1996). Through past learning experiences students formulate a unique lens through which to filter future ones and, therefore, view and respond to learning environments in different ways. As facilitators, then, we cannot assure how information can be understood or perceived because the individual has a unique relationship with the problem (Cust, 1996). Therefore, learning is the responsibility of the student and not the tutor, who can only provide the opportunity and facilitative environment to support optimum learning. This fits well with the philosophy of student-centred learning.

What is student-centred learning?

Student-centred learning (SCL) differs from traditional learning in two very important ways. First, the students are considered active participants in the learning process who both gain control over and are responsible for their own learning. Second, the teacher has to relinquish control over others and adopt a more facilitating role (Rogers, 1983). In theory, this requires the facilitator to form a learning partnership with students and to trust students sufficiently to achieve the learning outcomes (Johnson and Tinning, 2001). This necessitates a fundamental change in both traditional pedagogical beliefs (Haith-Cooper, 2000) and the trust/power relationship for both students and staff (Wilkerson and Hundert, 1997). Students' increased responsibilities include an individual and collective self-discipline to learn, an ability to negotiate and coordinate their own program of learning, and an ability to evaluate the extent and significance of their own learning (Barrows and Tamblyn, 1980; Rogers, 1983).

As facilitators, we are challenged first, and perhaps most intransigently, to achieve this level of empowerment within organisational culture and boundaries, learning outcomes and curriculum design. However, we also have to impart trust and decision-making responsibility to students and, subsequently, relinquish control of them ourselves. This can challenge expectations even within PBL formats where, for example, the decisions on how information is gathered may conflict with the philosophical perspectives of tutors (Creedy and Hand, 1994). At an extreme juncture, students may choose not to engage in the learning process, or be selective about what they learn. This can be a real challenge to the tutor as coercion, in any form, is not a recognised method in SCL philosophy (Brookfield, 1987). As facilitators however, we can ensure that the learning environment engenders self-directed, empowered adults, mutual respect among participants and that the exploration of new ideas is meaningful to the experiences of the learner. We can also ensure that the opportunity and choice offered within the learning environment is valued by students, as that greater flexibility can enhance the balance of power (Cust, 1996). In conclusion, however, as tutors in line with a student-centred approach, we may have to accept the student's own decision-making process above our own. Conversely, we also need to recognise that where learning is cooperative the needs of others may be compromised and, in such cases, enable a viable solution.

What is facilitation?

We have already discussed many of the principles underpinning facilitation. To summarise briefly, we know that facilitation is used in a constructivist educational philosophy with active rather than passive learners and is a skill necessary for enabling a problem-based, student-centred approach to learning (Haith-Cooper, 2000). We also know that facilitation requires an element of personal investment and change. Burrows, for example, defined facilitation as: 'A goal orientated dynamic process in which participants work together in an atmosphere of genuine mutual respect, in order to learn through critical reflection' (Burrows, 1997: 401).

Therefore, facilitation is person-centred, collaborative, a process of synthesis, of shared learning and a means of developing critical thinking. That said, however, the actual role of the facilitator remains elusive and only vaguely specified (Haith-Cooper, 2000). Rogers (1983: 189) maintained that a facilitator creates 'an atmosphere of realness, of caring and of understanding listening' and that this enhanced the student's learning environment. As a result facilitators have an active and supportive role to develop that is both genuine and empathic. This promulgates a more personal approach than necessitated in traditional teaching environments and, consequently, can result in facilitators' styles differing dramatically, which, conversely can have a profound impact on both the learning process and outcomes (Biley and Smith, 1999). As facilitators, then, we need to strive towards a style and skill base that promotes student satisfaction and meets individual and group needs while balancing this to maintain the boundaries and outcomes created by the organisation and curriculum in which we work. As such, the views of the students are crucial to effective facilitation not only for the purpose of participation and empowerment but also, fundamentally, for their voices to be heard.

In line with that thinking, the following sections on facilitation style and skills are emerging themes from students' views of their own experiences of tutor facilitation. Where appropriate this is integrated with existing research and literature. The issues raised reflect excerpts from the students' own words, but also encapsulate my own process of sense-making and representation. As such I set out only to offer you the opportunity to consider how participants, particularly in PBL tutorials, perceive and benefit from certain approaches and techniques in the hope that you will reflect on it.

Facilitation style

As already noted, the style or approach presented by the facilitator reflects their philosophical stance and their unique personality, thus there will always be elements of difference. These differences can either enhance or detract from the learning experience depending on the needs of the group, the ability of the facilitator to meet them, and the congruence between learning style and perception. In simple terms, as facilitators we need to ensure that we facilitate and not teach, enable students and not control them. This change in role is no easy task but is fundamental to becoming an effective facilitator. Johnston and Tinning (2001) argue that, by adopting a reflective approach, facilitators are offered an opportunity to explore their own actions and develop a level of self-awareness and responsiveness to others that can enable proactive change (Osterman and Kottkamp, 1993). Similarly, peer review systems and support from other tutors can enhance our understanding of how we actually facilitate (Johnston and Tinning, 2001). The group process itself can also enable facilitation by offering the opportunity for direct feedback from students and conseqently give them an opportunity to be heard. This not only offers a more equitable partnership but can enhance self-worth when student voices are valued.

Student perceptions of facilitation styles

Being in the group

Students suggested that the level of participation given to the group, including prompting, guidance and directiveness, was integral to both group function and individual satisfaction. Generally, active participation in the group enabled students to learn, while a more reserved role could be inhibiting and seen as purely observational.

> It's better [for the tutor] to be part of groups rather than on the periphery – it feels like being watched by a behavioural psychologist sitting there with a pad.
>
> Feeling like the tutor is an observer can inhibit the conversation/discussion – they observe but don't participate.

The level of participation and intervention was also noted as differing between tutors. Students felt that this negated effective group work and suggested that this could be a deliberate ploy to protect knowledge, due to a lack of guidance or individual differences.

> Tutors take different roles – some prompt and some tutors won't prompt and there are uncomfortable silences – I found this very frustrating especially when you had to go and find information and didn't know where to go to find it.
>
> Tutors seem to worry about being too directive – maybe tutors need to have guidance, some tutors don't say anything. Even when you ask them directly they say what do you think, [tutors] seem protective about knowledge.

Barrows and Tamblyn (1980) suggested that facilitators can create an imbalance in participation or direction within the tutorial group as they attempt to understand when and how to facilitate the learning process. Maudsley (1999) contended that this can result in tutor inactivity, while Drinan (1997) argued that facilitators can be over-directive and lapse into a teacher-centred mode. In either circumstance the result can be demotivating for students.

> Sometimes you go around in circles in the group and not understand what you have done, then get told to go away and look for it – I find this de-motivating, especially when it's something theoretical and concrete.

For facilitators this is further compounded by the fact that not only each group, but each individual group meeting can require a different level of participation to enable proactive movement. Therefore, facilitators have to both intervene at the crucial moment and intervene with a purpose, as comments that do not facilitate have little meaning to group members.

Cryptic comments are negative if you don't know what tutors are alluding to – what's the point?

Haith-Cooper (2000) and Maudsley (1999) agreed that preparation and practice is integral to effective facilitation. In theory then, learning can enable facilitators to become more critically responsive and meet perceived needs. Although this does not overcome the issue of personal differences, it may enable a more balanced approach to tutor activity within groups.

Being a resource

Students considered staff to be a valuable resource in learning. This seemed to have several strands. First, tutors were considered to have knowledge or experience to impart.

Grounding in reality is important – this is why tutors are important as a resource.

In this way then, facilitation would include not only active participation but the sharing of knowledge and experience. From both a cooperative, participative perspective and a human, honest and real one, being a resource would seem acceptable. However, from a teacher-centred versus student-centred one, this can cause a conflict between the expert versus facilitation role. This dichotomy has resulted in an ongoing debate between what Boud and Felletti (1997: 8) have termed 'facilitation and case expertise'. Engel (1997) for example, suggested that expertise lies in facilitation not knowledge, while Ryan (1997) and Barrows and Tamblyn (1980) contended that facilitators should be a resource as experts can inform knowledge and address errors in information, while conversely, non-experts may facilitate well but can allow incorrect information to be assimilated and important points to be missed. The students agreed with the latter point and stated that:

Tutors need to participate – offer their knowledge, involve themselves rather than analysing everything.
If you can get your answer then and there then why not – we identify the tutor as resource.

For the facilitators, as discussed previously, timely intervention is integral to effectiveness and decisions have to be made about when to offer information. Similarly, the content of knowledge given should enable, not inhibit, the problem-solving process. This can be a difficult task when balancing it with the student perspective as this may both reflect recognised need or, more contentiously from the tutor's view, could be seen as a push toward a more teacher-centred rather than student-centred mode of learning.

Being real

The students highlighted that 'personality is important', and that being approachable, enthusiastic, motivated and honest in group settings enabled learning. They also suggested that a positive approach enabled discussion.

If tutors are approachable, easy to talk to, people find it easier to talk. If there is some-body there where people are worried about saying the wrong thing the group tend to go quiet. People find it easier if tutors don't just disagree – to tell them that it's a valid point.

Rogers (1983) maintained that facilitators are real people and that being honest and forming genuine relationships in the learning situation was an important aspect of effec-tive facilitation. He also argued that positive regard, without conditions of worth, enabled facilitation. This non-judgemental stance has led to the profile of an effective facilitator being 'likened to that of a saint, unfazed by ambiguity, undaunted by student irritation or personal frustration' (Katz, 1995: 52). However, from Rogers' (1983) perspective, an effective facilitator is someone who feels able to be real, a person with fallibilities, within the learning environment and who can be honest about themselves and their limitations. The students seemed to corroborate this by suggesting that knowing the tutor created a more conducive environment, and that honesty was respected:

It's good when the personality of the tutor comes across – I've been in really bad groups and knowing about them makes you feel more equal, you can share experiences and it's safe to sort out groups.
It's okay[for tutors] to say no and be honest.

Students also noted that being responsive to both individual and group needs was important, and stressed that the individual still existed within the group milieu.

It's important to listen to and respond to group and individual needs. Individuals still exist in groups – each member may have different needs.

They associated this with being both valued and listened to and suggested that this encouraged higher levels of motivation.

If you feel supported and valued you feel more motivated.
Listening to students is important – sometimes you feel you are not listened to – it's horrible.

Rogers (1983) suggested that students' learning was more effective when they received high levels of understanding and caring. He also maintained respect, genuineness and empathy with the student resulted in greater problem-solving, more verbal responses, more involvement, more eye contact, higher levels of cognition and greater creativity. Effective facilitators, then, recognise and value the unique individual student.

Facilitation skills

So what are facilitation skills? To summarise, we know that part of the process is to provoke problem-solving and critical reasoning skills, to enable a structure through which students can learn to learn and develop lifelong study skills. We know that the process should be participative and cooperative with shared values, ground rules, responsibility and mutual respect. We also know that, consequently, the process empowers, is dynamic and that both individual and group needs should be met in line with the curriculum outcomes. Finally, we know that the effectiveness of the facilitation process is impacted upon both by the facilitators' skill base and learning and teaching philosophy and style. But that said, what do we actually do?

Student perceptions of facilitation skills

Focusing and clarifying

Students suggested that the ability of the facilitator to focus and clarify was integral to effective facilitation.

> You can't see wood for trees when you are in a group – you get tied up in the detail of it. [You] can't make sense of where you are going with it; [you] need someone to clarify it.
>
> We needed someone to link thinking and get discussion going. You need the tutor to facilitate discussion in the group, make the links and focus thinking in the group.

Seemingly then, the tutor has an important role to clarify the purpose and direction of the group to maintain focus and discussion. Barrows and Tamblyn (1980) suggest that tutors facilitate discussion by orientating and guiding, clarifying, identifying shared learning objectives and enabling interaction with the problem. Whereas this, in itself, is a complex task, facilitators are also challenged to integrate this with the learning outcomes of the course, the organisational expectations and the individual and group objectives. Also, as discussed earlier, a key success factor in facilitation is timing and, thus, when to clarify or focus is a crucial question. Bentley (1994: 57) argues that, 'true learning takes place when we move from a place of confusion to clarity'. Therefore, as facilitators we have to decide at what point to clarify to enable discussion and creative thinking for the students.

Challenging

Barrows and Tamblyn (1980: 83) suggest facilitators enable learning by, 'leading questions, challenging thinking, and raising issues and points that need to be considered'. The students' views supported this and they contended that tutors should try,

> challenging information and giving feedback – irrelevance should be challenged.

Generally, students appeared to consider that challenging was a fundamental skill, but also noted that the way in which facilitators challenged was essential to success. In basic terms students felt that a constructive approach was necessary and that comments students made should be valued, even if wrong. As a facilitator then, we have to challenge information and working patterns in groups, but do so in such a way as to encourage and motivate, not negate participation.

Providing feedback and summing up

Finally, students agreed that regular feedback and summing up within the group process enabled facilitation. As mentioned earlier positive feedback was considered essential and this was linked to feedback on content, knowledge and group processes. In the first instance, students felt that this motivated them and assured their understanding.

> Feedback gives you encouragement – feels like you made a good job of it.
> Providing positive feedback motivates.

In the second instance the feedback was more integral to group functioning and more formal.

> Periodically have reflection sessions on group dynamics – needs to be formal.

Students considered the facilitator role to encompass some responsibility for resolving group issues and considered reflection as a sound method. Correspondingly, from the facilitators' perspective, it can be difficult to decide how much to facilitate change in group dynamics and, indeed, whether the main responsibility lies with the facilitator or with the student participants. Haith-Cooper (2000: 270) contended that facilitators did have to intervene and that, 'by focussing on group interaction intervention levels will be individual to the group's needs'. As such, if facilitators are attuned to the dynamics within groups, intervention levels can be adapted to meet the groups' recognised needs. The students also noted that resolution of difficulties in a group was a shared responsibility, albeit with strong support from the facilitator to enable reflection.

> I think it's got to come from reflection in the group [sorting problems out].

As a final and more general point the students agreed that facilitators could provide the opportunity for students:

- to summarise and present key issues;
- to explain and discuss with others;
- to discover and explore personal meaning and develop tools for lifelong learning;
- to evaluate feedback about their learning and enable them to reflect on their own learning;
- to see how they are progressing toward meeting the objectives.

They also suggested that organisational issues (e.g. photocopying facilities and room availability), staff availability and library facilities were important and valuable tools in enabling learning. Ryan (1997) noted that sufficient library resources and time to explore and assimilate were necessary to enable deep understanding. This is therefore a valuable organisational consideration when considering developing a PBL curriculum.

Conclusion

To summarise, then, the facilitator's role is both multiplex and dynamic. Its complexity is compounded by the individual learner, the group and its associated relationships. As such, within any situation, the skills and styles adopted to enhance learning can change. Moreover, basic strategies and techniques can be learned and developed to meet perceived needs but, fundamentally, how you facilitate is intrinsically linked to who you are. This, in itself, can provide diversity and choice for both students and facilitators and, therefore, provide the flexible and adaptable approach necessary to meet the demands of a more person-centred learning environment.

References

Barrows, H.S. (1986) A Taxonomy of Problem Based Learning Methods, *Medical Education*, 20, 6, 481–486.

Barrows, H.S. and Tamblyn, R.M. (1980) *Problem-Based Learning, An Approach to Medical Education*, New York: Springer.

Bentley, T. (1994) *Facilitation: Providing Opportunities for Learning*, London: McGraw-Hill.

Biley, F.C. and Smith, K.L. (1999) Making Sense of Problem Based Learning: The Perceptions and Experiences of Undergraduate Nursing Students, *Journal of Advanced Nursing*, 30, 1205–1212.

Boud, D. and Felletti, G. (1997) *The Challenge of Problem Based Learning*, 2nd edn, London: Kogan Page.

Brookfield, S.D. (1987) *Developing Critical Thinkers: Challenging Adults to Explore Alternative Ways of Thinking and Acting*, Milton Keynes: Open University Press.

Burrows, D.E. (1997) Facilitation: A Concept Analysis, *Journal of Advanced Nursing*, 25, 396–404.

Creedy, D. and Hand, B. (1994) The Implementation of Problem Based Learning: Changing Pedagogy in Nurse Education, *Journal of Advanced Nursing*, 20, 696–702.

Cust, J. (1996) A Relational View of Learning: Implications for Nurse Education, *Nurse Education Today*, 16, 4, 256–266.

Drinan, J. (1997) The Limits of Problem Based Learning. In Boud, D. and Felletti, G. (eds) *The Challenge of Problem Based Learning*, 2nd edn, London: Kogan Page.

Engel, C.E. (1997) Not Just a Method but a Way of Learning. In Boud, D and Felletti, G. (eds) *The Challenge of Problem Based Learning*, 2nd edn, London: Kogan Page.

Haith-Cooper, M. (2000) Problem Based Learning within Health Professional Education. What is the Role of the Lecturer? A Review of the Literature, *Nurse Education Today*, 20, 267–272.

Johnston, A.K. and Tinning, R.S. (2001) Meeting the Challenge of Problem Based Learning: Developing the Facilitators, *Nurse Education Today*, 21, 161–169.

Katz, G. (1995) Facilitation. In Alavi C. (ed.) *Problem Based Learning in a Health Sciences Curriculum*, London: Routledge.

Maudsley, G. (1999) Roles and Responsibilities of the Problem Based Learning Tutor in the Undergraduate Medical Curriculum, *British Medical Journal*, 318, 657–661.

NCIHE (1997) The Report of the National Committee of Enquiry into Higher Education (The Dearing Report), London: HMSO.

Osterman, K.F. and Kottkamp, R.B. (1993) *Reflective Practice for Educators: Improving Schooling through Professional Development*, Thousand Oaks, CA: Corwin Press.

Rogers, C. (1983) *Freedom to Learn for the 80s*, New York: Macmillan Publications.

Ryan, G. (1997) Ensuring that Students Develop an Adequate Knowledge Base. In Boud, D. and Felletti, G. (eds) *The Challenge of Problem Based Learning*, 2nd edn, London: Kogan Page.

Wilkerson, L.A. and Hundert, E.M. (1997) Becoming a Problem Based Tutor: Increasing Self Awareness Through Faculty Development. In Boud, D. and Felletti, G. (eds) *The Challenge of Problem Based Learning*, 2nd edn, London: Kogan Page.

6

Developing students' skills in groups and teamworking: moving experience into critical reflection

Peter Hartley

Introduction

Despite the increased application of group methods in HE teaching, it is still well worth asking what (and how) students learn from these group activities and projects. And it is also worth asking how group projects can be best managed by teaching staff. The rhetoric of 'developing our students' teamworking skills' is now writ large in virtually all course descriptions. But what does this rhetoric actually mean? Do we have clear models of group progression and improvement that we can apply with our students, or do we have to adopt a more speculative and inquiring approach?

This chapter argues that much of our current knowledge about group dynamics (and most of the models of group behaviour that we offer to students to help them think about their interactions) has been derived from non-educational contexts and we need to adopt a much more tentative approach when we view student groups. In other words, we have fairly limited evidence about how student project groups really 'work'. However, we can turn this situation to our advantage by involving students in inquiry into their own group processes and use this as a vehicle to develop their critical and reflective skills. This chapter aims to show how we can do this by focusing upon a few critical questions about group behaviour, analysing examples of relevant research literature on group dynamics, and highlighting implications for our educational practice.

The development of group work with students

In my early university career in the 1970s, many colleagues regarded me as rather strange (some things don't change). While they were running seminars and tutorials, I was experimenting with group exercises and projects, inspired by writers such as David Kolb (and particularly by the first edition of his book of experiential exercises on organisational psychology, now in its seventh edition – Osland *et al.*, 2000). Nowadays, of course, small group activities are commonplace in university education. A number of factors have influenced this change in the UK, not all educational. For example, dramatic expansion in student numbers has pushed many lecturers to adopt small group methods. A mix of educational and political/economic pressures has put increasing emphasis on transferable or employability skills such as teamwork. These pressures have also affected higher education in many other parts of the world (Hartley, 1997). But have these changes in educational focus and activity outlined above resulted in valid and practical procedures that lecturers from *all* subject disciplines can use confidently with students to develop their teamworking skills?

The rhetoric of 'developing our students' teamworking skills' is now in virtually all course descriptions. Does this describe a systematic and evidence-based strategy to develop specific skills and understanding or is the reality rather more haphazard? How are these skills developed and assessed? At its worst, the rhetoric may conceal some exaggerated or even ill-conceived claims. And this is not just an issue in the UK. For example, Allen and Plax argue that 'participation in small groups is an integral part of the educational experience in the United States' (Allen and Plax, 1999: 493). They survey research evidence on the impact of group work in the educational context. While concluding that what they call 'co-operative learning groups' do enhance students' 'critical thinking, relationship and team-building skills' (ibid.: 510), they also suggest that a number of important questions remain essentially unanswered. For example, they question how much we know about the 'influence of participation in classroom groups on participation in other types of group experiences throughout one's life' (ibid.: 511). Yet, this transferability of skills and understanding is regarded as almost self-evident in many course descriptions.

We can question the extent of transferability and worry whether students' teamworking is advancing at quite the rate that the course documents suggest, without implying that we have not made significant progress. As one indicator of progress, we do now have some very useful and well-written textbooks, handbooks and guidelines to support our group teaching with students (e.g. Jaques, 2001; Tiberius, 1995) as well as some very useful case studies of good practice that illustrate the benefits and pitfalls of group learning (e.g. part 2 of Boud *et al.*, 2001). But are the guidelines always built on sufficiently robust theories of student groups to develop our students into the role of 'critical and reflective practitioners' that many educational developers currently advocate? These handbooks on groups often use models or approaches based upon notions of team-building which have been developed in commercial or industrial contexts. These can be controversial and/or contested. For example, Hayes distinguishes four main approaches to team-building in the organisational literature and then goes on to propose another based upon concepts of social identity. She also quotes a recent survey of studies on team-building interventions in commercial/industrial contexts which concluded that they had mixed success rates, largely because they tended to ignore 'the external and organisa-tional context in which the team was operating' (Hayes, 2002: 77). So, how can we develop our students' awareness and skills in ways that recognise the complexities of 'real' group dynamics but do not distract from their main subject focus? That question is the main focus of this chapter.

An important caveat – this chapter will concentrate on project groups, where students are put together to investigate a problem or case study and report back, either to the tutors or external client or some mixed audience. Of course, there are all sorts of permu-tations of this, ranging from simple problems over a week or two through to the semester or year-long experience with very formal assessment. This focus ignores some important group activities in the classroom that are well discussed elsewhere (e.g. Jaques, 2001; Light and Cox, 2001). The truly effective course design offers a balance of activities right across this range.

My argument is that we need to appreciate and value what students can learn from pro-ject group participation but also recognise that our current understanding of student group dynamics (and therefore the potential and limitations of generalisation or transferability of skills) is both partial and tentative. As a result, we should not be 'teaching group dynam-ics' but, rather, enabling our students to develop their own critical enquiry into the nature and processes of project groups. This means that students must have opportunities to experiment with and reflect upon their own experiences and then contrast those experi-ences with other models/situations. And we can do that without diluting or distracting from the main discipline knowledge and skills which those students need to acquire. This does *not* mean that all students and their tutors need to become social science researchers regard-less of their subject discipline. But it does mean that we all have to take seriously and reflect to some extent upon the group dynamics which actually affect us all in a work sit-uation. This is particularly true as modern HE institutions live in turbulent times where organisational change and restructuring are commonplace.

This chapter discusses the nature of student groups and their similarities to and differ-ences from the groups usually cited in the small group research literature. I look at some fundamental questions about group dynamics that raise practical questions (and raise important implications for project design) which students and tutors can use to extend their understanding of group processes. These questions cannot be exhaustive within the confines of a single chapter but they illustrate approaches and main issues. These exam-ples also highlight some areas where the advice in many current student guides is not very helpful and may even be misleading. After my discussion of each question, I make some suggestions for teaching practice in terms of two aspects:

- what we can do as tutors to sensitise students to these questions and difficulties;
- ways we can encourage students to critically reflect upon their own group processes.

How are student groups like other groups?

We cannot assume that student groups always operate in the ways that 'textbook small groups' do. Most small group research has been done on a limited range of groups in particular contexts. For example, many studies have looked at groups in commercial organisations. These groups often have an appointed leader, a status hierarchy and members with different functional roles. None of these features apply in the same way to student groups, and attempts to build groups with different roles may not work if the members do not have the necessary commercial or technical experience.

In some senses, all groups are similar in that they all have to find ways of solving problems, making decisions and getting along with one another. However, the differences in types and contexts might be more important than the similarities.

We need to question what are the important similarities and differences between student groups and other types of groups such as workgroups or sports teams. And, of course, these groups exhibit important differences that may not always be fully recognised. For example, teambuilding texts often draw analogies between the successful workgroup and the successful sports team. Some organisational analysts are sceptical about this comparison and Robbins and Finley describe it as a 'myth'. They suggest that sports teams are 'really entertainment teams who can perform very well under enormous stress' (Robbins and Finley, 2000: 193–4). Although they are typically composed of people with different roles and expertise, and have a common goal of winning, they are led by the external coach, often in extremely authoritarian and hierarchical fashion – a style of leadership that Robbins and Finley describe as 'the old-fashioned way' (ibid.: 194). They also have rather limited autonomy and are unlikely to create an atmosphere where members are encouraged or tolerated when they make mistakes. Yet, it is the opposite of many of these characteristics – participative leadership, member autonomy, and support for mistakes – which are often cited when describing progressive and successful work teams. Another important difference is the nature of rewards. Sports teams tend to live under very strict time constraints whereby losing the game is an immediate mark of failure. They may not have the opportunity to improve and try again, which many organisational teams can do.

So Robbins and Finley suggest that: 'Sports teams are dominated by superstars who take the lion's share of rewards, with journeymen and practised team members scrambling to pick up the scraps' (ibid.: 194). This is hardly the portrait of team performance and group loyalty that is often advocated by organisational analysts. And nor is this the co-operative and supportive team we would hope that our student groups can become.

What we can do as tutors

In virtually every subject area, we can point to examples of different ways of organising teams which have subject relevance – from the scientific, computing, healthcare or engineering team working on a new invention or project implementation through to different practices in creative writing or the arts, such as the common practice in the American media of using teams to write shows rather than the single creator/writer more common in the UK.

Encouraging students to reflect

As part of this process, why not ask students to make a specific comparison between their present group and some other group or team they have been involved in (such as a sports or work team), and ask them to explain the differences? Then ask them to find some research on this other type of group and apply it to their experience.

How do student groups develop?

Virtually every textbook commentary on the processes of group development mentions the model first popularised by Tuckman and Jensen, based on a review of all the studies he could find at the time of writing (1977). He proposed that groups go through five main phases – forming, storming, norming, performing and adjourning (many textbook accounts list only the first four phases from his earlier survey of studies published in 1965). When a group is brought together for the first time, members feel uncertain, both about what they have to do – the task they have to perform – and about themselves and the other members. This period of forming is followed by a phase of conflict (storming) where members argue about the nature of the task and where interpersonal conflict is also likely to appear. Assuming the group survives this phase, then they move into a process of norming – achieving agreement about the task that has to be performed and also coming to agree upon their respective roles and group procedures. Only when the group has worked successfully through these three phases can the group really get down to productive work and effective interactions (performing). If the group has to come to an end (the project or task is finished and there is nothing else to do) then there is a period where the members prepare to wind up and depart (adjourning).

There is no doubt that this model does apply to many groups and there is research evidence to support this. However, does it apply to all groups and, more specifically, does it apply to all student groups? Several student guides imply that it does. But there is also research evidence to suggest that groups can go through different life cycles or variations of this one (such as avoiding a storming phase). And if students are taught that Tuckman's is *the* model of group development then they may adopt a rather blinkered view of their own processes. I remember one student group a few years ago who apologised to me that they had not 'stormed' and wondered how they could have 'gone wrong'. In fact, they were a remarkably effective team based on existing friendships who had simply adopted very mature and effective decision-making procedures – they had 'jumped' to performing very quickly and very efficiently.

Despite the ubiquity of the Tuckman model, research evidence on the stages that real student groups confront is remarkably thin on the ground. And there is some evidence that argues for a very different sequence. Gersick found that her student groups went through a process of what she called 'punctuated equilibrium'. Her research found 'no universal sequence of activities in the groups studied – nor was group progress steady and gradual'. But she did find 'remarkable convergence in the times that groups formed, maintained, and changed their interaction patterns' (Gersick, 1990: 100). All her groups almost immediately established a 'framework of "givens"' about their situation and about how they should behave. This framework was usually not discussed explicitly or at any great length. Members very quickly settled into an almost implicit consensus about the nature of the task and the way they were going to work – equilibrium emerged quickly, often at or after the first meeting. The group worked on this basis for the first half of their time together (phase 1).

However, this equilibrium was then 'punctuated'. About halfway through their life cycle, each group underwent a 'transition': the group 'explicitly dropped old approaches and searched for new ones' (p. 101). This transition seemed to occur as the group members became concerned about the deadlines and how much (or how little) progress they had made. So there was a 'major jump in progress' at this midpoint. This was followed by a 'second period of momentum' (phase 2), and then a final burst of 'completion activities' in the last few meetings.

At this midpoint transition, groups can and do make quite dramatic changes to the way they work. In one of her examples, the group decided at this midpoint that the instructor was 'right after all'. They had initially rejected his analysis of the case study and had been working on it from a different perspective. So the meetings in phase 2 had a completely different agenda to those in phase 1 and the structure of the group also changed – a new leader emerged who took the group through to the end.

This model is very different to Tuckman's model of progressive development and Box 6.1 highlights some of the most important differences.

Box 6.1 Comparing models of group development

Tuckman's model	Gersick's model
Over time	
Phases or stages unfold over time, depending on leader and member behaviour. Subsequent phases build upon what has gone before.	Very different behaviours in different groups but common phases linked to the group's overall timescale.
Stages	
5 phases or stages:	2 main phases with major transition in the middle:
Forming: uncertainty over task; tentative behaviour between members	*Phase 1*: group adopt framework very early which takes them to halfway point
Storming: conflict over task and between members	
	Transition: halfway through the time period, members become very aware of deadlines and re-assess their progress and the way they work
Norming: roles and task agreement emerge and are accepted	
Performing: the group works effectively towards completion	
	Phase 2: new framework adopted
Adjourning: members split up	
	Completion: final burst of activities just before deadline
The link between time and stage	
No clear link between the stages and the group's overall timescale	Very clear link between the stages and the group's overall timescale
Conflict?	
Conflict likely or inevitable	Conflict not inevitable

And how do staff use these models? If we believe that our groups follow the Tuckman stages, then we may decide to act in particular ways (there are detailed recommendations for groups that follow these stages, as in Wheelan, 1999). For example, we might decide to leave the groups to their own devices for a while so they can settle down and 'form'. But if we believe that our groups follow the Gersick stages, then we might decide to talk to them very early on to see if their initial framework is going to help or hinder.

What we can do as tutors

What do we tell our students about group development? Left to their own devices they will almost certainly come across Tuckman as it features in so many texts about groups and project management. So shouldn't we be offering them at least two different models?

Encouraging students to reflect

Why not ask students to make a specific comparison between their present group and two different theories of group development? An obvious comparison would be Tuckman and Gersick as described above but there are other variations (see Hartley, 1997). One challenge is to ask students to identify specific behaviours or incidents that support their analysis (as Gersick does, pages 102ff.).

What roles do we need in student groups?

Various popular models of effective management teams suggest that they need a particular combination of individual roles, as in Margerison and McCann's team management wheel (Margerison, 2002). Probably the most widely used in educational contexts is the model from Meredith Belbin (1993). A questionnaire from one of his earlier books allows you to assess your own profile (Belbin, 2004).

Belbin proposes eight team roles. These roles include the innovator, who tends to offer new ideas, the teamworker, who is particularly good at personal support and helping others, the completer, who is very strong on meeting schedules and targets and focusing upon deadlines, and the chairperson, who is good at organising and allocating roles. This model was developed from observations of teams of managers on residential courses and is now used by a number of organisations for both training and selection. The ideal group will have all of the roles represented or be sufficiently aware of its strengths and weaknesses to overcome any limitations in the role distribution. Belbin suggests that most individuals will be particularly strong on one or two roles, and probably particularly weak on one or two others.

Although Belbin claims that there is strong empirical evidence to support his model, a number of critical articles have appeared. Some of these have questioned the precise statistical model that he uses to allocate scores to particular types (a useful summary of this debate can be found in Hayes, 2002). Other analyses have questioned the precise links between role distribution and overall group effectiveness and whether the roles can be quite so clearly distinguished in practice. Whatever the outcomes of these debates, we can certainly argue that the relationships between group effectiveness and particular role distributions have not been extensively studied in higher educational contexts. We can invite students to explore and experiment with these systems as a way of expanding their insights into group behaviour in different contexts.

What we can do as tutors

We can use systems such as Belbin's in various ways, as in the following examples.

We can use these systems to illustrate the range of activities that need to go on in successful groups without going into individual role analysis. For example, we can ask student groups how they are going to ensure that the group will stick to deadlines (the completer-finisher role function) or meet necessary quality standards (the monitor-enhancer role function).

We can select/create our project groups using these systems. This raises important issues of individual privacy and 'social engineering' which we do not have the space to explore here but which are receiving increasing attention (e.g. Harriman and Hartley, 2003). To avoid unnecessary personal intrusion, we can do this anonymously and also involve students in the process. For example, we have asked students to summarise their profile on the front of a Post-It note and put a private identifier on the reverse (such as a nickname and 4-digit number – just make sure they also write this down privately as well so they don't forget it!). The Post-Its can then be shuffled into small groups in public view or by the students themselves using criteria such as Belbin's specifications for a well-matched and successful group. The groups can be announced using the private identifiers and then it is up to the group members whether they reveal their role details to each other or not. Offering groups this choice is an interesting way of inviting discussion on how we expect others to behave – how do 'labels' or other expectations influence our behaviour?

Encouraging students to reflect

We can encourage students to complete questionnaires such as Belbin's and use the results to consider their own behaviour in groups and comment on the other members' behaviour. An important caveat is to emphasise that we cannot simply rely on a self-report questionnaire to reveal the truth about our social behaviour (as Belbin himself emphasises – he talks about the problem of individuals who may not have a very accurate perception of themselves). There are now several systems freely available on the web that students can use to identify their profile – another important caveat is to ask students to consider the evidence that these systems claim to support their validity.

Can student groups become teams?

We can also question whether all working groups become 'real teams'. In other words, how many of the project groups we set up actually achieve the highest levels of team performance, and how can we tell when a group has reached a sophisticated level of teamworking? One well-known analysis of organisational teams draws a very clear distinction between working groups, where members participate in order to share and coordinate information and decisions but where there is little or no shared responsibility, and four different types of team (Katzenbach and Smith, 1993). The pseudo-team call themselves a team but make little attempt to coordinate what they are doing or establish collective responsibility; the potential team is trying very hard to become a team but is usually or often unclear about its goals and purposes; the real team are jointly committed to a common purpose; and high-performance teams not only have members who are committed to common task goals but are also deeply committed to each others' personal growth and development. These various stages of team imply different levels of performance although the pseudo-team typically performs worse than a working group, according to Katzenbach and Smith.

What we can do as tutors

When we set up our group projects – both in terms of the overall task and the reporting and assessment requirements – we can make it more or less likely that students will need to engage in 'genuine collaboration' or simply allocate tasks to different members that are then pursued independently (as in the definition of the 'working group' above). Does the task encourage or demand genuine interdependence?

Encouraging students to reflect

Why not ask students to make a specific comparison between their present group and the different descriptions of types of groups/teams in Katzenbach and Smith or other similar characterisations of effective teams?

Conclusions

Much of our knowledge about group dynamics (and most of the models of group behaviour that we offer to students to help them think about their interactions) has been derived from non-educational contexts. And many of these models are contested in the research literature, as I have shown in the examples above. This has important practical implications for the ways we tutors work with project groups as well as the types of critical reflections that we might expect students to produce. If we believe that our groups behave in a particular way over time then we will intervene (or not) in particular ways.

We can use this situation to our advantage if we adopt an 'inquiry-led' approach to the dynamics of our student project groups. Rather than relying on textbook guides, which may only set out one theory or approach, we can (and should) invite students to adopt a more critical and analytic approach, encouraging strategies where they compare their experience with a range of models and evidence from other contexts.

References

Allen, T.H. and Plax, T.G. (1999) 'Exploring Consequences of Group Communication in the Classroom: Unraveling relational learning'. In Frey, L.R. (ed.) *New Directions in Group Communication*. Thousand Oaks, CA: Sage.

Belbin, R.M. (1993) *Team Roles at Work*. Oxford: Butterworth-Heinemann.

Belbin, R.M. (2004) *Management Teams: Why They Succeed or Fail*, 2nd edn. Oxford: Elsevier Butterworth-Heinemann.

Boddy, D. (2002) *Managing Projects: Building and Leading the Team*. Harlow: Prentice Hall.

Boud, D., Cohen, R. and Sampson, J. (2001) *Peer Learning in Higher Education: Learning from and with Each Other*. London: Kogan Page.

Gersick, C.J.G. (1990) 'The Students', in Hackman, J.R. *Groups That Work and Those That Don't: Creating Conditions for Effective Teamwork*. San Francisco: Jossey Bass.

Harriman, S. and Hartley, P. (2003) 'Social Engineering in Student Groups'. Paper to Institute of Learning and Teaching (ILTHE) Annual Conference, Warwick.

Hartley, P. (1997) *Group Communication*. London: Routledge.

Hayes, N. (2002) *Managing Teams: A Strategy for Success*. London: Thomson.

Jaques, D. (2001) *Learning in Groups*, 3rd edn. London: Kogan Page.

Katzenbach, J.R. and Smith, D.K. (1993) *The Wisdom of Teams: Creating the High-performance Organisation*. New York: HarperCollins.

Light, G. and Cox, R. (2001) *Learning and Teaching in Higher Education: The Reflective Professional*. London: Paul Chapman.

Margerison, C.J. (2002) *Team Leadership: A Guide to Success with Team Management Systems*. London: Thomson.

Osland, J., Rubin, I. and Kolb, D. (2000) *Organizational Behavior: An Experiential Approach to Human Behavior in Organizations*, 7th edn. Englewood Cliffs, NJ: Prentice Hall.

Robbins, H. and Finley, M. (2000) *Why Teams Don't Work: What went Wrong and How to Put it Right*. London: Texere.

Tiberius, R.G. (1995) *Small Group Teaching: A Trouble-shooting Guide*. London: Kogan Page.

Tuckman, B.W. (1965) 'Developmental Sequences in Small Groups'. *Psychological Bulletin*, 63, 6, 384–99.

Tuckman, B.W. and Jensen, M.A.C. (1977) 'Stages in Small Group Development Revisited'. *Group and Organizational Studies*, 2, 419–427.

Wheelan, S.A. (1999) *Creating Effective Teams: A Guide for Members and Leaders*. Thousand Oaks, CA: Sage.

7

Learning-to-learn online: fostering student engagement with online pedagogies

Gwyneth Hughes

Introduction

No one working in Higher Education today can doubt that we are working within a culture of instability and change. Strategies to accommodate the increasing numbers and diversity of students have been emerging over the past decade, resources have dwindled and at the same time there has been a rise in internet connectivity and digitalisation of knowledge. In this climate e-learning has been flourishing and, with the increasing use of Virtual Learning Environments (VLEs), online learning is now becoming almost mainstream, especially as a supplement to campus-based learning.

The increased use of networks and digital resources has brought with it a range of new problems both technical and pedagogical, but it is the technical concerns that have often gained more attention. Less obvious are the new teaching and learning skills that are required as the curriculum shifts online. While there is awareness among lecturers and support staff that students require help with technical skills for online learning, there is less clarity over the new learning processes that are required. New online pedagogies can be especially confusing for many campus-based students, who, unlike distance learners, are not as familiar with autonomous, flexible and reflective learning, especially if there are contributing social and educational disadvantages (Hughes and Lewis, 2003).

The Learning and Teaching Support Network's Imaginative Curriculum project (LTSN Generic Centre, 2002) proposed a view of the curriculum that emphasises the learning processes and structures as well as the content that is to be learnt. Designing or redesigning an online curriculum gives teachers an opportunity to consider more carefully the processes of learning, which are often taken for granted in a face-to-face environment. This chapter focuses on the process of learning online and the resources available to help online learners, e.g. tutorials on web searching. Two key questions are: how can we embed learning-to-learn online skills into the curriculum?; and how are learners best encouraged to use learning-to-learn resources?

This chapter will explore these questions in three sections:

- What new learning skills do students need to learn online?
- Why are some students more successful than others in learning online?
- How can lecturers and curriculum designers ensure learners gain 'learning-to-learn online' information and skills?

What new skills do students need to learn online?

Many programmes in Higher Education incorporate core skills either as add-on or as an embedded activity and may include learning-to-learn skills (e.g. time-management, note-taking, information literacy, group work, reflection, receiving feedback, critical thinking, research and presentational skills). These complement other skills such as IT skills, employability, numeracy, reading and writing skills and a range of study skills guides are available to address all these areas (e.g. Brown and Hood, 2002; Cottrell, 1999; Freeman, 1991). Learning online requires many of these skills, but sometimes in a different form, and there are new learning-to-learn approaches that need development.

New learning-to-learn online skills include:

- participating in asynchronous online communities;
- participating in synchronous 'chat' activities;
- working co-operatively and collaboratively online;
- searching for and selecting appropriate electronic resources;
- avoiding electronic plagiarism;
- taking online self tests/assessments;
- interacting with online tools and simulations.

Let us consider each of these in turn.

Participating in asynchronous online communities

Research into the use of online 'discussion' or computer conferencing indicates advantages and disadvantages of this learning method compared to oral communication. Text communication allows learners to spend time reflecting before composing messages and there is a permanent record for future reference and revision. However, many learners are reluctant to join in conferences, although they may learn vicariously, and many have difficulty expressing academic ideas in this medium (Light and Light, 1999; Salmon, 2000).

Salmon (2000, 2002) has proposed a model for the developmental stages through which a learner needs to pass in order to become a successful and contented online participant in computer conferencing. A good online tutor or e-moderator is essential to support learners through these stages, starting from Stage 1, and Stage 5 is the 'ideal' situation that tutor and learners should be working towards:

Stage 1: Access and motivation
Technical support is needed for setting up and accessing the system; tutors are welcoming and encouraging.

Stage 2: Online socialisation
Technical support is needed for sending and receiving messages; tutors provide bridges between cultural, social and learning environments.

Stage 3: Information exchange
Technical skills include searching for information while tutors facilitate tasks and monitor information overload.

Stage 4: Knowledge construction
Tutors facilitate active learning and debate in the conference, while the need for technical support is reducing.

Stage 5: Development
Students become more critical of the tutor and/or the conference and they may start up and moderate conferences themselves.

Salmon suggests that it is the e-moderator's role to take learners through the five stages with the accompanying technical support. From this model it is clear that acquisition of the technical skills for sending and receiving messages is not, in itself, enough to promote learning. Learners need to learn online socialisation skills, how to exchange information, and how to build knowledge through debate, critique and development of the contributions of others. Reaching the highest level would mean that learners are able to facilitate conferences for themselves and reflect on the processes of co-operative work.

Pincas (2000) identifies some additional skills for online communication such as being able to give messages appropriate subject headings, using the 'reply' function to keep the 'thread' of conversation going without digressing and keeping messages brief and to the point.

Participating in synchronous 'chat' activities

The potential of 'chat' rooms for learning online is underdeveloped, perhaps because of the more frivolous connotations of this term. Nevertheless, synchronous communication can be as valuable as asynchronous communication if the boundaries of both time and topic are clear. Salmon's model applies to synchronous communication as well as asynchronous. However, the protocols for online communication that is immediate, fast and live may be different and because messages are inevitably very short, it is easy for the 'conversation' to move off task. The moderating skills needed to keep the discussion focused yet free enough to develop learners' ideas are not to be underestimated.

Working co-operatively and collaboratively online

McConnell defines co-operative learning as 'working together on some task or issue in a way that promotes individual learning through processes of collaboration in groups' (2000: 8).

This could include file sharing online and/or communicating in online groups. Collaboration is sometimes distinguished from co-operation in that students work on solving problems together with a high degree of interaction and may submit joint work for assessment as well as individual pieces.

Online groupwork skills include: agreement of how to respond to others, management of the group and the pacing of the work, giving feedback or submitting joint assessments, etc. (McConnel, 2000).

Searching for and selecting appropriate electronic resources

The use of electronic resources provided by the Joint Information Systems Committee (JISC), the HE Academy subject centres and the Resource Discovery Network (RDN) and a vast collection of websites is expanding in Higher Education. Reading lists now contain web addresses and many learners will search the web for information whether instructed to or not. Awareness of information searching skills has grown and there are plenty of websites and resources to guide learners.

But it is not enough merely to direct students to the resources, learners need information literacy skills to enable them to organise and apply the information they find (Peters, 2003). Assuming students have basic library and IT skills they need to build on these by developing the following seven steps:

1   recognise information need;
2   distinguish ways of addressing the gap, e.g. electronic, books, etc.;
3   construct strategies for locating, e.g. search engines;
4   locate and access, i.e. navigation skills;
5   compare and evaluate, i.e. select based on quality of information;
6   organise, apply and communicate, e.g. report on findings to other students;
7   synthesise and create, e.g. for an assignment.

This 7-step model (Peters, 2003) is reminiscent of Salmon's 5-stage model and learners need to be coaxed through the different levels in a similar manner. Those who do not move beyond level four may resort to plagiarism.

Avoiding electronic plagiarism

Electronic plagiarism is one consequence of a 'cut and paste' culture that has developed from use of online resources combined with a lack of skills in how to evaluate and apply information.

On the one hand, our online learners are being encouraged to share information electronically for communication/conferencing where cut and paste is a useful tool, while on the other hand cutting and pasting plagiarised material into assignments is not acceptable. No wonder there is confusion about how electronic resources are best used.

The JISC Plagiarism Advisory Service (2003) offers advice on how to prevent plagiarism by writing careful learning outcomes and assignments. For example, the guide by Carroll and Appleton (2001) recommends that information skills be included in learning outcomes and that students are encouraged to critically evaluate web material and synthesise the material in such a way that merely copying and pasting chunks will not suffice.

Taking online self tests/assessments

Computer-based assessment (CBA) has been established for some time but now VLEs provide facilities for easy development and distribution of online assessments.

Online assessment is often used for objective testing or short answers to relieve marking loads as the marking is done electronically. CBA can also be used for self-assessment tests. Computers can also assist in the assessment of higher order skills such as application, analysis, interpretation and evaluations. In the latter case assignments are still likely to be printed off and marked by hand in the conventional manner (Joliffe *et al.*, 2001), hence the term computer-assisted assessment rather than computer-based assessment is often used to describe these activities.

While learners need to become familiar with any online testing system and be aware of any time constraints that have been set, I am not convinced that there is any immediate learning-to-learn need that arises from online assessment. However, for longer assignments application of web resources and web searching may be required, and skills mentioned above would be relevant. In addition, self-testing is increasingly common in online environments and learners need to be encouraged to make good use of any feedback on incorrect answers rather than focus on final scores.

Interacting with online tools and simulations

The potential for use of online tools and simulations is under-developed in Higher Education (Riley, 2003) and the skills required are likely to be context dependent and thus are beyond the scope of this chapter.

Why are some students more successful than others with online learning?

In any learning provision it soon becomes apparent that some learners are more successful than others and there is no reason why learning online should be any different. It is less clear which students adapt well to change and which do not. Researchers have been investigating the experiences of online learners for several years and we are beginning to find some answers.

I have written this chapter as a response to one such study which I carried out at a new university with a relatively short history of online learning development (Hughes and Lewis, 2003). Students in three different campus-based modules were interviewed about experiences of online learning. The main cause of dissatisfaction for many students was their lack of awareness of how to make the most of learning online. Although all three module tutors provided students with technical guidance on working online, they did not cover learning-to-learn online skills. This meant that while some learners quickly became aware of the potential benefits of online working, others could not see the advantages of online communication and interaction. Their frustration and confusion was a result of their lack of learning-to-learn online skills.

To understand which students were most affected by lack of learning-to-learn skills, we categorised students according to achievement and satisfaction with the learning experience as follows:

- Model – high achievement, high satisfaction;
- Disenchanted (resistant achievers) – high achievement, low satisfaction;
- Maladaptive (resistant non-achievers) – low achievement, low satisfaction;
- Fanatic (none in our study) – low achievement, high satisfaction. (Adapted from Lee, 2001.)

We then looked at the educational backgrounds and ICT experiences of the students in each category. Model students were the most motivated and educationally advantaged learners who were able to explore for themselves how to learn online without help. Disenchanted students were motivated, but did not have a good experience of learning online and defaulted to more familiar learning approaches such as face-to-face group work. This resulted in a positive achievement. The Maladaptive students rejected online learning without finding another way to succeed. The latter group tended to be particularly disadvantaged learners e.g. those with dyslexia, English as a second language and those with low confidence and/or limited IT backgrounds.

Because the study showed that the processes of learning online were more important than the acquisition of technical skills, we concluded that if students are given help in learning-to-learn online then more of them might be enabled to become model students.

How can lecturers and curriculum designers ensure learners gain learning-to-learn online information and skills?

Lecturers are not always aware of learning-to-learn online skills despite recognition of the need for new IT skills development. Nevertheless, many lecturers do bring learning-to-learn skills into their classroom teaching and the ways of addressing learning-to-learn are no different online.

Possibilities include:

- directing students towards generic support materials;
- providing learners with learning-to-learn instructions that specifically address the course requirements;
- embedding learning-to-learn online skills in courses.

Let us consider each in detail below.

Directing students towards generic support materials

Advantages: very easy to do.

Disadvantages: the materials may not be appropriate for your students' needs and may rely on learners' ability to assess their own needs and select an appropriate level of support.

There are some useful resources on using the web that are freely available for students. Examples include:

1   The Resource discovery network has made a series of discipline specific tutorials freely available on the web at www.rdn.ac.uk (accessed 27 November 2004).
2   The Sheridan Libraries of The Johns Hopkins University provides advice on evaluating the quality of websites 'Evaluating Information Found on the Internet' at www.library. jhu.edu/researchhelp/general/evaluating/index.html (accessed 10 December 2004).

Note that web tutorials often have a technical focus and do not necessarily cover pedagogic issues. For example, the tutorial on how to use WebCT at www.webct.com/oriented (accessed 27 November 2004) goes through the mechanics of how to send a message but does not cover how to use asynchronous discussion as a learning aid.

Thus, while it is tempting to rely on generic resources it may be better to focus much more specifically on your course and learner requirements.

Providing learners with learning-to-learn instructions that specifically address the course requirements

Advantages: avoids the problem of student assessing their own need first.

Disadvantages: may be seen as supplementary to the course and ignored by the learners who most need the skills. Instructions would be time-consuming to produce.

Online learners are inevitably bombarded with lists of instructions of a technical nature such as how to log onto the system and passwords etc. Learning-to-learn instructions can also be included in course handbooks. Examples could be:

- how to work collaboratively;
- internet protocols;
- what to include in online communications;
- avoiding plagiarism;
- how to select and use appropriate electronic resources.

The instruction can be tailored for the nature and level of the course. However, long lists of instructions and guidance notes can be daunting and thus self-defeating and a more structured approach is worth careful consideration.

Embedding learning-to-learn online skills in courses

Advantages: learning-to-learn is not an 'add-on' so all students will get the opportunity to gain new skills. There is the possibility of scaffolding students' online learning experiences to build up the relevant skills gradually.

Disadvantages: some course redesign may be needed to embed learning-to-learn activities or reflection on skill development.

I would argue that embedding skills is the most effective way of ensuring our learners learn to learn online so I shall look at this in more detail. I have already referred to Salmon's 5-stage model for developing online communication skills and her work on designing 'e-tivities' or online activities (Salmon, 2002) provides some good examples of how to embed online learning skills. Although these e-tivities are written for potential online tutors, because they are based on a generic model, they can be re-used by adapting and integrating such activities into any course. In an illustration using Salmon's model, I shall not only present some of her examples but also include examples from other online courses.

Stage 1: Access and motivation

I have found that this stage is usually pretty well covered with the instructions for using the technology to log in. The final step usually asks the learner to send an introductory message to demonstrate that they have arrived online. Protocols can also be introduced here such as style and language use. The example below shows how a tutor embeds guidance for taking part in a synchronous online 'chat' seminar into the activity:

> tutor>>one note on using the chat room . . .
> tutor >>when i or anyone else uses dots like this . . .
> tutor >>it means we continue a sentence . . .
> tutor >>and every one else can relax.
> student >>I get it . . .
> student >>and will try to type quickly
> tutor >>don't worry about spelling
> > > (From MSc in Architecture online course
> > > Hughes and Tucker, 2002)

Stage 2: Socialisation

If this stage is not addressed then inexperienced online learners are likely to be unsure about a commitment to online participation and may become passive or 'lurk' online or may cease to log in.

Salmon suggests an e-tivity that could address the issue of how much time to spend online.

E-tivity 2.4

Purpose: to contribute to an enticing stage of activity.

Task: send a postcard to E-tivity 2.4 saying something of interest that is going on in your part of the world. Keep it brief, no more than you would write on a postcard. You may say something about your favourite food – what you can see from your window – something you have discovered recently on the internet.

Respond: look through other people's contributions. Spot someone who has something in common with you and someone who has a difference and comment on both (Salmon, 2002: 54).

Another method for encouraging socialisation is to have a practice area or 'playground' or 'café' where participants can try out sending messages. Anonymity can be built in to help users overcome fear of appearing naive or foolish while they are learning new skills and protocols.

Stage 3: Information exchange

Many learners will happily offer information to others or answer questions while others may be less certain of the value of giving or requesting information, especially when they are accustomed to the tutor being the source of knowledge, not their peers. They may also be uncomfortable with uploading work for peer comment.

Salmon suggests making the information exchange explicit.

E-tivity 3.7

Purpose: being encouraging about the process of exchanging information without being the source of information.

Task: what would you do and why if you saw the following message in your conference: 'I'm trying to find out whether the term moderator meant the same in every learning culture?' Post your reply to *E-tivity 3.7*.

Respond: to other contributions aiming to get more information by asking a question or adding some other point and inviting comments (Salmon, 2002: 70).

Stage 4: Knowledge construction

The example below shows how skills of reflecting on and critiquing other learners' contributions and use of clear subject headings are embedded as part of the online activity.

Activity 1

Based on your reading and your experience, make a list of some of the potential values in using a particular learning technology and make another list of possible constraints.

Send these lists to the discussion forum with an explanation of how you arrived at these values and constraints. If you agree/disagree with a message that has already been posted send a reply to this message, add your dis/agreement and your reasons why. Start a new message only if you are raising a new issue.

Give your message a subject heading that tells others which technology you are referring to, e.g. computer conferencing (Application of Learning Technologies Course, UEL (Hughes and Mottley, 2002)).

Stage 5: Development

Salmon's model was designed for Masters and Professional level students and it may be that you would not expect your learners to interact at this level by moderating themselves. There are plenty of good ideas in her books if this stage is appropriate for you.

The model can be very useful to give a structure to learning-to-learn online skills development and similar steps for other online skills, such as information searching, can also form a basis for a plan to embed learning-to-learn online. However, I would emphasise that such linear process models do have limitations in that not all learners will proceed through distinct stages: they may jump a stage or need to return to review earlier stages in an iterative process. Thus, it is important that you have good awareness of the background and experience of your learners. Continual evaluation will help and action can be taken if, for example, your learners are not progressing to more advanced stages or if some learners find the activities too trivial.

Conclusion

To draw together the above, I conclude the chapter with a checklist for including learning-to-learn online skills in your curriculum (see Table 7.1).

Online learning is still a new area and I do not claim to provide all the answers but, rather, to offer suggestions as to how you might build up your students' learning-to-learn online skills. Improving student learning in a new medium will come with experience

Table 7.1 Checklist for learning-to-learn online skills

Steps	*Examples*	*Tick when completed*
1 What new learning approaches are you introducing to your students?	e.g. Computer conferencing	
List the new online skills they will need, both technical and pedagogic.	e.g. How to send a message; how to exchange information online	
2 Decide how to enable students to gain new learning-to-learn online skills.	e.g. Direct to resources; provide instructions; embed activities that develop learning-to-learn skills	
3 Explain the benefit of working online – particularly for campus students for whom it may not be obvious. Make the learning process transparent.	e.g. Discuss this during an induction session	
4 Evaluate your course to ensure that disadvantaged students are not being further disadvantaged by lack of support with learning-to-learn skills.	e.g. Ask students to reflect on their learning-to-learn online skills	

but greater awareness of the processes of learning online for both tutors and learners will help provide a smooth journey for all.

References

Brown, K. and Hood, S. (2002) *Academic Encounters: Reading, Study Skills and Writing*, Cambridge: Cambridge University Press.

Carroll, J. and Appleton, J. (2001) *Plagiarism: A Good Practice Guide*, JISC. Online. Available at: www.online.northumbria.ac.uk/faculties/art/information_studies/Imri/ JISCPAS/site/guide2.asp (accessed 30 November 2004).

Cottrell, S. (1999) *The Study Skills Handbook*, Basingstoke: Macmillan.

Freeman, R. (1991) *How to Study Effectively*, Cambridge: National Extension College.

Hughes, G. and Mottley, J. (2002) *Application of Learning Technologies*. Short course run by University of East London. Online. Available at: www.uel.ac.uk/lds/staff_ development/accredited_courses.htm (accessed 30 November 2004).

Hughes, G. and Tucker, S. (2002) *How Do I Learn Online?* Paper given to ILT Web Users group: Milton Keynes.

Hughes, G. and Lewis, L. (2003) Who are successful online learners? Exploring the different learner identities produced in virtual learning environments, in Cook, J. and McConnell, D. (eds) *Communities of Practice. Research Proceeding of the 10th Association for Learning Technology Conference*, Sheffield: University of Sheffield and Sheffield Hallam University.

JISC Plagiarism Advisory Service (2003) Online. Available at: http://online.northumbria. ac.uk/faculties/art/information_studies/Imri/JISCPAS/site/jiscpas.asp (accessed 10 December 2004).

Joliffe, A., Ritter, J. and Stevens, D. (2001) *The Online Learning Handbook*, London: Kogan Page.

Lee, M. (2001) Profiling students' adapting style in web-based learning, *Computers in Education* 36, 121–132.

Light, P. and Light, V. (1999) Analysing asynchronous learning interactions: Computer-mediated communication in a conventional undergraduate setting, in Littleton, K. and Light, P. (eds) *Learning with Computers: Analysing Productive Interaction*, London: Routledge.

LTSN Generic Centre (2002) Online. Available at: www.ltsn.ac.uk/genericcentre/index. asp?docid=16893 (accessed 26 March 2004).

McConnell, D. (2000) Implementing Computer Supported Cooperative Learning, 2nd edn. London: Kogan Page.

Peters, J. (2003) *Information Literacy and HE: What is the Connection?* ILT Members-only area paper. Online. Available at: www.Ilt.ac.uk (accessed 12 March 2003).

Pincas, A. (2000) New literacies and future educational culture, *Association for Learning Technology Journal* 8, 2, 69–79.

Riley, D. (2003) Simulation modelling: educational development roles for learning technologists, *Association for Learning Technology Journal* 10, 3, 54–69.

Salmon, G. (2000) *E-moderating: The Key to Teaching and Learning Online*, London: Kogan Page.

Salmon, G. (2002) *E-tivities: The Key to Active Learning Online*, London: Kogan Page.

8

Working with blended learning

Jo Smedley

Introduction

This chapter explores the nature of blended learning, emphasising how a blended learning approach using human and technological components can overcome the respective limitations of face-to-face and e-learning. The roles and responsibilities of learners and tutors in a blended learning experience are highlighted, with particular emphasis on the design issues of a blended learning course. Finally, a set of case studies demonstrate blended learning in action and provide evidence of the diversity of the student experience that can be achieved via the creative use of this combinatorial style of learning.

Learning, e-learning and blended learning

One criticism of traditional education is that, from an early age, we are trained to be dependent learners, expecting to learn when we are told to. This chapter is based on the assertion that students learn best when exposed to a rich variety of learning experiences, where assumptions are challenged and knowledge is reframed.

E-learning has been defined as: 'instruction that is delivered electronically through the internet or an intranet, or through multimedia platforms' (Bosman, 2002). The interest in e-learning stems from the drive to find faster and smarter ways to learn. It is more about the 'learning' and design of the content so that people learn well, rather than the 'e', the technology, i.e. the way that e-learning is delivered. E-learning is capable of delivering a large amount of information but to be successful it must both deliver richly varied content and provide richly varied learning processes. The major benefit of e-learning is that it removes structure in both time and place, which is replaced through a variety of study materials and activities (Cox, 1999).

Attention has recently been re-focused on the 'blend' for learning (Rosenberg, 2001), often a mix of face-to-face, online and paper-based materials, with anecdotal and researched information building a strong case for this approach. While e-learning offers many benefits, effective training must include a combination of modes, or 'blended learning'.

Blended learning means different things to different people (Broadbent, 2002). Many people hear of 'blended learning' and think classroom + technology = blended. But blended learning can encompass more than just this scenario. It allows organisations to gradually move learners from traditional classrooms to e-learning in small steps, making change easier to accept. Working in a blended environment enables tutors and designers to develop the skills needed for e-learning in small increments. Training professionals can move small sections online as they develop the necessary e-learning skills. Cost and resources are also a driving factor. Blended learning allows organisations to develop materials and supplement or complement existing courseware rather than replace it.

Roles and responsibilities within blended learning experiences

The 'people' aspect of e-learning is often disregarded. Blended learning needs to engage with these new human challenges and to place people at a much higher priority level than technology in the mix.

E-tutors are the key to success. A tiny proportion of the population are happy to learn alone. For the rest of us, we need the human touch and trainers are central to making e-learning work. Successful e-tutoring or e-moderating (Salmon, 2000) involves the revisiting of practised teaching styles and the willingness to adapt to the opportunities that technology provides for teaching the learner. An e-tutor monitors their students learning and emails them to encourage them to 'keep learning'. Students encouraged in this way often don't wait, and start setting deadlines themselves (Salmon, 2000).

For e-learning to succeed, students need to become independent learners, being provided with a detailed structure to aid them in their work. Well-structured, flexible e-learning courses recognise that students cannot instantly acquire these skills and need to be helped. Learner motivation plays an important role in learners completing their e-courses. Sometimes this can be external but the strongest motivation comes from an internal desire to complete a learning journey once it has been commenced.

The learner should be foremost in mind throughout the design of e-learning, keeping the schedule as compact and concise as possible. One of the most important steps is to clearly outline the module, the teaching and learning style, the curriculum content and any resources that the student will require to complete the course successfully. It is insufficient to merely modify traditional delivery methods to accommodate this new learning approach.

Introduction to the case studies

The most effective way of informing about new developments is to demonstrate them in action. The following case studies provide examples of three blended learning situations using a different mix of components in each case. I was the tutor in each blended learning situation together with additional roles of course designer and developer. This gave me direct insight into the very different set of challenges and outcomes posed by each blend. The case studies provide a snapshot from these experiences with the aim of encouraging others to experiment and have a go!

Case study 1: Tutoring Online, National Extension College, Cambridge, UK

Since it was established in 1963, the National Extension College (NEC) has pioneered the development of flexible learning for adults and is actively developing innovative materials and systems for open and distance learning opportunities. During 2000, the skills and practice of online pedagogy were identified as a suitable area for development, with educational and business approaches in mind.

Course development on Tutoring Online commenced during 2000. This was an online course aiming to help participants to develop the pedagogical skills required to tutor online, to assist in developing the technical skills required and to consider ways that this practice might enhance current tutoring practice.

The initial course, produced in 2001, was written by several educationalists with considerable experience of tutoring and producing materials for distance learning rather than e-learning specifically. They placed emphasis on encouraging reflective practice by the students. Prior to the commencement of the course, written materials were provided to students to enable them to make themselves familiar with the contents. These materials were contained in a folder and consisted of a course overview, six units of content, a course review and also some additional material providing guidance on computer housekeeping, computer safekeeping and using search engines.

The course was scheduled to run over a 10-week period, with some initial and final parts of the course with a scheduled duration of a week while the middle sections, focusing on the more theoretical aspects, had an expected duration of two weeks. Self-assessed questions existed within each of the six sections, with some set up as threads on the asynchronous conference. Students were expected to contribute to these threads and respond to other students' contributions within a regular timeframe. The tutors were expected to provide regular input and to summarise the comments as a form of finishing off the discussion topic, highlighting particular aspects that had been discussed and dealing with specific queries.

The assessment for this course required the development and submission of a portfolio to demonstrate the confident use of skills associated with e-moderating using a VLE, developed on a section by section basis during the course. It was anticipated that students would supplement their ideas with references to directed discussion from the conferences, chats, the course review and the students' individual learning journal. The first and second presentations were unaccredited. However, the third presentation was accredited by City and Guilds and was commercially available. The course was also available under licence for anyone wishing to use the material as a resource for delivery by tutors provided by the purchasing organisation.

An example of the NEC in-house virtual learning environment used for the first three presentations of this course is given in Figure 8.1. The VLE enabled asynchronous (conferences) and synchronous (chat) interaction facilities, with folders for course materials, learning links, messages, a notice board and share files. An email was sent to each respective tutor whenever an event occurred within the

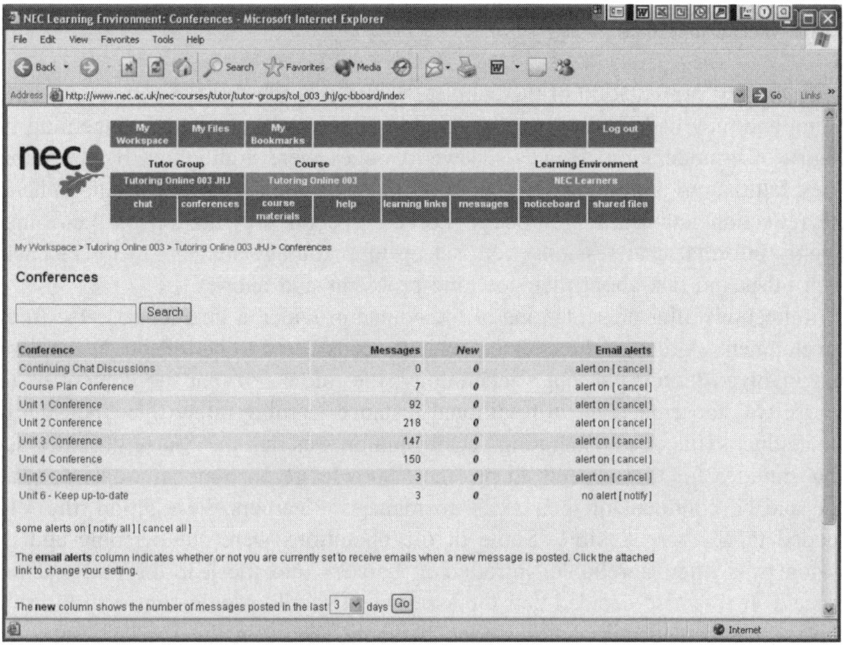

Figure 8.1 A page of the NEC VLE 2001–2002

VLE that involved one of the students in their group, e.g. adding a message to the asynchronous conference, submitting a piece of assessment.

The tutors

I was one of the two e-tutors providing guidance and support to learners throughout all the presentations of the course discussed here. We had both worked for NEC since the mid-1990s on various other projects and were asked to be involved due to our experience in e-learning. We were also involved in a consultant capacity with the course development enabling participation in reviewing and refining the course over several student cohorts.

The learners

Learners on the first two pilot presentations were part-time NEC tutors, encouraged to see the programme as an opportunity for their continuing professional development. There were approximately ten students in each e-group. In return for their participation in and reflections on the embryonic courses, they gained new and valuable skills in e-moderation. The third presentation involved paying participants.

The outcomes

After the first presentation of the course, the students felt that the course was interesting and they had acquired a considerable amount of knowledge concerning the theory of e-moderation. However, several issues were highlighted by the tutors. They felt that an opportunity to regularly interact within the group would enhance the reflection and learning process. For the second presentation of the course, weekly informal chat sessions were set up to encourage students to interact with each other and talk about their learning problems and queries.

Reflections after presentations of the course provided a broader base for future development. Although the course itself was considered to be reflective, academic and involved learning through technology, the tutors felt that the content of the course was too embedded in traditional distance learning rather than focusing on the distinct skills of e-moderating. Their opinion was that the course provided few opportunities for the students to put their knowledge on e-moderation into practice and be confident of their skills to manage e-learners. In addition, the VLE needed to be more flexible. Some of the operations were cumbersome and the system was often unreliable, introducing barriers into the learning and teaching process. It was also decided that the assessment should provide an opportunity to apply the newly acquired knowledge to some aspect in the students' work or learning, rather than merely being a series of general reflections.

Following all these comments, the course material was substantially revised to accommodate a significantly greater amount of practical activity (Tutoring Online, 2002). The third presentation of the course continued to receive favourable reviews from the students with more positive comments from the tutors, who commented that, although further development was required, the course was much improved. In particular, they felt that the increased student involvement had considerably enhanced the course with the participating students being encouraged to practise their e-moderation skills.

Tutoring Online has continued to develop and is now proving to be very successful with steadily rising numbers of students. Successful students have access to an alumni conference enabling them to access discussions on e-experiences, etc.

Case study 2: 'Online Learning', University College Worcester, UK

At University College Worcester, the Learning Paradigm (Gallop, 2002), taken from the Learning and Teaching Strategy, states that: 'courses are being designed and documented in terms of what students have to do in order to learn, rather than in terms of what teachers do to teach.'

During the academic year 2001/2, Online Learning was a Level 2 module providing 15 credits within the degree structure. The 12-week module was studied by two groups of students between February and May 2002. One group was based at the Worcester campus (Group A) during a regular weekly morning session while the other group was based at the Hereford campus (Group B) during a regular weekly evening session. The module content was taught to the groups in parallel to enable comparison in outcomes and to allow students to interchange groups if they so wished.

Group A involved 24 students who met for a weekly timetabled lecture and practical session while Group B, involving 10 students, were taught through three traditional scheduled lectures with the rest of the sessions using online delivery. The module content consisted of theoretical (weeks 1–6) and practical aspects (weeks 7–12). For assessment, students were required to submit an essay based on theoretical aspects of online learning and to develop an online learning package using a multimedia package (Toolbook). In addition, they had to provide an individual diary of reflections on their learning during the course. The study here focuses on Group B although comparison will be made with Group A with regards to assessment outcomes.

An e-learning blended approach was used in the design with the lecture sessions providing information on course content, encouraging group interaction and identity to take place. The same lecturing materials (PowerPoint slides) were used for both groups A and B. Scheduled weekly chat sessions were used to support an asynchronous conference containing module material and information. The course materials consisted of an online learning handbook highlighting the issues of learning online and a paper-based study pack with supporting information for research, e.g. websites, electronic library materials. It was anticipated that the practical sessions would require more face-to-face interaction and therefore regular sessions were timetabled for week 1 (to commence the module and establish group interaction), week 7 (to conclude the theoretical aspects and commence the practical) and week 10 (to provide support on practical aspects). During weeks 7–12, students were also offered additional one-to-one tuition in the use of the software package as well as telephone support during specified hours.

The standard VLE tool used at UCW was BSCW (Figure 8.2). To enable synchronous activities and to ensure secure assessment facilities, the IT service at UCW added additional features to the standard student interface login for module participants.

The tutor

From 1997 to 2002, I was a Senior Lecturer in Information Technology at University College Worcester, UK. As course developer and tutor, I provided guidance and support to learners throughout the presentations of both versions of this module.

The learners

The majority of the students in this group were mature students studying part-time. The gender mix was approximately equal and all of the students were familiar with being tutored through lectures and tutorials. One student had previously had some experience of learning using technology. Several acknowledged that they were keen

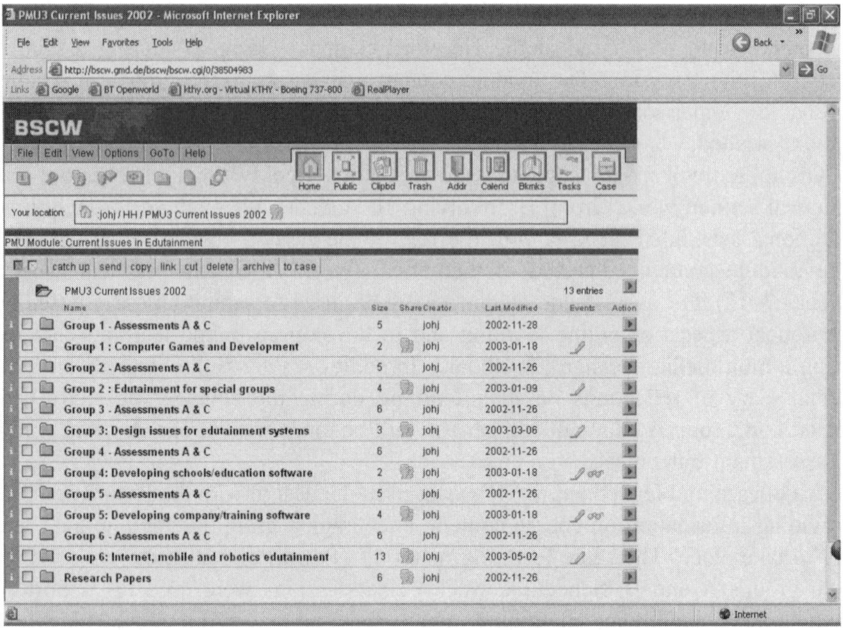

Figure 8.2 The BSCW VLE

to learn but were apprehensive whether the virtual environment would prove to be a barrier to their learning rather than an aid. The students were informed of the style of learning prior to them deciding to study for the module in this form. Approximately half of the group indicated that studying in this form was much more convenient and enabled more regular participation given their family and other responsibilities.

The outcomes

The first session with Group B was a face-to-face session where all information relating to the teaching and learning style was provided to the students. They were also given a general introduction and overview to the content of the module.

The first online session took place during the scheduled timetable session in week 2 of the module. It had been anticipated that some students would use the College facilities at Hereford while others would use their own home-based facilities. However, in practice, the vast majority of the students worked at home for the online chat sessions. The online chat sessions aimed to mirror the face-to-face sessions, i.e. the students would read and prepare questions from the lecture material and then pose their queries through the chat facility.

After the first chat session, student feedback was obtained regarding the student learning experience and the suggestions were used to inform the teaching for the next online session (Hamilton-Jones, 2003):

- Students requested that the lecture materials should be available for longer periods of time prior to the online chat session, giving them the opportunity to undertake more preparation. It is often assumed that in face-to-face (f2f) classes prior circulation of lecture notes encourages non-attendance at f2f sessions, whereas in this instance it had entirely the reverse effect!
- The lecture materials were revised to encourage further student participation as the flow of communication appeared to be dominated by the tutor with the students contributing little. Questions were added after every 5/6 slides in the PowerPoint presentation, designed to make the students reflect on the material, consider the question and then apply the information. This produced a much richer source of communication from the students with reduced tutor contributions. During this development, there was a marked difference in student motivation and learning between the groups.
- The timetabled sessions were of 3 hours' duration. However, in practice, students found it difficult to maintain interest after 1.5 to 2 hours. A shared 'plan' for the session was set up and a 'chatroom agenda' was devised. This was developed and refined over the rest of the online sessions.

Following these revisions, the course continued to develop well. The students became more confident in learning and communicating online with some volunteering to take leading roles in the communication.

At the beginning of the practical part of the course in week 7, the group met face-to-face to assess progress and to provide an introduction to the practical knowledge required. It had been anticipated that another group session would also take place in week 10 but, surprisingly, the students elected to continue to study the rest of the course in online mode. A number of the students made use of telephone support and one-to-one sessions for additional support. The students were now fully confident with learning online and demonstrated considerably more willingness to explore with their learning than the students in Group A.

The results from the assessments produced an interesting outcome with Group B gaining a significantly higher average mark than Group A. This was probably due to several factors in Group B:

- It contained more mature students who are traditionally more motivated to learn.
- The students had read through the theoretical information prior to the lectures and then discussed the questions, gaining a deeper level of understanding.
- The students had to work harder individually to complete any gaps in their knowledge.
- The students had a better group identity and supported each other more obviously than Group A.

From feedback, the majority of students in Group B indicated that the learning experience had been more challenging than had been initially expected. Most indicated that they would study another module using this learning approach.

Case study 3: current issues in edutainment, Halmstad University, Sweden

This involved a module that is part of an innovative undergraduate Informatics degree programme entitled Edutainment Software Design (ESD) held at Halmstad University, Sweden. The aim of this programme is to train systems developers for the edutainment sector and promote a reflective and participatory learning style throughout (Svane *et al.*, 2001 and 2002).

'Current Issues in Edutainment' is a final-year (senior level) 10-week module, providing 10 credits, running from November to January in each academic year. An important aim of this module is to encourage students to reflect on the curriculum of the course, using their more developed reflective and questioning skills as the basis for further exploration as well as broadening student awareness of current research issues pertaining to edutainment systems development. Upon completion of the module, students have read 30 to 45 research articles (at least 500 pages of text) and have had lectures on academic writing, the review process, peer reviews and other issues pertinent to the area. During the research on this module, students have typically added five or more 'individual' articles to their theoretical framework. Teaching involves lectures, tutorials and face-to-face seminars as well as online activity. All students are Swedish although they are all able to converse fluently in English, both verbally and in writing. This was a familiar situation in this degree as these students had often been taught by international lecturers throughout their three years of study. The VLE used in this case study was BSCW (see Figure 8.2).

The module commenced with a lecture in which students were provided with the module content. Then they were randomly divided into groups comprising of five or six students and presented with their topic/theme for investigation, together with an outline of the assessment requirements. During most weeks, students had opportunities for only short visits (15 minutes per group) to interact with the campus-based teacher and were encouraged to use the VLE to facilitate interaction with both tutors, with other groups, and for comparison of work. Early in the module, all groups had a discussion session on campus with both tutors. Each meeting included a review of group progress to date and instructions on how to use the VLE for individual and group work.

Module assessments included:

- individual research paper, focusing on any of the areas within the specified topic;
- group research paper, focusing on the given theme;
- individual reflective diary, outlining the group dynamics throughout the writing process;
- five reflective (group authored) critiques reviewing the other groups' research papers.

For feedback, all students received a full critique of individual and group papers from both tutors. They also received a shorter, written comment on their reflective diary, which contained each student's own reflections on their experiences from start to finish.

The tutors

This module provided an opportunity to team-teach on a module with a moderate number of students, involving online and face-to-face delivery. I was one of the two module tutors providing guidance and support to the learners with my colleague based in Sweden while I was based in England. This required the design and development of a workable learning and teaching blend, given the pattern of visits to Sweden, and the nature of the student support required. Both of us had been involved in the development of innovative curricula and reflective learning styles over several years (Hamilton-Jones et al., 2001; Svane et al., 2001; Hamilton-Jones et al., 2003).

The learners

There were 35 final-year students studying this module. Due to the distinctive nature of the degree programme, they were acknowledged as 'different' from traditional student groups as they were accustomed to questioning and seeking innovation at every opportunity, as well as being encouraged to develop and use reflective learning skills throughout their course.

The outcomes

Writing research papers is not an easy task and certainly posed a challenge to the ESD students, even though the students possessed massive experience of questioning, reasoning and reflection. Although this was the third year this group had worked together, the enthusiasm for module methods and concepts was still evident.

The initial part of the module was regarded as 'difficult' by quite a number of students, who had anticipated a more prescriptive dialogue from the tutors. The first few meetings set the scene for future development and, gradually, the students gained confidence in their more analytical role and their work developed.

The reflective component of the module proved to be an exciting opportunity for members to bond more closely and to learn about themselves and each other. Some student groups divided their group papers into sections and subdivided group tasks in a similar way. Moreover, some students noted the process of learning about group dynamics per se, and about the group as individuals.

Another factor that had not been anticipated by the tutoring team was the difficulty these students experienced in reflecting 'on demand'. On several occasions, they had been exposed to similar activities, but they had never before used a Virtual Learning Environment (VLE) for such work. As the module progressed however, the students' apprehension receded and their reflective diaries came to be just as valuable for individual insight as was intended. However, the initial hesitancy in reflective productivity caused us to ponder further on how reflective diaries could be used and what further factors needed to be considered. While reflection on command presented the Swedish students with a major challenge, working in their second language did not present too much of a barrier to learning.

Initial, overall findings included:

- Students felt apprehensive at the start of the module as they indicated they were expecting a more prescriptive input. This had delayed the start of the paper production process. Following the initial meeting, some of these reservations appeared to be resolved as the speed and intensity of work quickened.
- Students made little interactive use of the VLE, except as an electronic library, despite receiving guidance and practice on its use. This was understandable for *within* group communication but it was anticipated that use *between* the groups would have been greater. This could have been due to this being the first time the VLE had been used in a module, despite the students' informatics background.
- A significant number of students provided diaries with purely descriptive content, giving an account of contributions rather than reflective learning experiences. This was worrying and different from what we had anticipated.
- Those students that had reflected analytically had begun to see the relevance of the component parts of the ESD course and, in verbal feedback, indicated that they felt that this module had prepared them well for the dissertation which followed during the spring semester.

From this experience, some questions came to mind:

Did the ESD students need a tighter course structure?
This was frequently commented on, especially during the first weeks when students had not fully grasped what was required.

Did they need more guidance on undertaking research?
Maybe, although the research skills flowed once they had become more confident in their handling of the information.

Did the students find the peer-group part of the reflective process threatening?
This would be surprising as these students have experienced over two years of reflecting on their own and others' learning.

Was the blend appropriate for the course?
Although the initial hesitation caused us some concern, the student response was that the blend worked well for them. Further explorations on 'blend' will be developed based on these module experiences.

We shall review and refine the module content and operation over several cohorts, taking the results of our deliberations into account in subsequent development.

Acknowledgements

I would like to acknowledge the assistance and support of the following in preparing this chapter:

National Extension College, Cambridge, UK
Sue Carr (Administrator, Tutoring Online)
Anna Peachey (Consultant, Tutoring Online)
Karen Saunders (E-learning Development Manager)

Halmstad University, Sweden
Ulf Ivarsson (Director of International Office)
Torben Svane (Associate Professor, Dept. of Information Science, Computing and Electrical Engineering)

University College Worcester, UK
Rowland Gallop (Director of Learning and Teaching Centre)
John Peters (Deputy Director of Learning and Teaching Centre)
Helen Hill (IT Service)
Grants from the Learning & Teaching Fund

Aston University, Birmingham, UK
Roy Smith (Director of Combined Honours)
Miranda Cleal, Sue Perry and Lindsay Batt (Combined Honours)

References

Bosman, K. (2002) *Simulation-Based e-learning*, Syracuse University, Instructional Design, Development & Evaluation. Online. Available at: www.web.syr.edu/~kjbosman/Project8Product.doc (accessed 30 March 2004).

Cox, P. (1999) *Online Learning: Old Wine, New Bottles or a New Way to Learn in a Post-Modern Society?* Online. Available at: www.nw99.net.au/papers (accessed 30 November 2004).

Gallop, R. (2002) *The Learning & Teaching Strategy 2002–2005: Learning Paradigm.* Online. Available at: www.worc.ac.uk/LTMain/Strategy/2002-2005/paradigm.html (accessed 30 March 2004).

Hamilton-Jones, J. (2003) 'What Makes a Good e-Learner?' Discussion paper presented at ILTAC 2003, University of Warwick, UK. Online. Available at: www.aston.ac.uk/combhons/jo/publics.html (accessed 30 November 2004).

Hamilton-Jones, J. and Nixon, J.C. (2001) 'Who Survives the Double Degree?' Paper presented at the International Conference for Lifelong Learning, University College Worcester, UK, July 2000. Online. Available at: www.aston.ac.uk/combhons/jo/publics.html (accessed 30 November 2004).

Hamilton-Jones, J. and Svane, T. (2003) 'Developing Research Using Reflective Diaries'. Proceedings of 32nd ASEE/IEEE Frontiers in Education Conference, Boulder, CO, November 2003.

Hamilton-Jones, J.K., Lewin-Jones, J.J. and Nixon, J.C. (2003) *Developing Online Learning and Monitoring for International Students*, Small Grants Award Final Report submitted to UKCOSA, September 2002. Summary reported in World Views, *UKCOSA Magazine.*

Rosenberg, M. (2001) *E-Learning; Strategies for Delivering Knowledge in the Digital Age*, McGraw-Hill, New York.

Salmon, G. (2000) *E-moderating: The Key to Teaching and Learning Online*, Kogan Page, London.

Svane, T. and Hamilton-Jones, J. (2002) 'Establishing International Co-operation in Edutainment Software Design: Some Experiences'. Proceedings of 33rd ASEE/IEEE Frontiers in Education Conference, Boston, MA, November 2002.

Svane, T., Aderklou, C., Fritzdorf, L. and Hamilton-Jones, J. (2001) 'Knowledge by User Demand and Self-reflection: New Models for Teaching and Assessment in Edutainment Software Design'. Proceedings of 31st ASEE/IEEE Frontiers in Education Conference, Reno, NV, October 2001.

Tutoring Online (2002) *Course Handbook*, National Extension College, Cambridge, UK.

Note
J.K. Hamilton-Jones is now J.K. Smedley

Facilitating students towards self-directed learning

Julie-Anne Regan

Introduction

This chapter summarises results from a year-long study, which examined students' perspectives of self-directed learning (SDL). The results raise important issues regarding the process of becoming an independent learner. I have come to view this process as a continuum from directed learning to self-directed learning. Studies have shown that this development can be painful without guidance (Taylor and Burgess, 1995; Hurd, 1998; Lunyk-Child *et al.*, 2001; Hewitt-Taylor 2001) and I argue that this pain is unnecessary.

Initially, I identify the aims of the study and the rationale for the research design. My review of the literature about SDL then defines key terms and provides an overview of research undertaken in the area of the development of autonomy in learning. Although my study focuses on the experience of nursing students, this literature review suggests that my results and implications can be applied across the HE curriculum.

My discussion of the study's results is structured around the five research questions:

- What do students understand by the term SDL?
- How effective do students feel SDL is?
- What support do students perceive as necessary for effective SDL?
- What do students feel are the barriers to SDL?
- What motivates students towards SDL?

In each instance, I discuss the findings and identify implications for practice. Finally, I offer a summary of good practice in developing students towards SDL.

Background and aims

This work started from my concern that SDL was becoming an increasing feature of nurse education, without any clear evaluation of its effectiveness. There is a wealth of literature on SDL from the teaching perspective but very little from the students' per-spective. I felt there was an expectation that students could direct their own learning just because they were in Higher Education, despite the recognition that this is perhaps one of the most significant differences from their past learning experiences (Marshall and Rowland, 1998). There is also concern elsewhere in Higher Education that the constant drive to reduce contact hours is not necessarily in the students' best interest, at a time when the academic profile of the students is changing (Ottewill, 2001; Hurd, 1998).

Anecdotal evidence from students during teaching sessions and tutorials suggested that students were not clear about what was expected of them with regard to SDL. Many were not confident about the process of directing their own learning or the skills needed for util-ising such an approach effectively. Students were not convinced that SDL was beneficial to them but, rather, they saw it as an institutional strategy for coping with increasing num-bers of students. It was also apparent that lecturers were inconsistent in their approach towards SDL, especially regarding the level of guidance and support they were willing to offer students to facilitate the process of them becoming independent learners.

Therefore, the overall aim of this investigation was to gain a greater understanding of the nature of SDL from a student perspective. I anticipated that such an understand-ing would inform teaching practice by academic staff, support curriculum policy by the institution, and thereby improve the learning experience for the students.

Research design

The investigation, which had two distinct phases, was carried out with students on a pre-registration Diploma in Nursing programme. The first phase used two focus groups (12 students) to explore the topic. The results from this phase were then used to generate a questionnaire that tested the level of agreement within a larger sample. The question-naire was piloted with six students and, in the main study, 97 students responded. Respondents were asked to rate their level of agreement or disagreement on a 5-point Likert-scale, to a series of statements generated from the focus groups. The question-naire and full set of results are available on the accompanying website but the shorthand version of each statement can be seen on the result tables within this chapter.

The literature on self-directed learning

The term self-directed learning has become synonymous with other pedagogical terms such as autonomous learning, self-managed learning, lifelong learning and independent learning (Souto and Turner, 2000). These various terms can be confusing for lecturers, not least because the reality of the concepts can vary from institution to institution, or even department to department, and vary still further from the theoretical view of the concept. Boud considers that, despite the array of terms, the common goals are to: 'develop independence, self-directness and responsibility for learning' (Boud, 1981: 11).

Souto and Turner also consider that the various terms are interrelated and describe 'a trend towards encouraging more independent modes of study' (2000: 385). Because I wanted to know what students thought SDL was, I had loosely defined it, for the purpose of the study, as any learning outside of direct classroom contact.

The term SDL can be problematic in that it may provide a philosophical dilemma for some lecturers. The term implies students will direct the content of their learning as well as the process and therefore issues such as preparation, guidance and supporting students with SDL could be seen as 'paradoxical' (Taylor and Burgess, 1995: 87). Robbins (1988) considers that SDL should not be bound by rigid course competencies or outcomes but, for some professional programmes, such rigidity may be perceived as essential. I would suggest that a certain degree of rigidity about outcomes would apply to most programmes in Higher Education. Because of the theoretical debate about SDL, it is difficult to find a consensus in the literature about good practice in facilitating this process. However, there is an increasing trend towards the view that some preparation is required, particularly in relation to the skills of retrieving and critiquing information.

Hurd (1998) considers that, if you claim to provide choice, then you cannot compel people to become autonomous learners if they feel that approach is not right for them. However, SDL has long been associated with Higher Education and the characteristics of a graduate and I believe that the ability to direct one's own learning is a worthy and realistic aim for all students. True self-directed learning necessitates being able to identify your own learning needs. Baume and Baume (1997) argued this was problematic in the early stages of developing SDL skills. Taylor and Burgess (1995) argue that preparation is essential for effective facilitation of SDL skills and that viewing SDL as a way of reducing contact time may be a false economy. In summarising the literature on skills for SDL, Dunlap (1997) identifies the following as necessary:

- The ability to identify and define a problem/learning need.
- The ability to identify, find, use and critique resources for solving the problem or meeting the learning requirement.
- The ability to capture and apply information from resources to the problem or learning need.
- The ability to critique information, skills and processes used to solve the problem or meet the learning requirement.

(Dunlap, 1997: 2)

Clearly, the majority of students will not possess these skills as they enter Higher Education and some preparation is essential. Developing these skills will take some time so the nature of SDL may need to change as the student progresses.

Studies that have evaluated students' perceptions of SDL have found that anxiety, frustration, confusion and anger are common feelings for students at the start of their course (Taylor and Burgess, 1995; Lunyk-Child et al., 2001; Hewitt-Taylor, 2001). These lessen in the second year and only a minority express these feelings by the end of the course. For many students, their previous experiences of teaching and learning may have required little or no independent learning and a significant change will be needed. Some students feel more ready for changing their approach to learning at the start of their course than others do. Fisher et al. used a 'Readiness Scale' and found it 'aided in the assessment of students' attitudes, abilities and personality characteristics, necessary for self-directed learning' (Fisher et al., 2001: 516). In addition to being ready for the change, students will want to be convinced of the benefits of change. Akerlind and Trevitt argue that by discussing SDL as an approach to teaching and learning and giving students the opportunity to explore the 'advantages and disadvantages of the traditional and innovative approaches', student resistance to the change may be lowered (Akerlind and Trevitt, 1999: 101).

Lecturers generally seem supportive of SDL, recognising the benefits of lifelong learning for individuals themselves and society as a whole. In some institutions, the increased use of SDL could be seen as 'releasing' staff for research activities or enabling larger numbers of students to be catered for. Jordan and Yeomans (1991) found that while staff may believe SDL to be a positive development, introducing it in a context of timesaving can become a barrier to change. If lecturers are to facilitate the development of their students into self-directed learners, they need to understand SDL from the students' perspective, rather than from the organisation's perspective. Therefore, the results of this study will be of interest to everyone involved in this process.

Results and discussion

What is self-directed learning?

When I first asked this question in the focus groups, students were very reluctant to describe it in definite terms but they certainly understood the goals of independence, responsibility and developing the skills for lifelong learning. These themes were also evident in the second phase, as can be seen in Figure 9.1.

Few students felt they had complete freedom to learn what they wished but did indicate freedom to decide when, where and how much to learn. Students considered that learning to supplement the taught sessions, as guided by the lecturers or the curriculum, was still SDL. It could be argued that the term self-managed learning is a more accurate description than SDL (Hammond and Collins, 1991). Students in the focus groups did not think lecturers had clearly defined SDL for them but that it was expected they would 'do it' from the beginning of the programme.

Students in the focus groups were scathing about the possible motivation for SDL within their programme. There was a consensus that SDL was given as a 'cop-out' or to cover staff shortages. Fortunately, only 22.7 per cent (n = 22) of respondents to the questionnaire agreed that it was a cop-out and only 38.1 per cent (n = 37) that it was given to cover staff shortages. However, lecturers should not be too complacent about this and should take care in how they refer to time set aside in the programme for SDL.

This study confirms the need for programme teams to arrive at a consensus of what they mean by SDL. Hewitt-Taylor (2002) comments that lecturers and students find it difficult to define SDL particularly where the philosophy is incongruent with the realities and expectations of the programme. There needs to be an agreed terminology which accurately reflects the nature of SDL on that programme, so that lecturers can feel comfortable explaining it to students and making their expectations clear and unambiguous.

The goal you and they are striving towards is that of a self-directed, independent learner. Discussion about the developmental approach towards that goal should be an integral part of the programme, as part of learning to learn in Higher Education. This development can be monitored through level descriptors, as described by Moon in Chapter 10.

Akerlind and Trevitt (1999) suggest lecturers provide students with supportive evidence from the literature and previous students in an attempt to persuade them of the benefits of this change in approach. If students are less likely to resist the change at an emotional level, they may not find the change as painful. In other words we must not assume that students will see SDL as a benefit, we have to sell it.

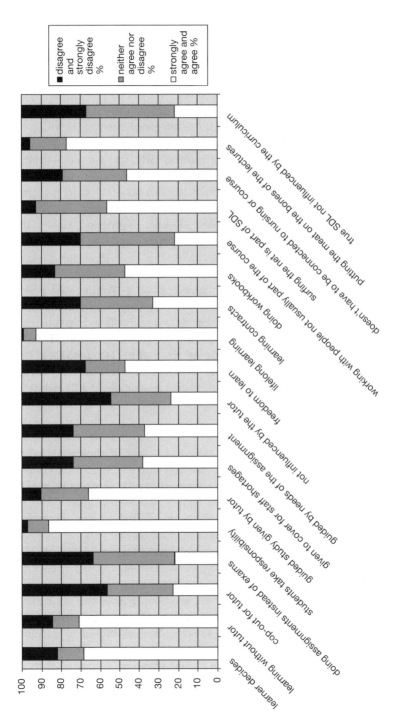

Figure 9.1 What is SDL?

How effective is SDL as a method of teaching and learning?

There was a strong consensus within both sample groups that individuals' characteristics play an important role in determining the effectiveness of SDL. A total of 90.7 per cent (n = 88) of students agree that the effectiveness of SDL depends on the individual. Eighty-four per cent (n = 80) of students agreed that the individual has to be self-disciplined for SDL to be effective, and 78.4 per cent (n = 76) agreed that SDL requires more motivation than more traditional methods of teaching and learning, in order to be effective. It could be argued that SDL should be an optional method of teaching and learning, depending on the individual's propensity to such a method. In reality of course, it is not so.

What is really worrying is that, in this sample of students, SDL was *not* seen as effective for the majority of students; 70.1 per cent (n = 68) agreed that most students do nothing during time allocated in the programme to SDL. The need for more guidance and feedback is a theme that continues throughout all sections of this study. Without it, it appears that SDL is not effective for many of these students, particularly early in the programme; 77.3 per cent (n = 75) of students agreed that SDL can be de-motivating if you 'don't know where you are going with it'.

If SDL by students is to be facilitated by lecturers, there needs to be an acceptance that the effectiveness of SDL requires guidance, particularly in the early stages of the development process. Not giving guidance at this stage can de-motivate students and lead to anger and frustration (Baume and Baume, 1997). Hewitt-Taylor also found that students 'considered SDL required some guidelines to be successful' (Hewitt-Taylor, 2001: 501). We need to direct students initially on what to learn, suitable sources of information, and the depth of knowledge and understanding that is expected. Almost half the respondents would like to see SDL used less in the Common Foundation programme (CFP) and more in the branch programme. This equates to less in the first year and more in the second and third years.

For students functioning at the 'directed' end of the continuum, SDL is not the most effective strategy for teaching and learning. This needs to be considered carefully when deciding what aspects of a programme should be covered in contact time. Of course, there is no guarantee that students will learn more effectively in the classroom but over 50 per cent of students in this study felt they learnt more in a classroom with a lecturer and other students than through SDL. The key to effectiveness surely lies in developing students to enable them to make more effective use of time allocated to SDL.

Using a readiness scale (Fisher *et al.*, 2001) has obvious benefits for assessing students' starting point on the continuum and would indicate what development is required before SDL can be viewed as an effective approach.

Another implication for practice is workload calculations of lecturers. In my department, teaching workload only includes classroom teaching. Therefore, if students are seeking guidance and support during time allocated to SDL, that is not classed as teaching. This implies that SDL does not require lecturer input and could support the view that you leave them to their own devices, regardless of the effectiveness, or not, of such an approach. Therefore, if a department does adopt a supportive approach to SDL, policies affected by that decision would need to be reviewed in the light of changing practice.

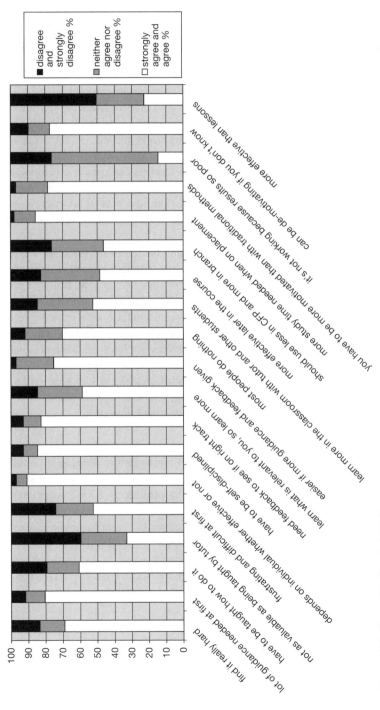

Figure 9.2 How effective is SDL?

What support is needed for SDL to be effective?

There was a high level of agreement with most of the ideas generated from the focus groups. Students need to feel confident in their ability to effectively direct their own learning, according to 97.9 per cent (n = 95) of respondents. With widening access it could be argued that many entrants might not have had a successful experience in compulsory education, hence the non-traditional route to HE. If this is the case, lack of confidence is likely to be an issue for such students.

Students were very clear that tutorial support is needed to ensure the effectiveness of SDL. The attitude of the lecturer in supporting SDL is also crucial. Students felt tutors needed to be more available, welcoming and willing to offer guidance and feedback. For a significant number of this sample, more training in the skills needed for SDL was an issue. However, this does not apply to all students and reflects the extremely varied background of entrants to this programme. A limitation of the study is that, to ensure complete anonymity, no biographical data was collected. Such information would have been useful in discerning patterns of age, gender and educational background in relation to the need for skills training. If this training was targeted, each student may be able to receive more individual assistance.

One area of disagreement between the focus groups and the questionnaire respondents was in relation to the use of quizzes or tests as a benchmark. The focus group participants were all in agreement that such methods, if managed in a non-threatening way, really helped them to identify their learning needs and gauge their knowledge level against others in their group. However, only 46.4 per cent (n = 45) of respondents to the questionnaire agreed with this statement. The students in the focus groups identified specific lecturers who adopt this style, whereas respondents to the questionnaire may not have the same personal experience. This could account for the incongruence between the two groups.

The challenge for practice is ensuring the availability of welcoming lecturers, willing to give guidance and support to students. Providing guidance and support will certainly not produce the timesaving that may have been anticipated by policy makers and a more supportive approach may be resisted.

Assuming that everyone is supportive of this change in practice, I believe that support for SDL needs to be organised to ensure equity. If supporting students to develop into independent learners is not seen as everyone's responsibility, it can fall to a few willing staff.

Dierks (1999) outlines an approach that includes the provision of an 'Independent Learning Lecturer' who is available during times allocated to SDL. This could be an effective approach, if it was rotated among all the lecturers in the department, classed as workload and the rota clearly communicated to students.

Sobral describes a small group approach, with a lecturer acting as facilitator. These weekly groups allow students to share their knowledge and receive guidance and feedback from a lecturer. Students using this method reported an increase in efficacy and confidence with regards to SDL (Sobral, 1997).

A third option, which can be viewed as a compromise, is to incorporate guidance and feedback related to SDL, within all taught sessions. Although this means that students still do not have access to a lecturer during periods allocated to SDL, they do have guidance on what direction their SDL should be taking and an opportunity to discuss their learning at a later stage.

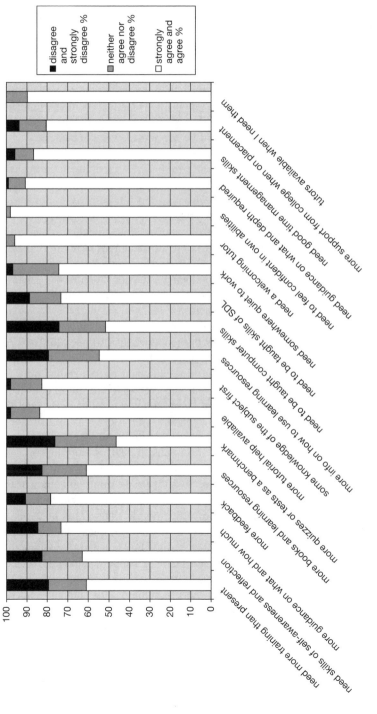

Figure 9.3 What do students need in order to direct their own learning effectively?

What barriers exist to effective SDL?

The statements receiving the highest level of agreement related to students' experiences of SDL in the clinical area. These will not be discussed here, as they are not relevant to all programmes. Apart from placement issues, students perceived the biggest barrier to be a lack of knowledge. This result reflects findings by Taylor and Burgess (1995) who also found that not knowing what to learn was one of the main problems reported by students. As can be seen in Figure 9.4, only 38.1 per cent (n = 37) of students agreed that too much SDL too early, is a barrier, which appears to contradict the previous point. However, 43.3 per cent (n = 42) of students responded using the 'neither agree nor disagree' option and only 19 per cent (n = 18) actually disagreed with the statement. I cannot account for this discrepancy but it could be the way it was phrased.

The theme of guidance and feedback features strongly in this section too; 83.5 per cent (n = 81) of respondents found that not being told if it was right or wrong was a barrier and 79.4 per cent (n = 77) found a lack of guidance to be a barrier. Self-confidence and lack of tutorial support are also seen as barriers but perhaps do not appear as strongly in this section. This leads me to believe that students recognise they can develop along the continuum without help, but the support and guidance of lecturers would facilitate that process significantly. The disinterest of lecturers in relation to SDL was found to be a barrier by 71.1 per cent (n = 69) of students and 68 per cent (n = 66) referred to a poor relationship with the lecturer as being a barrier. Such issues relate to previous discussions about the difficulties lecturers may have with guiding students with SDL and steps that can be taken to overcome them.

The profile of HE students is changing rapidly and many more students now have dependants and other commitments to balance with their studies; 81.4 per cent (n = 79) of respondents found family and/or social commitments to be a barrier to effective SDL. Students in the focus groups said that they used time allocated on the programme for SDL as a way of reducing childcare costs and/or an opportunity to engage in paid work to supplement their bursaries. With the continued emphasis on widening access and the likelihood of increased fees, more and more students are likely to be in this situation. Again, the underlying philosophy and expectations of SDL within individual programmes will determine whether this is seen as a barrier or a bonus. If SDL is truly meant to be self-directed, then spending that time working or caring for children is valid. If, however, the expectation is that students are using that time to fulfil the learning outcomes of the programme, then such commitments are seen as a barrier, as in this student group.

Not having access to learning resources out of office hours was seen as a barrier to SDL by 80.4 per cent (n = 78) of respondents. This is mainly a problem within smaller satellite sites – but also affected the main campus during holiday periods. Gradually, these issues are being dealt with but lecturers and learning support personnel need to work together to ensure such barriers are minimised.

There could be an argument for frontloading the programme with content delivered in a more didactic style and a limited amount of SDL. Incrementally, over the length of the programme, the balance could be reversed. This is already done to a certain extent by reducing the contact time allocated to modules at various academic levels. I would argue that there are further adjustments to be made, particularly in the first year.

Fallows and Ahmet argue that: 'Inspiring students to become independent and well-motivated learners is perhaps the key role of any educator' (Fallows and Ahmet, 1999: 1).

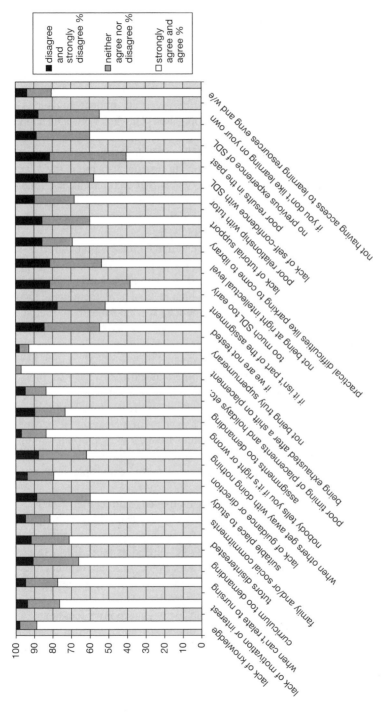

Figure 9.4 What barriers exist to prevent students directing their own learning?

Therefore, in addition to giving knowledge, guiding and supporting students, the lecturer also needs to find the key to motivating each student towards directing their own learning.

What motivates students to direct their own learning?

Although many motivators were identified within the focus groups, the majority of the discussion focused on the role of a 'good lecture' in motivating students to direct their own learning. The knowledge gained during the lecture gives the student guidance on what further knowledge they need to understand the topic area. This link between lectures and SDL was verified by the results of the questionnaire. One hundred per cent (n = 97) of respondents agreed that a good lecture motivates them to direct their own learning and 85.4 per cent (n = 82) agreed that a lively class discussion also motivates them. Combine that with an enthusiastic lecturer and it is obvious that lecturers have a fundamental role to play in motivating students to become independent learners. I believe that this link between directive approaches and the development of an independent learner does not receive sufficient attention in the literature on SDL.

Comments on the questionnaires suggest that 'big sticks and carrots' was not understood by many respondents and is therefore disregarded. Strict lecturers were seen as motivational in the focus groups but this was not supported by the larger sample. Likewise, the notion of a negative experience being motivational received a high level of agreement in the focus groups but not in the larger sample. On the surface, the idea was unpalatable to me but I have to admit the discussion within the focus groups was convincing and could have unduly influenced other participants.

It can be seen from Figure 9.5 that students are motivated by a range of factors, some of which would be seen as intrinsic motivators and others as extrinsic. Intrinsic motivation is described as reflecting a personal goal and deriving from an interest in the subject area; whereas extrinsic motivation is characterised by its instrumental form and reliance on external rewards and pressures (Entwistle, 1998). This view of a clear divide between the two forms can be viewed as over-simplistic (Iphofen, 1998), a view I would strongly support. Students indicated in the focus groups that different things motivated them at different times and in different subject areas and often there could be multiple motivators, both intrinsic and extrinsic.

In the focus groups, only one student said they were motivated to direct their own learning by group work and the student received a hostile reception from other participants. Given the trend towards Problem-Based Learning (PBL) in nurse education, I decided to include it in the questionnaire phase. Groupwork may be viewed as more likely to promote independent learning than lectures but this study would not support that view. Groupwork was viewed more positively in the larger sample with 53.1 per cent (n = 51) agreeing that it motivated them to direct their own learning. This does not compare favourably to the above figures relating to lectures and lively classroom discussions.

The theme of guidance, support and feedback continues in response to this question, as does the importance of the relationship between student and lecturer. These issues have been discussed in previous sections.

First and foremost, the successful lecturer needs to be aware of the fact that motivating students is a complex issue and there is no room for value judgements about what are

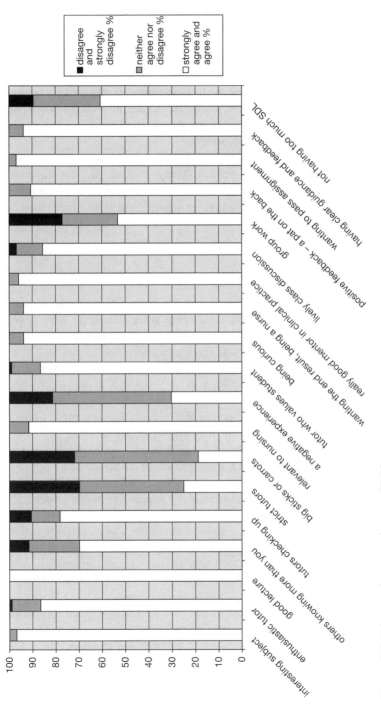

Figure 9.5 What motivates students to SDL?

good and bad motivators. When directing and supporting students in the process of becoming independent learners, the lecturer should endeavour to tap into as many motivational forces as possible. This will be particularly challenging if the topic area is of little interest to students or perhaps more difficult for them to see the relevance of. Creative and innovative ways of delivering the taught element of the topic will be needed in order to inspire students to direct their learning further.

Because what happens in taught sessions is so strongly linked to SDL, the quality of the taught sessions must be a priority. There is the temptation to think that the same lesson plan can be utilised for future groups, with some minor tweaking. This temptation must be resisted as the consequences spread beyond the taught session itself. There needs to be due consideration given to the feasibility of swapping modules on a regular basis to provide a new perspective and fresh ideas.

Groupwork and PBL are discussed in other chapters but the results of this small study surely indicate that pause for thought is needed. Many students are not motivated to direct their own learning by working in groups. This can be improved by ensuring students receive adequate preparation for effective groupwork and skilful facilitation by appropriately trained facilitators.

Conclusions

The small sample group limited the extent to which the study addressed the research questions but I believe the methods used to collect and analyse the data were appropriate. Further research is needed, both in terms of a larger sample and the need to examine the views of students other than those studying nursing.

My main conclusions from this study raise important questions for SDL across the HE curriculum and can be summarised as follows:

- The process of facilitating students to become self-directed learners needs to be as carefully planned as the subject content of the curriculum.
- Lecturers must take an incremental approach to developing independent learners, offering more direction at the start of the programme until students are better equipped to assess their own learning needs. Lecturers can direct students to what they need to know, the depth of knowledge and understanding required and offer students the opportunity to feedback on their learning.
- For the majority of students, guidance, support and feedback is essential for effective SDL, especially in the early part of the programme. Failure to facilitate SDL in this way can be viewed as a barrier to becoming an independent learner and causes the student unnecessary anxiety and distress.

Finally, this study indicates a strong link between SDL and tutor-centred approaches such as lectures. This link appears stronger than has previously been highlighted in the literature on SDL. Therefore, lecturers must strive to maintain the quality of the taught sessions, using student evaluations and peer review to ensure quality improvement and their own continued development.

References

Akerlind, G.S. and Trevitt, A.C. (1999) Enhancing self-directed learning through educational technology: when students resist the change, *Innovations in Education and Training International*, 36, 2, 96–105.

Baume, C. and Baume, D. (1997) The art of inspiring independent learning, *New Academic*, 6, 3, 2–6.

Boud, D. (ed.) (1981) *Developing Student Autonomy in Learning*, Kogan Page: London.

Dierks, A. (1999) Planning for independent learning, *Learning Resources Journal*, 15, 1, 15–18.

Dunlap, J.C. (1997) Preparing students for lifelong learning: a review of instructional methodologies, in *Proceedings of Selected Research and Development Presentations at the 1997 National Convention of the Association for Educational Communications and Technology*, held in Albuquerque, NM, 14–18 February 1997.

Entwistle, N. (1998) Motivation and approaches to learning: motivating and conceptions of teaching, in Brown, S., Armstrong, S. and Thompson, G. (eds) *Motivating Students*, Kogan Page in association with SEDA: London.

Fallows, S. and Ahmet, K. (1999) Inspiring students: an introduction, in Fallows, S. and Ahmet, K. (eds) *Inspiring Students: Case Studies in Motivating the Learner*, Kogan Page in association with SEDA: London.

Fisher, M., King, J. and Tague, G. (2001) Development of a self-directed learning readiness scale for nursing education, *Nurse Education Today*, 21, 7, 516–525.

Hammond, M. and Collins, R. (1991) *Self-Directed Learning: Critical Practice*, Kogan Page: London.

Hewitt-Taylor, J. (2001) Self-directed learning: views of teachers and students, *Journal of Advanced Nursing*, 36, 4, 496–504.

Hewitt-Taylor, J. (2002) Teachers' and students' views on self-directed learning, *Nursing Standard*, 17, 1, 25–23.

Hurd, S. (1998) Autonomy at any price? Issues and concerns from a British HE perspective, *Foreign Language Annals*, 31, 2, 219–230.

Iphofen, R. (1998) Understanding motives in learning: mature students and learner responsibility, in Brown, S., Armstrong, S. and Thompson, G. (eds) *Motivating Students*, Kogan Page in association with SEDA: London.

Jordan, S. and Yeomans, D. (1991) Whither independent learning? The politics of curricular and pedagogical change in a polytechnic department, *Studies in Higher Education*, 16, 3, 291–308.

Lunyk-Child, O., Crooks, D., Ellis, P., Ofosu, C., O'Mara, L. and Rideout, E. (2001) Self-directed learning: faculty and student perceptions, *Journal of Nursing Education*, 40, 3, 116–123.

Marshall, L. and Rowland, F. (1998) *A Guide to Learning Independently*, 3rd edn, Open University Press: Buckingham.

Ottewill, R. (2001) From dependence to independence: issues concerning student-managed learning time. Handout presented to the Institute of Learning and Teaching Annual Conference, York.

Robbins, D. (1988) *The Rise of Independent Study*, The Society for Research into Higher Education and the Open University Press, Buckingham.

Sobral, D. (1997) Improving learning skills – a self-help group approach, *Higher Education*, 33, 1, 39–50.

Souto, C. and Turner, K. (2000) The development of independent study and modern languages learning in non-specialist degree courses: a case study, *Journal of Further and Higher Education*, 24, 3, 385–395.

Taylor, I. and Burgess, H. (1995) Orientation to self-directed learning: paradox or paradigm? *Studies in Higher Education*, 20, 1, 87–98.

Part three

Enhancing student progression and development

10

Progression in higher education: a study of learning as represented in level descriptors

Jenny Moon

Introduction

Level descriptors are an expression of the expected learning achievements of students at different levels in higher education. In the United Kingdom (UK), there are three undergraduate levels and two postgraduate levels. This chapter is based on what is probably the most well-used set of English credit level descriptors in the UK – the SEEC Credit Level Descriptors (Southern England Consortium for Credit Accumulation and Transfer, 2003). These descriptors have formed a basis for development of most other descriptors in the UK and recently have been extended to encompass further education levels. Though the chapter is based on the SEEC version, the content of it applies to most other sets of descriptors because they use the same characteristics as a basis for their description. Some descriptors, such as those developed for the University for Industry (Jackson, 1999) have different emphases – but broadly similar content.

Level descriptors purport to demonstrate progression. Progression is demonstrated in the level descriptors as the expectation of increasing learning abilities in students, which corresponds to the provision of increasingly challenging work. The purpose of this chapter is to tease out some of what underlies the notion of progression in learning as described in the level descriptors. In pursuing the purpose we analyse the content of the level descriptors (i.e. the concepts of learning that are written into the descriptors). A by-product of this activity is the revelation of some of the issues and consequences that result from our adopted manner of describing higher education (HE) learning and teaching on paper. Pinning down something as abstract and genuinely mysterious as learning is difficult, but that is not to say that it should not be attempted. Having something is better than having nothing.

It is important, here, to recognise that the development of level descriptors is not and was not just a technical exercise about the meaning of words or the formation of an administrative classification as now they might appear. Level descriptors were developed as a result of the pooling of observations of academics who work with real students undertaking real programmes, watching the changes and developments in their learning over periods of time. As we show, descriptors are both a list of observations of pedagogical activity and, also, a list of skills and qualities that we have decided to expect in higher education students. On this basis, it is important to explain the processes involved in their construction. The first section of this chapter is, therefore, a brief account of the work on level descriptors that started in the mid-1990s (and in which the writer was involved).

Initial and later development of credit level descriptors

The initial development of level descriptors in the UK occurred as a part of two Department of Employment and Education credit development projects. The process involved meetings of academics who represented disciplines from 50 or so higher education institutions. The academics represented disciplines as diverse as medicine and art history and they discussed, argued and fought over the words that would describe what we might expect of students' work in higher education.

Some of the participants in the exercise of developing descriptors began with the idea that it would be possible to identify a neat progression wherein skills of manipulation of knowledge (analysis, synthesis, evaluation, application) could be exactly mapped in relation to years of study. This represented an incorrect reading of the message that Bloom (1956) was propounding – but is still perpetuated in some quarters. We also went through stages of talking of three-dimensional models or complicated computer graphics to depict the interacting factors that underlie progression. Eventually, there was a recognition that the outcome had to be simple enough to be used.

There have been a number of subsequent changes in form and format of the descriptors. Level M was split into Master's and Taught Doctorate levels as postgraduate programmes have increased. We now also differentiate between credit level descriptors for the description of modules, and qualification descriptors developed as part of the Framework for Higher Education Qualifications (QAA, 2002). Looking back at the changes now, it is interesting to note that none were as fundamental as the original work since none of the subsequent work has relied on direct observations of learners at work.

The content of level descriptors

Many academics discount the value of level descriptors. They see them as too abstract and generalised. They may acknowledge that the descriptors have value for administrative procedures and for giving value to learning in a credit system, but they do not see a role for them in 'real' teaching/learning situations (Moon, 2002a, 2002b).

However, there is another perspective from which level descriptors can be viewed. They provide a pooled expression of the views of a substantial number of experienced HE staff from many disciplines on progression and learning achievement of students in higher education. It is on the basis of this perspective that the current chapter rests. We assume that the elements that have come to be described in level descriptors are an expression of those elements seen as significant in the progress of a student's learning from the beginning of their contact with higher education to the point where they emerge with a qualification.

A rapid perusal of the descriptors shows a range of headings that run through the descriptors and that are consistent at each level. The system of headings helps in the use of the descriptors as progression in particular traits can be observed at any level. Deeper analysis of the descriptors, however, indicates that the actual headings are not always help-ful in that they contain quite a mixture of factors that relate to learning and the manage-ment of learning. For example, sometimes they refer to a student's process of learning ('can analyse'), and sometimes they refer to the context of learning or the management of the learning of a student (e.g. the level of guidance required). Sometimes, too, they refer to learning itself ('has comprehensive understanding of technique') and sometimes to the representation of learning in the fulfilment of a task ('can transform abstracts . . . towards a given purpose'). Essentially, level descriptors are made up of 'strands' of areas of development that follow through all levels. While these can be identified as separate, most are not independent – they interrelate. For example, a child of five can analyse (represented in one strand) – but what attaches the cognitive activity of analysis to a level of functioning is the complexity of the material that is analysed (another strand).

Strands in level descriptors

The strands in the level descriptors are listed below. They were teased out of the descrip-tors and subjected to continuous trial and error until they seemed to be sufficiently robust to support the discussion of progression that follows. As already said, many of these strands are not represented by specific headings in the descriptors. For example, strands such as those relating to guidance for students or student autonomy, are represented under several headings – not just one. Another factor that became evident in the process is that there is an obvious division between strands that refer to the context of the learning (its management or teaching) and the others that refer to learners' qualities and abilities (i.e. to do with learning processes). Level descriptors refer to a range of pedagogical activ-ities with implications for learning – not just learning itself. The strands are as follows:

Strands that relate to the context of the learning
- Change in the complexity of knowledge that is presented – the degree of challenge of the material of learning to the learner.
- Change in the complexity of tasks that the learner is expected to be able to tackle. This may be expressed in terms of the degree of predictability or structure in the task.
- Change in the support for or guidance given to learners – the degree of manage-ment of that learning or guidance in tasks and the amount of student autonomy allowed for or expected.

Strands that relate to the learner's qualities and abilities
- Learner's skills that are not directly related to the development of academic learning – these may be vocational or employability-related.
- The capacity of learners to be autonomous – the degree of the learner's responsi-bilities for her actions in the learning and tackling tasks in the context of formal education and/or in the workplace.

- The ability of learners to study, to research and to manage learning resources and information.
- Self-awareness, self-knowledge, self-management and the ability to evaluate own performance.
- The sophistication of the learner's skills of manipulation of knowledge (analysis, synthesis, evaluation and application).
- The capacity of the learner to deploy knowledge in tackling tasks/solving problems.
- The learner's range of knowledge and understanding of a discipline/disciplines.
- The learner's understanding of the nature of knowledge and knowing.

In the sections that follow, issues about the nature of the pedagogy described and underpinning theory within the strands are discussed. Clearly, there could be a great deal to say about all of these strands and just one or two issues are selected for comment in this chapter. In the review of the strands, below, the strands are often grouped because of particular relationships between their subject matter. The strand that most clearly stands alone is that concerning skills – and we start with that.

Learner's skills that are not directly related to the development of academic learning – these may be vocational or employability-related

More issues arise with the sections on skills in level descriptors than any other area. Many of the skills that we expect of students in higher education do not arise naturally out of disciplinary studies, but are expectations added to curricula. This explains some of the anomalies that arise with skills attached to level descriptors. One issue, for example, is how the 'level' of skill should relate to each education level. Should skills always be required to improve or is there a point of adequate competence that will suffice for the standard required for the whole programme? The expectation of progressive rises in skills at each level is an anomaly of the format of progression through levels and of the decision to mix skills in with other learning attributes in the same format. The presence of skills in this format can cause difficulties at accreditation boards, which may expect all descriptors to be reached in any module for any discipline. Correspondingly, some skills are central to a discipline (e.g. communication in journalism) and the quality of communication described for a given level of study then is likely to be too low.

It is possible that straightforward skills do not have a useful place in level descriptors as they are currently used. They might be better written in a more suitable format elsewhere, where actual skills are described in relation to particular disciplines and related to the level descriptors as appropriate. There are alternative sets of skill-descriptors which meet some, but not all of these issues.

Change in the support for or guidance given to learners – the degree of management of that learning or guidance in tasks and the amount of student autonomy allowed for or expected

and

The capacity of learners to be autonomous – the degree of the learner's responsibilities for her actions in the learning and tackling tasks in the context of formal education and/or in the workplace.

Throughout the level descriptors there are representations of the expectation that students will become more independent and correspondingly that there will be a reduction of guidance from those who are managing the learning. An example is: 'can take minimum responsibility for own learning with minimum direction'. This trend is used to shape the expectations of acquisition and deployment of skills, but also it describes the ability of a learner to manage her own learning and to deploy her ability to carry out tasks within higher education or in the workplace.

The descriptors imply that there should be a progressive shift from 'given' reading and reference lists, handouts and highly structured work, and a trend towards learners becoming increasingly self-sufficient and able to face the unpredictability of real-life learning. But independence needs to be fostered, and sometimes the implication of this is that there is less independence at first, while students are enabled to function autonomously. In such a manner the learner becomes independent while increasing her ability to tackle more complex material. There are many implications of this, particularly in the shift from FE (further education) to HE environments that face a growing number of students.

The ability of learners to study, to research and to manage learning resources and information

Closely associated with the expectation that students will become increasingly autonomous is the expectation that they will expand and improve their ability to access and efficiently use learning resources. Across the FE and HE span of levels, there is a broad range of learning resources that may be drawn on. However, information-seeking skills go well beyond the simple use of resources. To seek information in the academic context, students need to be able to identify the kind of information that they require – in effect, to frame the question that they are addressing. They need to be able to evaluate the source and the information that is available and (usually) transform it to match to the context in which it is to be used. In formal research at higher levels, they need also to be able to hold different ideas in mind, and reflect on their relationships and their place in support of the argument in hand. To function in this way, students need to be able to evaluate their developing work (see below), and to understand the disciplinary context and the nature of knowledge in the context of their work.

Self-awareness, self-knowledge, self-management and the ability to evaluate own performance

There are several reasons why self-awareness and self-management capacities (we will refer to these as 'self-capacities') should have a place in a set of level descriptors, though, if they were written at the present time, they would almost certainly include the word 'reflective practice' as well. First, expectations of increasing autonomy and a shift towards greater personal management of study would seem to require the learner to be able to judge her own abilities to manage herself in order to be able to make reasonable judgements about the quality of the work that she produces.

The second reason for the presence of these ideas has emerged in the employability agenda. There is a requirement that students maintain some sort of record of their personal development, and think ahead about career issues while they are in higher education. This has led to a range of activities generally included under the heading personal development planning (PDP) – see Chapter 11 for further discussion of this.

The third reason is not explicit in the level descriptors but rates as an area of useful underpinning theory. Learners who are self-aware in the realm of knowledge and cognitive functions (i.e. are metacognitive) are probably more effective in studying (Hadwin and Winne, 1996; Ertmer and Newby, 1996). There is, of course, a possibility that students who are good at study are more metacognitive. Such evidence may be particularly important in supporting the developments of reflective learning at the present time (Moon, 1999b).

There is probably further teasing out to do among these self-capacities. For example, to what degree is self-awareness related to self-management; is a self-managing learner better at managing self in other contexts than learning? There might be reason to use the notion of adequate competence – 'good enough' in this section. In addition, there is a relatively new field of literature that might usefully inform this strand – that of emotional self-management (e.g. interpreted sometimes as 'emotional intelligence' – Goleman, 1998).

Change in the complexity of knowledge that is presented – the degree of challenge of the material of learning to the learner

and

Change in the complexity of tasks that the learner is expected to be able to tackle. This may be expressed in terms of the degree of predictability or structure in the task

This study of level descriptors has indicated that reference to the context of learning in level descriptors is particularly important because it is the 'backdrop' against which all other progression occurs. For example, at level HE1, a learner 'has a given factual and/or conceptual knowledge base'; and at level HE3 'has an awareness of the provisional nature of knowledge'. As it is a 'backdrop' that becomes more complex, it sets up an increasing challenge to the learner, though at the same time the learner's capacity to deal with the challenge is increasing as well. The reciprocal relationship here is central to achievement in learning.

There are various other issues that relate to 'complexity'. For example, what do we mean by 'complexity' in the context of multidisciplinary programmes? How does complexity relate to the understanding of the range of knowledge in a discipline, in contrast to specialism?

The learner's range of knowledge and understanding of a discipline/disciplines

and

The sophistication of the learner's tools of manipulation of knowledge (analysis, synthesis, evaluation and application)

and

The capacity of the learner to deploy knowledge in tackling tasks/solving problems

and

The learner's understanding of the nature of knowledge and knowing

The discussion immediately above views the context of knowledge and tasks in terms of the challenge that they produce for the learner and we have suggested that level descriptors plot the way in which the material of learning within a discipline tends to be presented to a learner. In a reciprocal manner, this section teases out some lines of theory that appear to inform the descriptors and their expression of progression in learning. No theory is overt in the wording of the descriptors, but the following seem to be helpful:

- theory relating to the students' approaches to learning;
- the SOLO (structure of learning outcomes) taxonomy;
- theory relating to the development of thinking and the conception of knowledge;
- framework for levels of reflective writing (depth in reflective thinking).

These areas of theory are, themselves, substantially interrelated and in noting these areas, we are not denying the existence or value of others.

Approaches to learning

Much of the research on learning in higher education in recent decades is related to the concepts of approaches to learning. This work distinguishes different ways in which learners go about learning and uses the terms 'deep' or 'surface' to describe approaches (Entwistle, 1996; Marton *et al.*, 1997). The literature is well known. There are many implied references to this theory in the descriptors – particularly at higher levels where engagement with subject matter is stressed.

SOLO taxonomy

The SOLO taxonomy (structure of learning outcomes) is helpful in terms of tasks that students perform and the manner in which they become more able to work with knowledge using skills of manipulation of knowledge (Biggs and Collis, 1982). SOLO is presented as a sequence of stages that apply to any new learning. It seems useful to distinguish between the processing of ideas of relatively less sophisticated learners (e.g. in the FE levels) to those who are more sophisticated in the higher HE levels. For example, to operate the skills of manipulation of knowledge, there needs to be a general view of 'the whole' – which is implied only in the most advanced stages of the SOLO model. In accordance, FE level descriptors do not separate skills of manipulation of knowledge (unlike the HE descriptors). In effect, a deep approach to learning will need to be taken in order that ideas can be related to the whole in the more advanced stages of the SOLO model (Moon, 1999a).

Development of thinking and the conception of knowledge

Throughout the higher education level descriptors are phrases that relate to the work of several groups of researchers who were interested in the progressive development of thinking and understanding of the structure of knowledge (e.g. in references to provisionality, predictability of knowledge, the development of criticality and so on). Perry (1970) was the most well-known of these researchers, though more applicable is Baxter Magolda (1992). Although they used different vocabulary, these researchers were working with similar ideas. Their work suggests (in simplistic terms) that in early stages of understanding of knowledge, learners believe that knowledge is certain (i.e. 'facts are facts') and any problem has a definite solution so long as the solution can be found. They believe that good authority figures 'know'. Later there is recognition that sometimes there may be more than one 'right' view or solution to a problem. At this stage the notion of opinion is developed. In the highest stages in these schemes, there is recognition by learners that knowledge is not a 'given' commodity 'but must be actively constructed and that claims of knowledge are understood in relation to the context in which they were generated' (King and Kitchener, 1994: 66).

Framework for levels of reflective writing

New work on stages in the development of the ability to learn from reflection or reflective writing (Moon, 2004) seems also to underpin the level descriptors. The work is related to the other theoretical work mentioned above (Moon, 1999a, 2002a).

In the least sophisticated forms of reflective writing, material is described in a serial manner, without evidence of any real reflection (descriptive writing). With greater sophistication, learners question the events, evaluate their relationship to them and mull over meanings and interpretations. In the most sophisticated stages of reflective writing, there is full recognition of the constructed nature of knowledge. There is evidence that the learner recognises that there can be different frames of reference imposed; that different people may have different points of view; that states of emotion are cumulative. She will understand that the passing of time can affect initial interpretations and there is a questioning of the processes of reflection themselves. Well-conducted academic work recognises these factors that influence interpretation of observations. References in the descriptors to the sophisticated qualities of reflective learning tend to occur in the higher levels of HE learning.

Progression and pedagogy across the levels – some generalisations

In this chapter, level descriptors have been viewed as an agreed expression of academics as to the learning observed and some capacities that are required in current higher education. The headings in level descriptors are reference points that are valuable in the use of the descriptors, but it has been more useful to conceive of strands that relate to the context of the learning and to learner qualities and abilities. Any new development of level descriptions would do well to take note of the identity of the strands instead of the original headings.

Particularly helpful in thinking about the developing capacity to learn in the level descriptors is the range of theories identified in the section above. The consideration of the content of level descriptors shows that the descriptors are consistent with these respected theories and ideas. This could be either because the theories were at 'the back of the mind' of those who developed level descriptors, or because the observations of student learning are, indeed, explained in different ways by these (and other) theories and ideas.

The generic nature of the language of level descriptors is off-putting for many lecturers. The concept and evidence of progression becomes much more obvious when the generic language is translated into the language of the subject, discipline or programme. This process is now further aided by the identification of strands in the level descriptors. However, is it only staff who need to be aware of levels and progression? We might think of translating generic level descriptors for the use of the learners – so that they are brought into some of the mysteries of this thing in which they are involved – the progression of their learning through levels. Again, the identification of strands in the progression can help to clarify the activity.

The notion of progression is reflected within these strands in the increasing complexity (of context) or capacity (of the learner). However, it is also apparent that progression is different and has different qualities in different strands. On this basis, the progression of students in different areas is not likely to be consistent. What will tend to make it more consistent, is the clear interrelationship of development in the different strands (including those associated with the complexity of knowledge). Ironically, sometimes progression may be less about progress than about the role of limitations in pedagogy. A concept that seems to be useful to apply to this pattern is that of limiting factors in ecology (Odum, 1968). Taken in a simple manner and generalised, the concept suggests that it is the factor that is the least developed in the pedagogical environment at a particular stage, that is most likely to limit the development of the students at that stage in their progression. The seeking out of limiting factors at any level in student progression – probably in relation to a particular discipline or programme – could be a rewarding and different approach to the improvement of student learning.

References

Baxter Magolda, M. (1992) *Knowing and Reasoning in College*, San Francisco, CA: Jossey-Bass.

Biggs, J. and Collis, K. (1982) *Evaluating the Quality of Learning*, New York: Academic Press.

Bloom, B. (1956) *Taxonomy of Educational Objectives*, New York: Longmans-Green.

Entwistle, N. (1996) Recent research on student learning and the learning environment, in J. Tait and P. Knight (eds), *The Management of Independent Learning*, London: SEDA-Kogan Page.

Ertmer, P. and Newby, T. (1996) The expert learner, strategic, self-regulated and reflective, *Instructional Science*, 24, 1–24.

Hadwin, A. and Winne, P. (1996) Study strategies have meager support. A review with recommendations for implementation, *Journal of Higher Education*, 67 (6), 1–17.

Goleman, D. (1998) *Working with Emotional Intelligence*, London: Bloomsbury.

Jackson, N. (1999) *Continuing Development Awards Framework: Draft Design Principles for Application in Higher Education*, Sheffield: University for Industry.

King, P. and Kitchener, K. (1994) *Developing Reflective Judgement*, San Francisco, CA: Jossey-Bass.

Marton, F., Hounsell, D. and Entwistle, N. (1997) *The Experience of Learning*, 2nd edn, Edinburgh: Scottish Academic Press.

Moon, J. (1999a) *Reflection in Learning and Professional Development*, London: Kogan Page.

Moon, J. (1999b) *Learning Journals*, London: Kogan Page.

Moon, J. (2002a) *The Module and Programme Development Handbook*, London: Kogan Page.

Moon, J. (2002b) *How to Use Level Descriptors*, London: SEEC, SEEC Office, University of East London.

Moon, J. (2004) *A Handbook of Reflective and Experiential Learning*, London: Routledge Falmer.

Odum, E. (1968) *Ecology*, New York: Holt, Rhinehart and Winston.

Perry, W. (1970) *Forms of Intellectual and Academic Developments in the College Years*, New York: Holt, Rhinehart and Winston.

QAA (2002) QAA website for all documents including the Framework for Higher Education Qualifications, online, available at: www.QAA.ac.uk. Accessed 11 December 2004.

SEEC (2003) *SEEC Credit Level Descriptors 2003*, London: SEEC, University of East London.

11

Developing the Keynote Interactive Guide to Personal Development Planning

Jenny Phillips

Introduction

The *Keynote Interactive Guide to Personal Development Planning* was developed as part of the Keynote Project, funded under the HEFCE Fund for the Development of Teaching and Learning (FDTL) Phase 3. This 27-month consortium project commenced in May 2000, and was led by The Nottingham Trent University in partnership with The London Institute and The University of Leeds. The overall focus of the project was key skills, graduate employability and lifelong learning, primarily in the Materials Technology sector. A number of practical resources for staff, students and employers were produced by the project team and refined in response to an extensive pilot at several institutions. The Guide to PDP complements the other project outputs, which include a Work Placement Guide for staff, students and employers, an Audit of key skills, and a Guide to Good Practice in key skills development.

This chapter describes the development of the Keynote Guide to PDP. It first discusses the national context that led to the inclusion of a PDP guide as a priority for the Keynote Project. It then outlines the development, evaluation and redesign of the Guide, focusing on choice of technology, content and usability issues. The final section looks at approaches to integrating PDP within different subject areas, and discusses some key issues arising from the alternative models.

National picture

The concept of Personal Development Planning is based on a long history of encouraging reflection and recording of students' learning and achievement in both Secondary,

Further and Higher Education and into employment (Jackson, 2001). National initiatives such as 'Higher Education for Capability' and 'Enterprise in Higher Education', along with extensive examples of good practice at an institutional level, paved the way for the Dearing Report recommendation that all Higher Education institutions develop a Progress File consisting of two elements, a 'transcript recording student achievement' and 'a means by which students can monitor, build and reflect upon their personal development':

> The second element of the File would include material which demonstrated progress and achievement in key and other skills and recorded informal and work-based learning. The File would need to be structured to enable students to manage the information they want to record, store and update.
>
> (Dearing, 1997)

The Dearing report also predicted that IT would play a key role in ensuring the success of both elements of the Progress File.

The Quality Assurance Agency in Higher Education (QAA), through a process of consultation, produced a policy statement to implement this recommendation, setting standards and deadlines for all Higher Education institutions (QAA, 2000a). The policy defined a Progress File as consisting of two elements: Student Transcript (addressed centrally by most institutions) and Personal Development Planning (PDP). The deadline for achievement of its objectives across the whole system and for all HE awards was set at 2005/06. The extensive list of papers, project reports and case studies that informed the policy illustrates its position as a culmination of existing work in this area, outlining a common route forward for the diverse initiatives already under way:

> There is nothing new about the basic activities on which PDP is based. The process of reviewing (revising) what has been learnt in order to crystallise newly acquired knowledge and consolidate understanding and then identify and rectify gaps and deficiencies is central to effective student learning. PDP simply captures the intellectual capacities, skills and behaviours that underlie these processes and uses them to help people review and evaluate their overall development in a structured way.
>
> (Jackson, 2001)

The policy explicitly states that it is not its intention to over-write this good-practice ('the new criteria are not intended to constrain existing practice or local initiatives'). While setting out the minimum necessary for compliance, the Policy Statement leaves the actual method of implementation open to interpretation and the impetus for under-taking PDP is placed very much on the student. Institutions are held responsible for making information on PDP available in a coordinated way: in material supplied to applicants, through the programme specifications, and in the HE Transcript. They are also required to explain the rationale for PDP and to provide students with 'opportunities for PDP at each stage of their programme'. However, the policy emphasises that it neither requires nor recommends that PDP should be made a compulsory element: 'The ultimate responsibility for deriving benefit from PDP should rest with each student' (QAA, 2000a).

With this in mind, we set out to find a way of supporting PDP that would successfully engage the interest of students.

Initial planning

Having gained an understanding of the national policies and how they developed, we next undertook a survey of key PDP initiatives within Higher Education, aiming to clarify the issues involved in putting the policy into practice. This research highlighted the resource implications of developing a complex PDP system using specialised software, as well as the inherent difficulties of managing cross-site implementation.

It prompted a careful consideration of our goals and limitations. We were committed in the project bid to 'develop a student progress file to enhance students' ability to record and articulate their achievements'. However, this was only one of several outputs of the Keynote Project, and it was not possible to dedicate significant resources, for example to support a team of programmers. The project team were primarily academics with limited technological expertise and we had less than 18 months in which to develop, pilot and deliver the outcome.

We considered our options. Producing a Personal Development Plan template that the students could personalise would involve using database technology to allow students to save and recall their information. A less high-tech approach would be to develop an Interactive Guide to PDP. Information would be presented as web pages, with linked MS Word documents that the user could edit and save either to disk, or on their own computer. These recording, planning and reflection documents would form the basis of the individual's PDP.

We felt that this approach would be more achievable within the context of the Keynote Project. It also tied in with a strongly held belief, backed up by research (Edwards, 2001), that the *process* of personal development planning was more important than the *product*. Providing the student with guidance, support, information and inspiration was therefore a greater priority than producing a visually appealing means of documenting the outcomes.

Having decided on the approach, we then focused on the content and structure of the Guide. We referenced the Leeds Faculty of Engineering Progress File and consulted the Centre for Academic Practice (CAP) and the Student Skills Training Programme (STRIDE) at the Nottingham Trent University who were beginning work on a generic, paper-based Progress File. One of the employers collaborating on the Keynote Project, R.R. Donnelley, provided a copy of the Development File used by its employees. This well-written document was extremely useful, with particular relevance to the Career sections of the Keynote PDP.

Box 11.1 Advantages of approach taken

- Can be accessed and used by students at any institution with fewer logistical problems.
- Open access, anyone can download.
- Encourages autonomy.
- Ownership of PDP, lifelong learning.
- Achievable within timescale and funding constraints.
- Doesn't demand significant future resource.
- The files could be made available for customization.

We wanted to produce a guide that would encourage a holistic approach, facilitating personal development planning in relation to course-related learning, skills development, career planning and extracurricular contexts. We aimed to give students the framework in which to diagnose their strengths and weaknesses; think carefully about the skills, qualifications, and experience they have and what they will need to gain; be able to gain the maximum benefit from their time in HE and make informed choices about their future; and to begin a process of recording, planning, goal-setting and reflection that would serve them well in their chosen careers. Box 11.2 shows the contents of the original pilot version of the PDP.

The next stage was to design the interactive presentation of the material. Macromedia Dreamweaver was used to create the main pages of the Guide, which could be navigated in a non-linear manner, like a website. These contained information, tips, guidelines and links to resources. A series of templates and quizzes were created as locked MS Word documents with editable areas.

We based the visual design of the Guide on the Keynote Logo, with menus allowing access to all the pages from anywhere in the Guide. We aimed to make the site appealing by using moving images, titles that zoomed in on each page and several different photographs.

The pilot

We realised early on in the project that the success of the Guide would depend less on the document itself, and more on the way it was implemented. Therefore, we sought

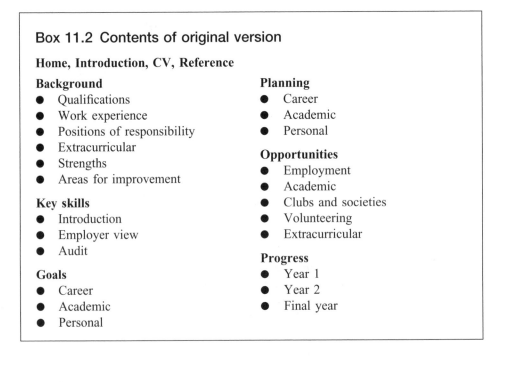

Box 11.2 Contents of original version

Home, Introduction, CV, Reference

Background
- Qualifications
- Work experience
- Positions of responsibility
- Extracurricular
- Strengths
- Areas for improvement

Key skills
- Introduction
- Employer view
- Audit

Goals
- Career
- Academic
- Personal

Planning
- Career
- Academic
- Personal

Opportunities
- Employment
- Academic
- Clubs and societies
- Volunteering
- Extracurricular

Progress
- Year 1
- Year 2
- Final year

detailed information from the participating institutions prior to piloting the PDP Guide. It was vital to understand the context in which the PDP would be introduced: how our version would fit in with other initiatives at the institution; what policies were in place locally; the nature of the support structure; its place within the curriculum.

For the institutions involved in the pilot we produced several different versions of the Guide, tailored specifically to the course on which they would be used. For example, the 'Opportunities' section was changed to include information on institutional clubs and societies and local organisations. Other changes included altering the terminology used to fit in with existing institutional protocol – for example, changing Personal Development Planning to Personal and Professional Development; altering the 'Progress' section to follow the years of a postgraduate or non-sandwich course and including extra document templates supplied by the course team.

The customised draft versions were piloted in nine institutions between January and April 2002. The sample included 182 undergraduate and postgraduate students, as well as 12 academic and careers staff. Advice was also sought from specialists in disability awareness. The level and source of support for students using the Guide varied between the different institutions. The reaction was overwhelmingly positive, with 88 per cent of students and 83 per cent of staff finding the Guide either 'very useful' or 'quite useful', and 80 per cent of students saying they intended to continue using the Guide. We also received a wealth of information on the content, structure and usability of the Guide.

Further valuable feedback was gained from conference workshops where groups of staff were given the opportunity to interact with the Guide. The reaction was generally very positive, and several requests for further information were received with the expressed intention of considering using the Guide as a basis for implementing new systems of supporting PDP. In particular, we received some useful guidance on the accessibility of the Guide for dyslexic students.

Analysis of the feedback from the pilot and other sources led to an intensive period of review in which the Guide was completely restructured and redesigned.

Restructuring

The pilot indicated the need for better information to accompany the PDP Guide (only 7 out of the 12 staff were familiar with PDP as a concept). An extensive introductory section was written setting the Keynote PDP Guide within the context of other national initiatives and describing the results of the pilot study. It also provides guidelines for staff on customising, integrating and evaluating the PDP Guide.

The *Introduction* for students contained within the PDP Guide was expanded in the final version to include guidance for mature students. Some of the pilot users indicated that they felt the examples in the Guide were aimed at younger students, and did not apply to those returning to Higher Education having already experienced a career. The aim of the *Introduction for Mature Students* was to illustrate how these different experiences could be used equally effectively in the process of personal development planning.

In order to make the Guide easier to navigate and more user-friendly, a *Site Map* and list of *Downloadable Documents* were included. Quotations from students who took part in the pilot stage were used to illustrate the sections. The quotations chosen were primarily positive, but gave a realistic view of the effort involved in engaging in the process of reflection and goal-setting as well as the benefits.

We took the best ideas from the different pilot versions and used them in the final generic Guide. The end result was hugely improved by the input received from diverse sources. This included feedback from students, academic staff, careers staff, the Learning and Teaching Support Network (LTSN) Subject Centres and Generic Centre, conference delegates and colleagues from across the sector. The opportunity to develop the Guide in a truly collaborative manner as part of the FDTL Project was a significant advantage.

The *Key skills* section was extended and positioned at the beginning of the Guide and examples of job adverts and quotations from employers were included. We felt it was important to include the employer perspective upfront in order to further contextualise the idea of PDP. In the *Background* section, *Positions of responsibility* was subsumed into the other headings to avoid duplication, and the forms were developed further to include more examples and prompts.

Box 11.3 Contents of final version

Home

Introduction
- Intro 2 – How to use
- Intro 3 – Why bother?
- Intro 4 – Introduction for mature students

1 Key skills
- Skills intro
- Skills list
- Employer perspective
- Job adverts
- Audit – Word Doc

2 Background
- Qualifications – Word Doc
- Work experience – Word Doc
- Extracurricular – Word Doc
- Strengths – Word Doc
- Areas for improvement – Word Doc

3 Learning style
- Learning styles quiz – Word Doc
- My learning style

4 Goals
- SMART
- Career – Word Doc
- Academic – Word Doc
- Personal – Word Doc

5 Planning
- Career – Word Doc
- Academic – Word Doc
- Personal – Word Doc
- Financial – Excel Worksheet

6 Opportunities
- Employment
- Academic
- Volunteering
- Extracurricular

7 Progress
- Learning logs
- Year 1
- Year 2
- Placement year
- Final year

8 CV
- Preparation – Word Doc
- CV
- Covering letter – Word Doc
- Interviews – Word Doc
- Links

9 Reference – Word Doc
- **Docs** – List of all Word Documents and how to edit and save
- **And finally**

A new section on *Learning styles* created by the London Institute for its customised version was retained. This included a quiz to help students recognise their own approaches to learning. In response to valuable feedback from the LTSN Generic Centre's Advisor on Employability, information on SMART goal setting was added to the *Goals* section.

Advice on personal finance was added to the *Planning* section, with tips for financial planning and a downloadable budget sheet in MSExcel. The *Opportunities* section was rationalised, with the *Clubs and societies* section being merged into *Extracurricular activities*. It was designed to make clear the whole range of activities available to students, in order to allow them to develop their skills and employability strategically. Information on *Learning logs*, including a template was built in to the *Progress* section, and a new optional stage for students undertaking a placement was added.

The section that changed most as a result of the pilot feedback was the *CV* section. Demand was high for more information to be included and it was expanded significantly to include checklists, tips and planning tools to assist in writing a CV and covering letter, and attending an interview. In recognition of the many excellent dedicated websites available, a links section was included to signpost these. Concentration on this aspect was supported by a survey of employers and professional and statutory bodies looking at how PDP can be implemented 'to be of maximum value to students in recruitment processes and later career management' (Edwards, 2001).

Redesign

The major change between the pilot and final version in terms of design was the recognition of accessibility standards. The introduction of the Special Educational Needs and Disability Act (SENDA, see also Chapter 16) in 2001 had implications for all the Keynote Project outputs, including the PDP Guide. It dictated that no one should be discriminated against in any aspect of their education on the grounds of their disability, and made it unlawful for higher and further educational institutions to discriminate against a disabled person in the student services it provides or offers to provide. The requirement reinforced the Quality Assurance Agency's Code of Practice, which urged all institutions to ensure that 'electronic learning materials are fully accessible to disabled students' (QAA, 2001).

After much deliberation, we decided on an inclusive design for the Keynote Project outputs producing one version of the materials that would be accessible to all users. We studied the Web Accessibility Initiative (WAI) guidelines and read broadly on the subject – see our section of the website for further resources on this. We also took into account the feedback from the pilot on the usability of the original design. This had brought up issues such as the lack of visibility of certain navigation buttons on smaller screens or those set to lower resolutions, and the awkwardness of having to scroll through longer pages.

A clean, uncluttered style was adopted, with a single graphic image used throughout the site. The only other graphics used were the Keynote Project Logo and the Bobby and Lynx accessibility approved logos. All unnecessary, and potentially distracting, moving images were removed from the design. The animated menu buttons and headers were replaced by simple text links. This allowed them to be resized by the user, along with all other text on the site, using the view menu on the browser. We split the longer pages down into sections and made them narrower, so that scrolling would not be necessary in most cases.

The decision to break down the longer pages, together with the additional content meant that the navigational model of the pilot version was no longer practicable. There were many more pages in each section, and we decided to have the menu on each page linking only to the main sections and not to each individual page. Once within a section, a submenu allowed access to the pages it contained.

We took measures to make the pages translatable by screen-reader software for blind users, and to allow sight-impaired users to be able to use the site, referring to relevant guidelines (RNIB).We also followed advice on making the pages navigable by keyboard strokes for users without fine motor control or unable to use a mouse. To make the Guide as user-friendly as possible for dyslexic students, we re-examined the language used to ensure it was as clear as possible, and provided full descriptions of acronyms. As well as shortening the pages, we presented the text in two columns to facilitate scanning.

Making the site accessible for disabled users had several positive ramifications for all users. Download times were significantly decreased, with the typical page size in the new version just 7k (compared to up to 33k in the pilot version). This would be particularly important for students accessing the Guide on the Internet, using low-bandwidth connections. The site was also able to render comprehensively without Cascading Style Sheets,

---

Box 11.4 Suggested customisations

1   Use institutional logos.
2   Add an introduction to opportunities for PDP at your institution.
3   Provide details of the specific support mechanisms available to your students with contact details for named individuals.
4   Add details of relevant local or subject-specific links to the generic links in the Opportunities section. e.g. University Careers Advice, Student Union, Local Organisations, Local Radio and Newspapers, Local Voluntary Organisations, Committee and Course Representative Information, Subject Networks, Skills Courses.
5   Change Progress section from generic four-year sandwich course to reflect specific course.
6   Alter the suggested mentors in the Progress section to fit in with systems of support at your institution.
7   Incorporate specific reference to the Learning Outcomes of the course. Making these readily available may help students plan what modules to take to meet their skills development goals.
8   Include details of relevant skills modules, or courses offered by the Careers or Student Union.
9   Include timetable of dates for assignments and assessments.
10   Include lecture and seminar timetable.
11   Provide space for reflection on feedback comments from assignments, essays, and projects.
12   Include an evaluation form to collect student feedback via email.
13   Add examples relevant to postgraduate or mature students.

and on a greater number of browsers including older versions. Forcing us to focus on accessibility dramatically improved the design, navigation and overall usability of the Guide.

At the same time we began to look towards the end of the project and consider how the Guide could be given most longevity once the funding had run out. We felt strongly that our ability to produce customised versions for each of the pilot sites had made a significant impact on staff engagement and gained support for its use in a way that a generic version may not have. Staff valued the opportunity to contribute directly to the content and design of the Guide. But the time taken in making these multiple versions was significant, and it would not be feasible to offer this service to staff interested in taking up the PDP Guide after the end of the project.

The best way to emulate this positive feature was to make a generic version of the Guide available via the website, with an option to download the html files for the purposes of customisation. The effort expended in the drive to make the materials accessible came to fruition in an unexpected way as we realised that the very simplicity of the new version of the Guide was, in itself, an aid to its customisation. It made it possible for someone inexperienced in web-design to add or remove sections without needing to design buttons, or manipulate complex graphic menus. It also made it more likely that customised versions would remain accessible.

Comprehensive notes on how to customise the files using Dreamweaver were produced and added to the introductory section of the site. Once customised the PDP Guide can be made available to students via the institutional intranet, departmental website, integrated into a Virtual Learning Environment or distributed on CD Rom.

Integrating the Keynote PDP Guide

The introduction for staff includes advice on different models of integration for the PDP Guide based on QAA Guidelines (QAA, 2001). These include:

- support for the learner;
- support for learning;
- support for off-campus learning;
- support for extracurricular learning;
- preparation for employment/professional practice.

It also identifies several important issues that must be considered irrespective of the chosen model. Several of these are common to the introduction of any new initiative, for example: the importance of consulting staff and students at developmental stages to encourage local ownership; the need to raise awareness of the national agenda through newsletters and events; the key role played by effective staff development and the importance of embedding PDP into the ethos of Higher Education. Others relate to decisions about the nature of student engagement with PDP: whether it should be compulsory or voluntary; on what criteria it should be assessed or certificated, if at all. Finally, to the structure of support offered: for example the level at which it is introduced; how it can be built in to existing systems; and the need for support mechanisms to be well organised and clearly identified.

Evaluation is also covered briefly in the introduction and staff are encouraged to build an evaluation plan into the scheme. In considering how the impact of PDP on student learning, personal development and employability can best be measured, both the source and the focus of feedback are important. As well as involving teaching staff and students, specific input from placement tutors, employers, student reps, the student union and support staff can be informative. The focus of the evaluation should be on the learning outcomes and perceived developmental gains, not just the tools or the system.

Case studies: models of integration

1 University of Plymouth

In 2002, the Faculty of Land, Food and Leisure at the University of Plymouth introduced PDP into a modular degree scheme. Some 180 students engaged with the process of PDP in a compulsory first year information technology module. The eight-week module, which ran in the first semester, aimed to prepare students for their studies at university, through IT and study skills development and personal development planning. A customised version of the Keynote PDP Guide was made available on the intranet, via the student portal. It provided the structure for the module, giving access to relevant materials. The range of linked documents was expanded to include module information and exercises from other HE initiatives as well as many from Keynote. The development of IT and study skills were cohesively linked with the idea of PDP through a mixture of compulsory and optional exercises. The success of this approach is indicated by the proportion of students who chose to complete and submit additional voluntary exercises contained within the PDP (around 60 per cent did at least one extra item). The module carried 10 credits and assessment focused on the process of PDP, the level of engagement and the ability to use IT to create and manipulate materials.

Following this successful pilot, the Faculty decided to continue and expand support in this area, further integrating the process through the introduction of a core pathway focusing on PDP in the first year, and the development of a Portfolio in the second year.

2 Nottingham Trent University

The Institutional Learning and Teaching Strategy (2002–2005) at the Nottingham Trent University allows for departmental autonomy in the implementation of its target of introducing Progress Files for all students by 2005. Two areas are using the Keynote Guide to support PDP. In the School of Art and Design, versions of the Guide will be available for all students via the Virtual Learning Portal. Work is currently under way to develop a database, adding functionality to the Guide by allowing students to upload, store and recall information. The Faculty of Education has adopted the Keynote PDP on three of their courses, again making it accessible via the Virtual Learning Portal on the Faculty web server. It has been introduced within a level 1 first semester core module called ICT and Research Methods, which forms part of a suite of Personal Development and Planning modules. One advantage of this module was that it already had many sessions timetabled in a computer resource room. Students were instructed to hand in several completed *Background* documents. In addition they were asked to reflect on how useful they found the Personal Development Planner, the skills they had developed using it and how maintaining their Personal Development Planner can be used to support their course and future development. This has ensured that all students on the module have engaged to some extent with some of the initial audits of skills and started to think about future usage. Further plans to integrate the PDP into the course include on-going linkage to modules at level 2 (placement module) and 3 (career planning module).

Common themes

The evaluation of all these approaches brought to light some common themes:

- Spending time on briefing the students fully on the concept of PDP, its advantages, and what is expected of them is vital, whether in a large group context, in tutor groups, or in written form.
- Clear lines of support should be identified for the students' benefit, whether this is teaching staff, personal tutors, careers team or others.
- As early as possible within the first year is the ideal point to introduce PDP initially, transferring to higher levels as the students progress through.
- Tying PDP in with assessment is potentially useful to ensure initial engagement, although many students will be motivated to continue with the process once begun.
- PDP can successfully be used to bring together academic course content with IT, study and other key skills development and planning for employment.
- Offering a systematic means of saving the student's files – either to particular student areas or a database – is perceived as an important future development.

References

Dearing, R. (1997) Report of the National Committee of Inquiry into Higher Education (1997) Higher Education in the Learning Society, HMSO, 2 vols.

Edwards, G. (2001) *Connecting PDP to Employer Needs and the World of Work*, LTSN Generic Centre.

Jackson, N. (2001) *Personal Development Planning: What Does it Mean?* PDP Working Paper 1 version 4, LTSN Generic Centre, online, available at: www.ltsn.ac.uk/generic centre (accessed 30 March 2004).

QAA (2000a) *Policy Statement on a Progress File for Higher Education*, Universities UK, Universities Scotland, SCoP, the Learning and Teaching Support Network and QAA, online, available at: www.qaa.ac.uk/crntwork/progfileHE/guidelines/policystatement/contents.htm (accessed 27 November 2004).

QAA (2000b) *Quality Assurance Agency Code of Practice: Quality and Standards in HE*, online, available at: www.qaa.ac.uk/public/cop/copswd/contents.htm (accessed 27 November 2004).

QAA (2001) *Guidelines on HE Progress Files* (February 2001) Universities UK, Universities Scotland, SCoP, the Learning and Teaching Support Network and QAA, online, available at: www.qaa.ac.uk/crntwork/progfileHE/guidelines/contents.htm (accessed 27 November 2004).

RNIB Royal National Institute for the Blind – why make information accessible?, online, available at: www.rnib.org/seeitright/whyaccess.htm (accessed 27 November 2004).

SENDA (2001) *The Special Educational Needs And Disability Act* (2001), The Stationary Office, online, available at: www.hmso.gov.uk/acts/acts2001/20010010.htm (accessed 27 November 2004).

WAI, Web Accessibility Initiative, online, available at: www.w3.org/WAI/ (accessed 27 November 2004).

12

Learning about employability

Kathryn McFarlane

Introduction

This chapter starts with a definition of employability and an outline of why it is important. You will be set two challenges – initially, to consider what opportunities your students have to develop their employability skills and, later, to explore how you might build on these opportunities. Taking my own advice on board, I will give an outline of the existing approaches to enhancing employability at my own university, Staffordshire, and our plans for the future.

What is employability?

While DLHE (Destinations of Leavers from Higher Education – i.e. what a graduate is doing six months beyond graduation) gives us some indication of where a graduate starts in the labour market, it does not measure their long-term employability. How do we know that a graduate has the ability to find a job that is appropriate? How do we know that they can remain employable in the changing labour market of the future? As Arthur points out, we need to help people think about: 'Securing employment two, five or even ten years ahead, not by presuming where those people will be, but by helping them to remain employable' (Arthur, 2003).

ESECT (Enhancing Student Employability Co-ordination Team) offer the following definition of employability: 'A set of achievements – skills, understandings and personal attributes – that make graduates more likely to gain employment and be successful in their chosen occupations' (Booth, 2003: 4).

In my experience, employability-enhancing activities within HE are likely to develop the *skills, understandings and personal attributes* indicated by ESECT. These include:

● *Career Management Skills (CMS)* – ability to make and implement realistic and well-informed career choices.

- *Work-related learning* – the opportunity to engage in work- or community-based experience or projects.
- *Key skills* – the development of the generic and specialist skills sought by employers.
- *Entrepreneurship* – opportunities to develop these skills can also contribute to student employability in certain specific areas.
- *PDP* – underpinning all of the above is the opportunity for students to engage in Personal Development Planning (PDP) to enable them to articulate the learning that has taken place.

Why is it important?

Increased numbers in HE mean that graduates now face greater competition for jobs, and at the same time there is anecdotal evidence that increasing student debt means that many graduates are in more of a hurry to start their first job. Graduates not only need the skills to compete for traditional graduate jobs, they also need the skills to be effective in jobs that do not match the traditional definition of a graduate job. According to Hawkins *et al.* (1995):

> For most graduates, the routes into employment are also changing. The sight of a large recruiter taking on 300 graduates through the national milkround is already becoming scarce. The milkround to graduate training schemes still exists, but traditional positions will not absorb the vast numbers of new graduates. Instead they find themselves facing the challenge of a small business, or in positions previously filled by school-leavers. In even the larger companies, decentralisation often means that small company conditions exist.

The expectations of graduate recruiters have also changed. This can be seen simply by looking at application forms for graduate vacancies. These forms no longer ask for lists of qualifications, previous jobs and hobbies. Now most ask for evidence of skills and competences. Recruiters expect graduates to know not only what they have done, but also what they have learnt from it. According to the Council for Industry in Higher Education (2002): 'Our employers look for individuals who have some knowledge of the world of work, have reflected on their experiences and can articulate in a job interview what they have learned.' This view is further supported by research into the destinations of graduates by Careers Services (2002):

> The most recent labour market information appears to provide evidence that a degree on its own, without accompanying work experience, evidence of achievement, and/or transferable skills, is not enough. This is true especially against a backdrop of increasing participation in HE, and the provision of new and different course choices.

For some years now we have heard reports of changing structures in the labour market, and the end of reciprocal loyalty between employer and employee. While some would dispute this, the pace of change in science and technology has a continuing impact on careers and training within the labour market. This means that we need to develop graduates who have the ability to be effective career planners and decision makers, not just once when they graduate, but throughout their working lives.

Policy drivers

The Dearing Report (1997) supports the need for the curriculum to be more closely linked to employers. Dearing observed that there was a large gap between the demands of graduate employers for mature, 'work-ready' graduates with strong key skills, and the average UK graduate. He recommended that institutions should identify opportunities to increase the extent to which programmes help students to become familiar with the world of work and to help them to reflect on that experience (Recommendation 18).

This theme is continued and further developed in the more recent White Paper, The Future of Higher Education (DfES, 2003a), which has a focus on links between business and universities, and the development of vocational courses. This Paper supports the need to integrate employability within the entire curriculum, for example in paragraph 3.23:

> As well as improving vocational skills, we need to ensure that all graduates, including those who study traditional academic disciplines, have the right skills to equip them for a lifetime in a fast changing work environment. Therefore, we will continue to sponsor work already under way by HEFCE to integrate the skills and attributes which employers need, such as communication, enterprise and working with others, into HE courses, on a subject-by-subject basis.

Other policy drivers include the QAA benchmarks for university-wide employability, and QAA guidelines on PDPs. A detailed outline of the drivers for employability in HE is included in the ESECT Employability Briefings.

Employability audit

So, if enabling graduates to develop employability skills is so important, what are we doing about it, and how can we measure it?

The following activity asks you to consider your institution or department and try to measure its effectiveness in this area by placing it on a simple continuum (Figure 12.1). While no cohort of graduates will be completely at the 'virtuous' end of the continuum, the aim is to move your institution further in this direction.

> Graduates have developed skills, but are unaware of them; they may have work experience, but are unable to focus on what they have learnt from this; they lack career management skills.

> Graduates can articulate their key skills, reflect on their work and community related experience, and make realistic and well-informed career choices.

Figure 12.1 The Employability Continuum

Many careers advisers and tutors will tell you that while they organise careers events for students, gaining attendance and involvement is very difficult. Moving your institution along this continuum is not just about providing more programmes – it is also about delivering them in such a way that students are motivated to get involved. In my experience, many students are motivated by assessment, getting paid, and gaining an understanding of the requirements of employers (for example, would-be teachers and TV researchers learning that experience is needed). Developing employability needs to be seen as a continuous process throughout education (and in future employment via continuing professional development), not as a something to be 'bolted on'. According to Harvey (2003):

> At root, employability is about learning, not least learning how to learn. Employability is not a product but a process of learning for life. It is not about training for a job; rather it is about empowering learners as critical reflective citizens.

So, consider the following questions and try to place your institution, department or course on the employability continuum in Figure 12.1.

Employability questions

- What opportunities do your students have to develop specific and generic (or 'key') skills within the curriculum?
- Can the students outline what key skills they have developed?
- Do students have opportunities to gain work- or community-related experience (e.g. through projects, employer briefs or placements), either within the curriculum or through the institution more generally?
- Do they know about and use these opportunities?
- Can they articulate what they have learnt or how they have developed, as a result of these opportunities?
- Do students have the opportunity to develop their career management skills? Which means, do they know how to make effective career plans and how to approach potential employers?
- How effectively do they do this?
- Do students engage in PDP? How does this impact on the above, in terms of ability to articulate learning?
- Do students have the opportunity to develop their career management skills? Which means, do they know how to make and implement effective career plans, approach potential employers and target appropriate vacancies?

Developing employability at Staffordshire University – what do we do?

Like all good tutors, rather than just ask you to do an exercise and wait for the results, I am also going to do the exercise myself and share the results with you. While you may feel your institution is ahead of, or behind, Staffordshire University on the *Employability Continuum*, this outline will give you the chance to learn about our good practice and compare your experience with ours. I will start with our overall strategy, then focus on the employability-enhancing activities identified above. I have given more details of some initiatives and departments which may be of particular interest.

Institutional strategy

Our students have the opportunity to enhance their employability through a range of activities, some centrally organised and others embedded within the curriculum.

Since 2002, the University has been working to integrate and promote employability across the institution. At a policy level, the university's Learning and Teaching Strategy for 2002–5 included as one of its three goals: 'To enhance the employability of all our students, empowering them to take control of their career direction and personal development.'

A commitment to employability has been made in other policies, such as the University Plan 2003–8. Furthermore, the undergraduate curriculum is being redeveloped around a new Undergraduate Modular Framework, which includes employability in its Design Principles: 'All awards should enhance student employability, enabling them to identify and develop their key skills, work related learning and career management skills.'

To implement these policies, in 2003 a Student Employability Group was set up, comprising academic and service-based staff. This group has produced a University Employability Policy, with a view to providing consistent opportunities for all students to enhance their employability. Below is an examination of current practice in relation to key employability-enhancing activities, with reference to this Policy where appropriate.

Key skills

When delivering a training session for a group of lecturers on a postgraduate teaching course, I have on a few occasions used the following activity. I split the group in half, and while one half identifies the skills their students gain through studying their discipline, the other half considers the skills sought by graduate employers, and builds up their evidence by looking at graduate recruitment brochures. After about ten minutes, the two groups compare notes. Inevitably the two lists of skills have a great deal of similarities.

This activity shows that students do have opportunities to develop their key skills through their academic studies already. At Staffordshire University, we formalised this in 1999 by the development of a University-wide *Statement of Skills and Personal Characteristics*, against which all awards were benchmarked. Key skills continue to be developed and assessed as part of the eight generic (skill-based) Learning Outcomes which all awards adopted from 2004.

As well as integrating skills across the curriculum, much good practice exists in the university in terms of developing key skills through discrete modules. For example, a number of skill-related modules are available within Business. These include the *Personnel Management Workshop*, where students go through the entire recruitment and selection process, from analysing a vacancy, to producing an advertisement, to short listing and interviewing. Another example is the *Learning and Self Development* module, where students analyse their self development needs and maintain a Continuing Professional Development record and plan.

Some key skills modules are available centrally, for example the Information Service's *Information Skills* module. This module is aimed at first year students, and aims to enable them to develop the skills needed to access and make effective use of information in a variety of formats.

Bearing in mind that not all key skills are developed through academic study, the Students' Union has been active in offering students opportunities for skill development. The NSLP (National Students' Learning Programme) enables students to train other students in key skills, which range from revision techniques to time and project management. A Key Skills website has also been developed centrally, giving students and staff access to information and resources to develop skills.

Career management skills

The University Employability Policy required that all students should have access to career management skills (CMS) through the curriculum by 2005. This can be delivered by a variety of approaches, for example through discrete modules, integrated into different modules at appropriate levels, through PDP, or a blended approach combining a few of these elements.

In terms of curriculum provision, there is a centrally run Careers Module, and embedded modules delivered within a number of disciplines. The centrally run Careers Module was the precursor of many of the discipline-based Careers Modules, and it is described below as an example of this approach to developing CMS.

The Careers Module is delivered by the Careers Service, and is open to penultimate year students from any discipline. It aims to enable students to formulate career plans, to engage with the processes of graduate recruitment, and to develop the ability to take control of their career throughout their working lives.

The module currently follows the Watts model of careers education, illustrated below, and is being revised in line with the National Framework for Careers Education and Guidance 11–19 (DfES, 2003b) to create a seamless progression route for students.

Students are assessed by two pieces of written work that encourage them to focus on their development in relation to the 'circles' shown in Figure 12.2. After conducting a detailed self-analysis, they compare this analysis with possible opportunities in order to make realistic career decisions. They also produce applications targeted at appropriate vacancies.

This module has much in common with other Careers Modules run elsewhere in UK universities. Distinctive features are the opportunities students are given to make a commercial contact and to undertake a mock interview with personnel professionals from local companies.

A web-based version of the module has also been developed. The web environment gives users the opportunity to make the most of the wide range of careers material already available on the internet. Furthermore, the materials are accessible to academic staff and students across the university. This means that students can view the materials as they wish, and academic staff can use them as part of curriculum-based activities.

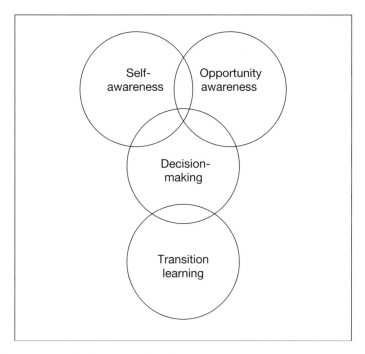

Figure 12.2 Watts model of careers education

Embedded Careers Modules have been developed to focus on the needs of students in specific disciplines. Careers Service staff have been keen to support and encourage these developments, because:

● The model is more sustainable – the Careers Service is not resourced to deliver a module to 3,000 second year undergraduate students.
● Academic staff have specific knowledge of their discipline, and can relate this to CMS.
● The involvement of other staff in the delivery of CMS leads to the development of new ideas and approaches.
● CMS can be integrated into students' programmes, rather than being delivered in isolation.

Tutors have adopted different approaches to the development of the CMS curriculum within their own fields, and below are some examples that illustrate these approaches:

● *Centrally run*: In the Humanities programme areas, most awards have the centrally run Careers Module as an option, and students are encouraged to take it up. Meanwhile staff within the department are developing and delivering employability modules and community and work-based learning modules.
● *Collaborative approach*: The Biology Department developed its own version of the Careers Module, *Professional Development.* There were many similarities with the Careers Module, but also some significant differences specific to the career

development needs of biologists. In this collaborative model of delivery, a careers adviser delivered some of the core lectures, while Biology tutors delivered tutorials and other sessions. The marking was done by tutors, and moderated by careers advisers.

- *Consultancy approach*: In the Business School, a tutor takes responsibility for delivering and assessing a Business-based version of the Careers Module. Following training (by acting as 'trainee' seminar tutor on the centrally-run Careers Module) she is fully conversant with the learning materials, and simply uses the Careers Service on a consultancy basis.

Outside the curriculum, students have access to the Careers Service face-to-face and via a website. In common with many other University Careers Services, the service provides clients with guidance to enable them to formulate and implement their career plans. This includes a drop-in system where students, graduates and potential students can have brief appointments with a careers adviser, without booking in advance. Longer, booked appointments are also available for more in-depth discussions. The service offers a range of information, speakers from industry and vacancy publications, as well as delivering a number of initiatives that are explored later in the chapter. The university also has a personal tutoring system, and through this students have access to academic guidance which, in many cases, also links to careers guidance and the development of CMS.

Enterprise skills

The University Employability Policy states that students will be encouraged to view starting and running a business as a genuine career choice, and where appropriate will gain access to practical support to make this happen. Currently, support for this is available both through and beyond the curriculum. The Faculty of Business and Law offers an *Enterprise Skills* modular pathway, open to all students in the university. Outside the curriculum, Enterprise Fellowships are available for students and staff, to help them start a business by providing expert help and a comprehensive support package. In addition, the HE Full Circle Project is currently working to raise the profile of enterprise through a variety of approaches, including a Summer School in Entrepreneurship, bursaries for graduates, and Enterprise Fests.

Work- and community-related experience

The University Employability Policy now requires all academic programmes to provide the opportunity for students to gain experience of the professional environment related to their field of study. This could be achieved through, for example, employer visits, project briefs set by employers or community organisations, employer-based mentoring, and placements.

This has already been happening for some time in many disciplines. In some areas, such as Social Work and Nursing, placements are a mandatory part of the course. Other areas, such as Computing, Business and Engineering, enable students to gain experience through a one-year placement between years two and three. A range of approaches has been adopted elsewhere in the university. Design students complete briefs set by employers. Biology students do a three-week placement at the end of their penultimate year, as part of a final year module. A work-based learning pathway is available in sociology, where students develop their awareness of and ability to liaise with community-based organisations and, in the final year, do a project in partnership with one of these organisations as an alternative to a dissertation. LPC students have mentors who are practising solicitors.

Outside the curriculum, Staffordshire University also provides a variety of centrally run opportunities which are available for students across the institution. Examples of these are outlined below.

Sponte, jointly managed by the Students' Union and the university (and funded by HEFCE), acts as the link between students and staff who want to volunteer, and volunteering opportunities in the community and further afield. As well as developing information sources and links with relevant organisations, *Sponte* provides training and support for volunteers, and opportunities to reflect on their learning through voluntary work.

Through another in-house scheme, students can act as *Student Ambassadors*, choosing from a range of activities to do with promoting the university, for example raising aspirations and promoting HE to pupils in Stoke-on-Trent schools.

The university is working towards providing enhanced support for students who are likely to experience disadvantages in terms of employability. Recent research by the Centre for Higher Education Research and Information points to the experience of 'disadvantaged' students in HE, in particular focusing on the difficulties they face when trying to enter the labour market. The researchers conclude that there is a need to focus employability resources more on meeting the needs of these groups.

Currently, a mentoring scheme is run through the Careers Service for students with disabilities. Through the scheme, students are matched with a mentor who is normally business-based and at management level. The student and mentor agree on a programme of activities that should reflect what the student hopes to achieve from the scheme. The programme is aimed at developing the student both personally and professionally, giving support and access to professional knowledge and experience. In the future there are plans to explore the possibility of a mentoring scheme open to a broader range of students.

While the experiences explained above enhance CVs and help to formulate career plans, they do not always provide any money. Workbank is a private employment agency that operates from within the university. It specialises in linking students to part-time work opportunities that fit around their studies.

It is not enough to provide opportunities for students to gain experience, they also need to be able to reflect on and learn from experience:

> As more and more students are graduating with some work experience, the focus is shifting from quantity of work experience to quality, from simply having some experience to learning something from it. Employers more and more want to see that graduates have had some work experience at university. What they value are graduates who have learnt through reflecting on that experience, so that they can articulate and apply what they have learnt.

With this in mind, the Work-Volunteer-Learn website was developed by the Careers Service. The site includes articles on work experience, case studies, skills resources, and work experience opportunities. It also includes an interactive profiling tool, which is being scaled up to become the basis for Personal Development Planning (PDP) in the university, explored below.

PDP

In line with QAA guidelines, the University Employability Policy also states that all students will have the opportunity to engage in a PDP programme by 2005. Core PDP elements will be available to each student, and they will be able to negotiate an individual programme tailored to their needs. In the light of increasing diversity in HE, this approach to PDP is intended to make degree studies more relevant to individuals and to enable them to take responsibility for their own development. Students will access PDP through the curriculum, through the personal tutoring system, and through a web-enabled resource.

Plans for the future

The University Employability Policy states that all students will have access to opportunities to enhance their employability, which will include work-related learning, developing CMS and key skills, and articulating their learning through PDP. This Policy is being implemented through Faculties, with central support from a Student Employability Group. The first stage of the implementation has been to deliver interactive sessions to enable academic staff to engage with the Policy. Following this, each Programme Area is conducting an audit, mapping existing practice to the commitments of the Policy. The audit will be used at an institutional level, to further disseminate good practice and to identify needs for staff development. The audit will also be used at a Faculty level to develop Employability Action Plans, which will outline strategies to build on the areas for development identified, and to share good practice across the Faculty. Monitoring and evaluation will be carried out at a Faculty level by Employability Co-ordinators and an Employability Working Group, and at an institutional level by the Student Employability Group. Beyond this, evaluation of the Policy will enable further plans to enhance student employability to be developed.

Moving along the continuum

This chapter started with a definition of employability, and an explanation of its importance in HE. Then readers were set a challenge – to identify the opportunities for students at their own institution or department to develop their employability. This was followed by an outline of a range of programmes and embedded initiatives at Staffordshire University. Whether you consider your institution to be ahead of us or behind us on the *Employability Continuum*, my second challenge to you is this. How can you build on the existing employability-related activities at your institution, and develop graduates who are able to take control of their own career direction in the labour market of the future?

And finally – the vision

I often explain career planning to students and potential students as being about having a vision; a vision of what career they will be doing a few years down the line, and of how it fits in with the rest of their life. To be an effective career planner, each student needs to identify the skills, experience, qualifications and training they need to make that vision a reality, work out the practicalities – then do it.

Moving your institution or department along the *Employability Continuum* works in the same way. Develop an 'employability vision' for your graduates – where will they be on that continuum, and how will they approach the labour market of the future? In the context of their specific disciplines and background, work out what skills, experience, training and resources your staff and students will need, in order to achieve this. Think about the practicalities – then do it.

References

Arthur, M. B. (2003) New Careers, New Relationships: Understanding and Supporting the Contemporary Worker, *Centre for Guidance Studies Occasional Paper*, University of Derby. Online. Available at: http://www.derby.ac.uk/cegs/publications/NewCareer Paper348.pdf (accessed 15 October 2004).

Booth, J. (2003) Good Learning and Employability: Issues for HE Careers Services and Careers Guidance Practitioners, *Briefings on Employability 6*, ESECT. Online. Available at: http://www.ltsn.ac.uk/genericcentre/index.asp?docid=19185 (accessed 15 October 2004).

Centre for Higher Education Research and Information (2002) *Access to What? How to Convert Educational Opportunity into Employment Opportunity for Socially Disadvantaged Groups*. Online. Available at: http://www.staffs.ac.uk/institutes/access/docs/Event7JB2.doc (accessed 15 October 2004).

CSU/AGCAS (2002) *What do Graduates do?* Online. Available at: http://www.prospects.ac.uk/links/WDGD (accessed 15 October 2004).

Dearing, R. (1997) *Higher Education in the Learning Society*, National Committee of Enquiry into Higher Education. Online. Available at: http://www.leeds.ac.uk/educol/ncihe/ (accessed 15 October 2004).

DfES (Department for Education and Skills)/Council for Industry and Higher Education (2002) *Work Related Learning Report*. Online. Available at: http://www.dfes.gov.uk/wrlr/ (accessed 15 October 2004).

DfES (2003a) *The Future of Higher Education*. Online. Available at: http://www.dfes.gov.uk/hegateway/strategy/hestrategy/ (accessed 15 October 2004).

DfES (2003b) *Careers Education and Guidance in England: A National Framework 11–19*. Online. Available at: http://www.connexions.gov.uk/partnerships/publications/uploads/cp/Careers_Education_11to19.pdf (accessed 15 October 2004).

ESECT Employability Briefings (2003) Online. Available at: http://www.ltsn.ac.uk/generic centre/index.asp?docid=19185 (accessed 15 October 2004).

Harvey, L. (2003) *On Employability*. Online. Available at: http://www.ilt.ac.uk/1603.asp (accessed 15 October 2004).

Hawkins, P. and Whiteway Research (1995) *Skills for Graduates in the 21st Century*, Association of Graduate Recruiters. Online. Available at: http://www.agr.org.uk/publications/reports_summary.asp?pubs%5Fid=58 (accessed 15 October 2004).

Law, B. and Watts, A. G. (1977) *Schools, Careers and Community*, London: Church Information Office.

Part four

Supporting and developing staff

13

Research into practice: learning by doing

John Shaw

Introduction

Although our main focus is on how students learn it is equally important to examine how we, as practitioners, learn about learning and what part educational research plays in this process. Research is something we, as university lecturers, are expected to do – but how do we learn from it and use it to improve our teaching practice? There is a large body of research available to the profession but important problems arise in the translation of this research into practice. One problem is commented on by Wankowski (1993): 'The most wasteful feature of the . . . research and practise of education is the gap between learning theories, their experimental findings and their application . . . this gap is widest at the level of HE.'

It must be a matter of concern that so many, in a profession that prides itself on teaching a rational, objective approach to subject matter based on a sound evidence base, are unaware of or ignore the results of this educational research. One important reason for this is suggested by Lambourn (1979): 'Teachers tend to disregard the research because it is not their own and therefore not immediately relevant and not arising from their daily work.' Thus, a primary focus must be on what makes teachers want to read and use this research.

Aims

This chapter's main purpose is to look at how we learn to improve our teaching and has three aims:

- to explore the role of educational research in providing a critical and challenging perspective on teaching practice while providing guidance on how to support learners correctly;
- to explore the benefits of action research and suggest that, in this field, it is as important to persuade teachers (and students) to research, and thus reflect, on their own experience, as to read the results of others' research;
- to look at some of the problems and skills needed to translate the research into action.

Case study background

In order to illustrate these themes and suggest a solution I will use as a case study some research that I undertook with a team of lecturers from a college, which had a degree franchised from my university. I was in the fairly unusual position of being employed by the university full-time but with a large part of my time purchased by a college to help run, and teach on, the first two years of the franchised degree course. We set up the research with a dual aim – to give the further education lecturers the experience of taking part in a research project and to choose an area that would have an immediate, identifiable effect on the college's learning process. The subject chosen was 'Widening participation – what causes students to succeed or fail?' and was eventually published in the SEDA (Staff and Educational Development Association) journal, *Educational Developments* one year later (Shaw *et al.*, 2001). It was based on exhaustively interviewing a cohort of students at the FE College to identify the phenomenological texture – thus building up a 'rich picture' of their learning experience.

The learning experience

First, it is important not to view the process as an exercise in 'rational-linear' or 'top-down' planning. It is a development process and thus requires space and time for reflection to find a meaningful and motivating area to research. I was using it to motivate a team of lecturers and started the process with a weekend development session on research methodology in an isolated farmhouse in Normandy. The team decided to work around the issue of widening participation. It seemed to them that there was not enough clarity on who we could widen participation to, what triggers caused non-traditional students to return to study, and what factors affect their ability to stay on the course.

An important aspect of this project for these lecturers was the opportunity to return to studying the work of educational writings in this area. Thus, the shared reading included: Brown and Scase (1994); Entwistle (1992); Bhachu (1991); Prosser and Trigwell (1999); Jarvis *et al.* (1998), who emphasised the complexity and paradoxes involved; and Barnett (1994), whose use of Habermas' term 'life world' to describe 'the total world experience' of learners was illuminating. Thus, from this first meeting arose the 'mission statement' which, in turn, led to the reading, the choice of subject, and a determination to succeed (particularly necessary in a further education college which is not a research-friendly environment).

Another lesson was the advantages of selecting a methodology of using intensive interviews, which could easily fit into the already well-established tutorial and induction systems for the non-traditional students this course specialised in. We started at induction when we issued a set of questions to new students, asked them to pair up and then interview each other. This not only gave us useful material for later interviews but also helped students get to know each other quickly. After looking at the results we 'fine-tuned' the questions for the first meeting with their tutors. This again had the additional benefit of making the personal tutorials more productive.

After three interviews of this kind, we had another meeting to review the results. Initially the responses looked depressingly conventional but then we met off-site, laid the answers on the floor, walked round them, reflected and produced our own individual summaries. What then emerged was that it was our prior assumptions that were blinding us to what the students were really saying. First, these 'non-traditional entry' students were not people who had no contact or understanding of HE. More than 90 per cent had either family or close friends who had experience of HE. What was happening was that these students had rebelled, feeling hostile to and dropping out of school, only returning when events pushed them to reconsider. Second, the students were not fixated on 'getting a career'; on closely examining their replies it was clear that they wanted to learn 'the knowledge', i.e. they needed to re-badge themselves as a 'proper academic'. They were not interested in careers advice or study skills support. The latter was a definite 'turn-off' as it suggested they weren't good enough and thus further lowered their self-esteem. I also strongly suspect that using what might be viewed as a 'non-rigorous' phenomeno-logical approach gave staff more power to question and revise their results, something that might not have happened with a more statistical approach.

Finally, something very interesting happened in the next round of interviews, which took place after Christmas – the students started to believe in themselves and their ability to complete the course. Thus, the first term was revealed as a time of peak anxiety. We already guessed that lack of finance, though a real problem, was not the key to students giving up. We found that key variables were (student responses are in italics):

● tutors showing interest in them as individuals *'when you stopped me and asked how I was doing I was just about ready to give up'*;
● students socialising, helping each other and discovering everybody else is just as anxious and unable to ask basic questions because *'they seem so stupid'*;
● getting early feedback from assessments which told them they weren't as bad as they thought – *'What my lecturer taught came up in the exams and I knew what to write – it was great'*, but note also the waste – *'I did all the assignments but didn't hand them in because they were rubbish'* and *'if I'd known I could do that well I'd have really gone for it!'*;
● staff taking the time to really explain the academic process and to produce feedback comments that students such as ours can really understand. *'Lecturers are talking about assignments, case studies and essays and I don't even know what the differ-ence is!'* How do students who haven't been in the traditional sixth form make sense of comments on 'balanced arguments' or 'critical evaluation' and 'depth'?

Action research and learning

At this point it must be emphasised that an important aspect of this rolling programme of interviews was that it was centred on action research. As Rapoport (in Susman and Evered, 1978) defines it, there are two main elements: it aims 'to contribute both to the practical concerns of people in an immediate problematic situation and to the goals of social science'; and it uses 'joint collaboration within a mutually acceptable ethical frame-work'. This, in turn, involves action *learning* which has three distinguishing features (Mumford, 1992; Vince and Martin, 1993):

● learning means learning to take effective action;
● learning needs to be expressed through actions on real work problems which must involve implementation as well as analysis and recommendations;
● learning is a social process in which individuals learn from and with each other.

It therefore means involving teachers in experiential learning (Kolb, 1984) and reflective practice (Schon, 1982). Thus, together, we applied our findings to our teaching and personal tutoring as a series of incremental steps, refining, discussing, questioning – and above all reflecting. Anyone who wanted to try a method for implementing the provisional findings was encouraged to experiment. An encouraging aspect was the increased demand for educational literature from the team during and after the research. This included reading and discussing current, relevant articles such as 'Strengthening action-research for educational development' (Cousins, 2000) which took on the criticisms of action research as having 'acquired a certain flabbiness', correctly pointing out that there were signs of a revival in interest because of its staff development potential and suggesting credible models of methodology.

Another benefit was that as the year progressed staff were spending more time explaining to the students why we were giving them particular types of assessment, planning more teamwork assessments, encouraging social events, improving the timing and content of our feedback to students. Retention improved by 30 per cent. Cynics may argue that this may be largely because of the extra attention paid to the students as a result of the research (it is almost impossible to isolate the influence of the observer on the experiment in this field) but this, in itself, is an argument for involving course teams in action research. The act of researching improves the performance of both the staff, who become 'reflective practitioners' (Schon, 1982), and students, who feel important and become more aspirational. So why not try to repeat this experience each year?

The other important aspect of this research was that the results forced us to re-assess some cherished beliefs – always a good 'rule of thumb' indicator that the research has come up with some worthwhile results. As mentioned earlier there was the realisation that although the students were typical non-traditional entry students in terms of age and ethnicity they did not come from families with no HE experience but had 'dropped out' of the education system some time in the past – often deliberately rejecting pressure to conform and enter HE. Second, they were not fixated on a career or a good job – they wanted 'knowledge' – to be 're-badged' as an academic. We were putting the cart before the horse by emphasising study skills early in the course. The conventional approach only served to make their self-esteem even lower by branding them as needing remedial help. It was only after they had achieved satisfactory results in their assessments that they would start a dialogue on how they could do even better by learning study skills from a position of strength. Note the transition;

From:
I don't feel like a proper student. I don't even know what a degree standard is. I'm going to try but I'm sure I'm not really clever enough.

To:
If I'd known I could do that well I'd have really gone for it.

Long-term effects

Finally, it had longer-term effects inside and outside the course. Inside there were structural changes to the tutorial system, induction, assignment and feedback design. Staff also reflected on and changed important assumptions about students and the way they behaved – being convinced during the process of the value of educational research. Outside, by being published and giving conference papers and presentations we developed a network of contacts which helped motivate, confirm and refine ideas of everyone in the network. What was fascinating was to see many other teams commenting on how they too had been thinking along similar lines. Also, it had the effect of raising staff aspiration levels dramatically: the other two main authors of this piece of research have since left their FE lecturers' positions – one to become SEDA's first-ever appointment of a development officer and the other to be an educational researcher at Kingston University.

So, in summary, from a fairly modest financial base and using existing resources and structures, we managed to complete a research project that motivated staff and students, showed clearly improved outcomes, helped other teams and discovered some interesting, unexpected results. The more crucial lesson was that this modest approach to educational research was the key to a major block to staff development in HE as highlighted in the quote from Lambourn. In the role as person responsible for learning development in my department, I have always been frustrated by the contrast between lecturers' eagerness to research their *subject* content and disdain for the research into their *job* content. This problem has often been mentioned in the literature, note the arguments of Wankowski and Lambourn already mentioned, which forcefully state that higher education is particularly prone to the 'this doesn't apply to me' attitude. It is Lambourn's quote, however, that provides the key to the answer – for, if the staff cannot be 'brought to' the extensive research that already exists to inform their practice – then the research must be brought to them – in the form of small, local action-research projects of their own.

Amateurs versus professionals?

One criticism of this approach is that for educational research to be effective it must be of a high standard. For example, at the 2001 ILT conference a keynote speaker stated firmly that staff should not be expected to research education but that this should be left to the experts – our role was simply to be well read in this area. The counter argument is that such implied criticism of 'amateur researchers' is misplaced, not least because it ignores the fact that there is already an extensive literature on nearly all aspects of our role as teachers which is being neglected by the majority of the profession. Research by Bennett (2001) exploring lecturers' attitudes to new teaching methods is relevant to this argument in two aspects. First, it shows that nearly all staff, when they need information, ignore the professional literature and go to their colleagues. There are advantages in this approach (Dougherty, 1999): the knowledge acquired in this manner 'relates immediately and directly to the personal objectives of the recipient, who is fully in control of the learning situation' (Bennett, 2001). However, it does also give rise to the problem of 'information dependence' which can be defined as: 'unquestioning conformity to suggestions made by highly regarded peers ... resulting perhaps in the application of inappropriate methods' (Cherrington, 1989).

This is known to be particularly problematic where people are faced with something they find threatening (Schachter, 1959). Thus, in a continuing environment of external pressures forcing rapid change on the profession, if we are to avoid demoralisation we need to persuade our colleagues to become true 'reflective practitioners' (Schon, 1982) who are thus equipped to take a proactive approach to change. In this process of 'reflecting' and 'selecting the appropriate technique' the local, small-scale piece of action-research is a very powerful way of persuading sceptical staff that educational research is relevant to their own practice. It allows us to retain the advantages of informal network transfers of knowledge while avoiding the problems of information dependence and thus inappropriate teaching methods.

Unfulfilled research

The experience of using action research also provides the key to another problem. This is the problem of research that is wasted because it is unused. Too much educational research is in a state of suspended animation as an unfulfilled ambition. It might be completed and published or presented but if it is not applied to improve the student's experience it has not fulfilled its true purpose. If we are honest we know that we often avoid the application of research because we know it can be difficult and frustrating. Course organisers need to be persuaded, staff motivated, logistics sorted and the possibility faced that it just won't work and you will look foolish in front of colleagues. It is tempting to leave the research as an academic exercise with just enough ambiguity to allow face-saving re-interpretations. The lessons from action research are that application requires ingenuity, creativity and, above all a supportive, non-judgemental team.

Creativity and ingenuity

These qualities are even more important when applying others' research, as it will inevitably need re-configuring for your own students' context. To give a short example; we were desperate to get good quality feedback from the students on our application of research to a HND Business course. The problem was that the students had been asked too many times to fill in feedback forms or questionnaires and were giving ritual answers. Therefore, we 'tweaked' one of the assignments for the 'Managing Activities' module which asked them to evaluate a business in terms of its operational processes – we instructed them to use the HND course as the production process in question. Once they understood that they were the output of this process they gained a new perspective on the educational process and produced a wealth of illuminating insights.

Some lessons

These are the same whether you use your own or apply others' research:

● create time and space for reflection;
● be prepared for your assumptions to be challenged – and don't accept the first interpretation of results;
● work with a team to develop creative methods of application – in a non-judgemental atmosphere;
● develop a methodology that works 'with the grain' of the course (and is not too intimidating for staff without strong numeracy skills);

- don't wait for lengthy analysis – try out different solutions;
- the more qualitative the methodology, the more systematic the approach should be;
- remember the process of developing staff into reflective practitioners is as important as the end result;
- small, incremental changes can be as important and successful as dramatic shifts;
- keep the process going, as in Kolb's reflective cycle – there's always something new to learn and the educational ground is always shifting.

Finally, note how each teaching situation is unique and each investigation and application will throw up some new unique insight. Lecturers' cynicism about others' research is, to some extent, justified as this research *is* never wholly applicable to your own experience – the field we work in is just too complex with too many variables and too much scope for subjective interpretation. To adapt Heraclitus, every time we step into the educational river the water has changed – no two classes, courses, colleges are the same; everything and everyone is changing. But what seems a problem for the professional researcher is, in fact, an opportunity for the potential legions of 'amateur' researchers.

Conclusion

This is not to say that we ignore the high-standard professional research in favour of an amateur approach. This is not a competitive situation – the staff who take part in these action research projects not only learn the value of their own educational research but they also begin to respect and read other colleagues' research. It is important that our profession does not retreat into two 'ghettos' – the active researchers and the teachers – when, in this field, the two groups have so much to gain by blurring the distinction between each other. All staff would benefit enormously by undertaking one action research project each year which allows them, as part of a team, to research an educational hypothesis, reflect and act on the findings. My guess is that this would result in an exponential increase in the demand for educational publications (and conferences). Thus, to return to the chapter title, 'learning by doing' has a double meaning – research is best appreciated by those who do it and research is not completed unless it is applied to improve the student's learning experience. So, let's all join in, and as Chairman Mao once declaimed, 'Let a thousand flowers bloom'.

References

Barnett, R. (1994) *The Limits of Competence*, Milton Keynes: Open University Press.

Bennett, R. (2001) 'Lecturers' attitudes towards new teaching methods', *The International Journal of Management Education*, 2, 1, 42–58.

Brown, P. and Scase, R. (1994) *Higher Education and Corporate Realities: Class Culture and the Decline of Graduate Careers*, London: UCL Press.

Bhachu, P. (1991) 'Ethnicity constructed and reconstructed: The role of Sikh women in cultural elaboration and education decision making in Britain', *Gender and Education*, 3, 1.

Cherrington, D. (1989) *Organisational Behaviour: The Management of Individual and Organisational Performance*, Boston: Alleyn & Bacon.

Cousins, G. (2000) 'Strengthening action research for educational development', *Educational Developments*, 1, 3, 5–7.

Dougherty, V. (1999) 'Knowledge is about people, not databases', *Industrial and Commercial Training*, 31, 7, 262–266.

Entwistle, N. (1992) 'Student learning and study strategies', in Clarke, B.R. and Neave, G.R. (eds) *The Encyclopaedia of HE*, Milton Keynes: SRHE and Open University Press.

Jarvis, P., Holford, J. and Griffin, C. (1998) *The Theory and Practice of Learning*, London: Kogan Page.

Kolb, D.A. (1984) *Experiential Learning: Experiences as a Source of Learning and Development*, Englewood Cliffs, NJ: Prentice Hall.

Lambourn, D. (1979) 'Seeing a model of learning', in *Proceedings of a Joint Conference of the Society for Research into Higher Education and Staff Development and Educational Methods Unit*, Manchester Polytechnic Conference Papers, No. 27.

Mumford, A. (1992) 'New ideas in action learning', in *Approaches to Action Learning*, Keele: Mercia Publications.

Prosser, M. and Trigwell, K. (1999) *Understanding Learning and Teaching: The Experience in Higher Education*, Milton Keynes: SRHE and Open University Press.

Schachter, S. (1959) *The Psychology of Affiliation: Experimental Studies in the Sources of Gregariousness*, Stanford, CA: Stanford University Press.

Schon, D. (1982) *The Reflective Practitioner: How Professionals Think in Practise*, New York: Basic Books.

Shaw, J., Hall, J. and May, S. (2001) 'Widening participation – what causes students to succeed or fail?', *Educational Developments*, 1, 4, 5–7.

Susman, G. and Evered, R. (1978) 'An assessment of the scientific merits of action-research', *Administrative Science Quarterly*, December, vol. 23, 582–603.

Vince, R. and Martin, L. (1993) 'Inside action learning: an exploration of the psychology and politics of the action learning model', *Management Education and Development*, 24, 3, 205–215.

Wankowski, J. (1993) *Reflections and Operational Prescriptions*, in Raaheim, K., Wankowski, J. and Radford, J. (eds) *Helping Students to Learn*, Milton Keynes: Society for Research into Higher Education and Open University Press.

14

Learning to teach with technology

Vivien Sieber

Introduction

Computers play increasingly important roles both in learning and teaching and in the administration of courses, assessment and institutions. Two distinct skills sets are needed to make effective use of information and communications technology (ICT) in teaching: technical competence with a range of applications (word processing, presentation, spreadsheets, database, internet, specialist applications, etc.) and an understanding of the pedagogy and learning and teaching issues surrounding the use of technology. This chapter explores a range of strategies institutions have used to help academic staff gain both technical competencies and the understanding necessary to promote the use of learning technologies.

Drivers for institutions to promote the use of ICT have been largely economic, resulting from reduced funding, increasing student numbers, and moves towards part-time and distance learning. Most teaching staff have increased administrative burdens and largely do their own word-processing and record-keeping, with limited administrative support. As computers become further embedded into our lives, these technical competencies become more important. But ICT competencies are not generally used as selection criteria for academics who are subject specialists with considerable expertise within a discipline. Until recently, few have received formal training in ICT, and the majority gained their skills by ad hoc means. Although most institutions offer training in basic competencies, the proportion of academic staff volunteering to attend this training remains relatively small. Later in this chapter, I describe some initiatives promoting the development of these skills along with successful, and less successful, examples.

Teachers also need to understand how appropriate use of ICT may enhance their teaching and how to develop electronic materials that promote effective online learning. I would argue that this is achieved by using computers to provoke interaction, utilising graphic and multimedia capabilities, giving a rich learning experience with feedback; rather than as essentially an electronic filing cabinet providing static lecture notes and handouts. With computers it is possible to show students *how* things work rather than telling them; even better, an environment and culture that enables students to work things out for themselves can be provided. Innovative use of technology in teaching has, until recently, relied on a few enthusiasts who have overcome the barriers to learning both about the pedagogy surrounding learning technologies and how to use the technologies themselves. Change has been more gradual than many pundits predicted – 'evolutionary' rather than 'revolutionary' (Seale, 2003).

Institutional recognition of the potential of ICT to cope with large classes, improve communication and enhance the learning experience along with potential economies of scale and increased competition has led to a range of initiatives intended to promote the use of ICT. Without appropriate support and training the potential of learning technology (LT) is not realised, leading to expensive mistakes. In terms of learning and teaching, it is more important to promote discussion, disseminate examples of good practice and encourage teachers to explore the potential offered by technology to enhance their teaching, rather than to provide technical training in isolation. Generally, academic staff are subject specialists and not specialist web developers.

This chapter explores the main barriers to using ICT encountered by academic staff, and to a lesser extent institutions, and describes a range of initiatives designed to overcome them. The main barriers are discussed under the following headings:

- technical issues;
- ICT skills for academics;
- issues relating to learning and teaching;
- staff development;
- dissemination;
- institutional support.

At the end of each section, I pose a number of questions/challenges you might wish to raise in your institution.

Overcoming the technical barriers

We are deterred from using technology if it does not work or requires considerable additional effort to make it work. Facilities and equipment must be available, and accessible, with supportive technical help. It is not reasonable to assume that everyone can find the CD-ROM drawer in any make of laptop or, indeed, that all laptops have floppy drives. Change is rapid within the IT industry, new products appear, others become obsolete and many are incompatible with one another. Often academics are nervous as they begin to use technology in their teaching. Having to organise the equipment is an additional barrier both in terms of the time needed to make the arrangements and contact time lost when things go wrong. It is embarrassing to delay a lecture when the data projector cannot talk to the computer and the class is waiting. Institutions must recognise and budget for the ongoing cost of providing technical support along with maintenance and upgrading of equipment and facilities. Ideally, technical support involves a supportive relationship between IT personnel and individual teachers. It is reassuring to know that willing help is available and we are then more prepared to take risks and try new things.

Institutions have limited budgets and are faced with relentless innovations provided by the IT industry. Few institutions can afford complete installations of new software upgrades but can maintain rolling programmes. New versions of software may require concomitant hardware upgrade, further increasing the financial burden. While programme upgrades can generally read files from their precursors, old versions are usually unable to open files created by newer programmes. Many of us have experienced the embarrassment of a PowerPoint presentation that does not work on the equipment available at another place. Frequently academics choose to work from home but then encounter problems where their home and work computers are set up differently. Technical support for home PCs is costly and may not be provided by an institution.

Key questions

- What level of technical support does your institution offer to support the use of ICT?
- What happens when something goes wrong?
- How does the level of technical support affect staff confidence and willingness to develop new methods?

What ICT skills does an academic need?

Major changes in computing and information technology are making a significant impact on learning and teaching. It is worth remembering that the world wide web is less than twenty years old (Berners-Lee, 1989) and the graphical user interface (GUI) of Windows and Mac operating systems nearly as new. Until recently, ICT was not part of the school curriculum, and universities would only teach those skills considered relevant to specific courses. The absence of coherent or systematic training meant that most people simply worked out a way of achieving their desired end-point, for example printing a document, with no opportunity to develop a deeper understanding of these applications and the commonality of skills across applications.

In response to the Dearing Report (1997), several universities included ICT skills audits in the learning and teaching strategies prepared for the Higher Education Funding Council for England (HEFCE) (2001–2) and invested in equipment and infrastructure. These audits showed broad similarities in that almost all staff used e-mail and word processors while about half used internet resources to support their teaching. My experience at the former University of North London showed that staff responded highly positively to learning more about the opportunities offered by ICT but cited competing pressures on time and lack of institutional recognition as the main constraints.

Pragmatically, all academic staff need a wide range of ICT competencies along with additional more specialised expertise to work efficiently in a modern university. The skills set described by the European Computer Driving Licence (ECDL) was introduced to provide a basic qualification for the 'man in the street' (www.ecdl.co.uk). The seven separate tests cover basic PC operation, file management, word processing, spreadsheets, database, presentation, e-mail and the internet. The training needed to pass these tests is essentially skill-based, and has the advantage of providing an overview of commonality between applications along with a basic background to computers.

ECDL has gained increasing credibility among employers as evidence of basic IT competence. A number of UK universities now include the ECDL within or alongside their undergraduate teaching. The National Health Service (NHS) has adopted ECDL as a reference standard and many universities operate schemes that enable staff to obtain the qualification.

There is controversy over the ECDL in HE. Some argue that parts of the syllabus, particularly databases, may be irrelevant to many. But information overload affects all disciplines, with search and evaluation skills becoming of primary importance to all academics. These are the skills we must develop in our students to prepare them for the relentless increase in information that technology makes possible. Passing ECDL 'databases' will not turn you into a skilled database programmer but it should teach you how a database is put together. Understanding these basic principles should, in turn, improve individuals' ability to interrogate a database (search). As most information systems, e.g. student record systems, within universities rely on databases, this should help academics with their administrative duties.

A second criticism of the ECDL is that the skills-based training provided is inappropriate to academic life, tending to rote learning which concentrates on only one way of doing anything without demonstrating flexibility or transferability of skills between applications. This view may depend upon the type of training available: trainer-led workshops, paper-based or electronic teaching materials. The tests themselves are independent of application – you can take ECDL in Welsh on a Mac.

I found the discipline of preparing for ECDL very helpful and learnt a range of new shortcuts. As a result of working through the tests, commonalities in the routines underpinning applications became more obvious. The skills required for ECDL Advanced are also highly relevant to academics, particularly 'Presentations' as lectures are frequently supported by visual presentations (www.ecdl.co.uk/advanced/presentation.htm). Again, I would argue that electronic presentations, basic web literacy and the ability to write simple web pages are both important and increasingly routine parts of an effective academic's life.

Skills training to achieve specific competencies may have negative connotations, especially within an academic environment (Partington, 1999). Staff appear reluctant to invest time developing basic IT skills partially because they do not recognise the potential gains in personal efficiency or the further capabilities offered. Perkins (as cited in Surry and Land, 2000) identifies three conditions that must be fulfilled for technology to be used effectively:

- it must be available;
- users must recognise the opportunities it offers;
- users must have the motivation to exploit these opportunities.

(Perkins, 1985)

Relating to my own experience – in the 2001 survey at former UNL, the overwhelming majority (95 per cent) of staff wished to learn more about ICT, but only 40 per cent expressed an interest in gaining a recognised IT qualification. Few of these academic staff joined the pilot scheme which provided web-based training materials, support and covered the costs of taking ECDL. Reasons given for not participating in the trial included: 'lack of time', and 'I already have a PhD and don't need it'. In contrast, the trial was popular with professional service area staff. Academic staff do not appear to appreciate the advantages associated with gaining basic IT skills in terms of improved efficiency and information management.

Surry and Land (2000) analyse Keller's (1983) ARCS model of motivation and identify four categories of motivation in relation to psychological conditions and application to technology:

- *attention-gaining* where staff lack knowledge or understanding of the opportunities offered;
- *relevance* where there is reluctance to invest time skills;
- *confidence* due to lack of technical skills, and so facilities and support are needed during the learning process;
- *satisfaction* which may be intrinsic: more effective use of IT and improved teaching, and/or extrinsic: institutional recognition, qualification.

Applying this model to ICT, efforts should be directed towards gaining staff attention by providing information and examples of the benefits of gaining basic IT skills. Once individual members of staff begin to develop an understanding of the potential value of increasing their personal ICT skills they generally become enthusiastic and spend time gaining these skills, however interactions with skilled trainers are frequently needed to develop this motivation. In turn, many will become enthusiasts influencing and teaching their colleagues informally. Most of us do not recognise the full capabilities of applications, often gaining useful tips in casual conversations with colleagues. For example, the 'comment' option in Word can be used to provide detailed feedback on documents sent by e-mail to colleagues and students. Most of us will work out how to use this tool once we know it exists and recognise its potential.

Key questions

- What level of training does your institution offer to help academics master ICT applications?
- How is this training perceived? And how well is it used?
- What mechanisms are used to involve academics in the development of ICT skills?

ICT in teaching and learning

ICT offers an increasingly wide continuum of opportunities ranging from basic IT skills described above to complex interactive multimedia, virtual learning environments (VLEs) and electronic discussion. In order to use technology effectively academic staff must develop a complex range of understanding, skills and competencies, broadly divided into pedagogic, learning and teaching issues, curriculum design, application of technology to learning and teaching and associated technical skills. Of these, technical skills are least important to the process of developing effective learning; paradoxically they also appear most popular to staff offered training. To enhance the learning experience, teaching related issues are significantly more important than technical skills. With ingenuity, simple technology can create effective teaching opportunities.

Following the Dearing Report (1997) increased emphasis has been placed on the active promotion of good practice in learning and teaching, academic and educational development within universities. Recognition of the importance of e-learning has also led to the development of centres supporting development and training in ICT. Although the location of academic and ICT development centres varies within institutions they have a common aim – to promote good practice in learning and teaching and the effective use of ICT. For example, Littlejohn *et al.* (1999) provide a case study of developments supported by the Centre for Academic Practice at the University of Strathclyde. The Teaching and Learning Technology Centre (TLTC) was set up at London Metropolitan University to promote the effective use of learning technologies in teaching by supporting training, pedagogy, curriculum, evaluation and technical developments. The unit is centrally funded by the institution and both training and development are free to staff.

Staff development used to concentrate on learning and teaching issues within subject or discipline (Thackwray, 1994; Partington, 1999); more recently, activities that generate development of generic issues have increased. Although basic ICT skills are generic, colleagues with limited experience of ICT show strong preferences for training to be organised and delivered within their discipline and feel less embarrassed working alongside their colleagues. In contrast, confident users of ICT do not appear to share this view and are happy to attend mixed sessions on advanced graphics, web authoring and multimedia training. However, opportunities to see discipline-specific and related examples are essential.

Historically, ICT in teaching and learning has been developed and promoted by individual 'enthusiasts' within departments. Some institutions, for example the University of East London, support named academics within departments, giving them the role of promoting ICT within their discipline. This approach has the advantage that developments are relevant and the e-protagonist already understands local conditions. For any new teaching tool to be adopted by academic staff and successfully introduced into delivery it must be 'owned' by the teachers who will use it, implying participation in the development process. Unless e-protagonists can access ICT expertise in their institution or nationally they may be isolated.

Key questions

- What level of support does your institution offer to help academics use ICT in teaching and learning?
- How is this support organised and disseminated through the institution?
- How are the enthusiasts encouraged and supported?

Pedagogy, learning and teaching

Opportunities to learn about pedagogy and teaching practice are now compulsory for most new staff in HE via postgraduate certificates. The role of technology and specific issues arising may be included in these courses, for example computer aided assessment. Institutions are offering an increasing variety of M-level modules and qualifications that explore learning technologies, on-line learning or computer mediated communication. Many are delivered virtually to give participants an opportunity to experience on-line learning as students themselves. The Open University, Sheffield Hallam University and the Institute of Education offer courses on managing electronic discussion groups (Salmon, 2003). Other less generic courses aim to develop participants' e-teaching expertise within their discipline.

Before technology can be used to enhance teaching it is necessary to learn about the range of opportunities offered by individual technologies and select an appropriate medium. PowerPoint is an excellent presentation package; with imagination it can be used to create animated presentations and even simple computer aided learning (CAL) materials delivered over the web (Mottley, 2003). Encouraging staff to audit their own skills during development sessions can provoke interesting discussion while encouraging attendance at training sessions. Once they begin to see how useful a programme may be, the motivation to take the time needed to develop these skills appears. It is often the basic file management skills that are missing; without these it becomes increasingly difficult to use more major programmes.

Perhaps one of the most important tasks is to specify a particular learning situation where the use of technology should improve existing practice and identify what technology could be used, where, and how. Given an individual scenario possible solutions may be identified and the optimum selected:

Example 1: supporting learners

Mature community workers (nurses, social workers) frequently study part-time, only coming to university for their actual classes. They are geographically dispersed and do not come into contact professionally with their peers between classes. Contact time between staff and students is also limited particularly in terms of informal interaction.

Electronic discussion using the internet either within a VLE or via discussion groups would provide these students with an opportunity to communicate between scheduled classes. They may also submit work electronically and receive peer or tutor feedback.

Further developments might include developing a web site to provide further information and opportunities of on-line feedback e.g. www.prescribing.info (accessed 27 November 2004).

Example 2: developing materials

Evaluation of a traditionally delivered course on International Purchasing and Supply management showed that students had difficulties learning the range of terms (Incoterms) required by the International Chamber of Commerce to ensure safe passage of goods between countries. These terms are an array of acronyms.

An interactive multimedia development was used, with a 'games' approach, where students were asked to complete a number of challenges – each a real scenario with photographs and sound of the teaching staff. Student feedback was very positive when this replaced the conventional lecture (Holley and Haynes, 2002). In this example, technology was used to present a rich learning environment which stimulated students to learn something inherently boring. Multimedia presented additional advantages in that the materials are illustrated with photographs from real haulage situations and students encouraged to compete with one another in terms of their performance during the 'games'. Evidence that this approach helps the, often disadvantaged, underrepresented nontraditional groups in HE is emerging.

Developing staff skills

To take an example from my experience, *Applying Learning Technologies* is a SEDA-accredited 20-credit module at postgraduate M-Level, aimed at experienced academics who wish to develop their understanding and use of technology in teaching and learning, delivered at London Metropolitan University. Sessions are a mixture of face-to-face and electronic exercises and discussion to provide an opportunity to experience virtual learning from a student perspective. For example, the electronic discussion following the first VLE session included:

> I also believe that the 'technology' often gets in the way of developing teaching. Students (and I) get bogged down in how to actually use the technology before we can use it as it is supposed to be used – i.e. as an aid or tool for teaching our subject. Sometimes it will be useful, but we should also appreciate that sometimes it will not be useful. I'm at the stage when I don't really know what will be of use and what won't!
>
> I agree with the comments about signposting. It seems even easier to get lost in e-teaching and go off at a tangent than it used to be when using 'old fashioned' libraries and books. Does anyone else agree?

The programme explores pedagogy, curriculum, learning and teaching issues, alongside technology. Individual ICT audits form the basis of discussion of the range of technologies available and used by staff and to identify scope for further personal development. The main assessment component is the identification, specification, design, implementation and evaluation of a learning technology (LT) intervention for the participant's own teaching. This process is managed by one-to-one tutorials and e-mail support from course tutors and specialist project management and development from learning technologists/multimedia developers. Despite low numbers taking the module and poor completion rates, the module has been influential in terms of promoting the effective use of learning technologies within the institution. Past participants continue to make advanced and innovative use of technology, to disseminate and promote good practice and continue further study for a PhD. Increasingly, staff are asking to take the module without having to do the associated assessment, in other words, they would like access to project management and support during their ICT developments. The cycle of specification, development and evaluation is similar to the individual learning cycle that each participant experiences. Feedback indicates that participants particularly valued the opportunities to: revisit learning theory; consider the learning and teaching issues raised by their own teaching; and develop their personal ICT and LT skills.

Using external expertise

Academic staff appear to value the opportunity to use expertise from specialist ICT within their departments. Bringing in an impartial, external protagonist to an academic department may help individual members (with a wide range of individual skills, interest and expertise) agree on a way to proceed. Increasingly, the most effective developments involve teams: academic, learning technologists, multimedia programmers, curriculum developers and learning and teaching specialists. Specifying the specific learning context and identifying possible technical and pedagogic solutions arise from formal and informal conversations between team members. Prototypes, possibly based on existing conventional teaching materials, are built rapidly to inform further discussion. Evaluation involving the end users, the students, is an integral part of the development cycle and informs the process. This cycle of specification, development and evaluation is stimulating and all members of the team learn both about the project itself and wider issues surrounding introducing LT into the curriculum.

The JISC funded 'Learning technology career development scoping study' (www.jisc. ac.uk/index.cfm?name=project_career) (accessed 27 November 2004) identifies a range of staff roles involved in developing LT materials that ranges from support staff, learning technologists, staff developers, academic staff and senior management. It is becoming increasingly important to collaborate and to recognise that, for example, building a website should be left to professional web developers. Innovation in the IT industry provides a number of applications which, while increasingly interoperable, require increasing expertise to exploit fully. Project management becomes particularly important where a complex range of expertise is required: graphics or animations experts will only be needed during the development phase, while experts in evaluation will be needed during the initial project specification and then at points throughout the project.

Effective learning relies on the appropriate use of technology in a given situation. Simply transferring traditional materials into electronic format, or making documents and presentations available from the web, fails to exploit the potential offered by learning technologies to promote a rich student-centred, interactive learning environment. Littlejohn (2002) and Dutton (1999) argue that the majority of on-line learning has been developed directly from traditional didactic models of information transmission. The true potential of ICT and computers in promoting dialogue between teacher and learner, Laurillard's (1996) 'conversational framework' is frequently not recognised. Littlejohn *et al.* (1999) suggest that limited understanding of pedagogy underpinning traditional didactic teaching also acts as a barrier to staff developing on-line learning materials. Moving from traditional lectures, where an academic 'expert' delivers to generally passive students, to the facilitation of learning where a group of academic subject-specialists, learning and teaching, and technologists collaborate in 'team teaching' to produce an active student-centred learning experience, is a daunting prospect for many academics.

On-line learning cannot be used effectively in isolation nor should the availability of technology drive change. Technology can provide solutions to specific problems encountered in identified situations but must be developed and introduced in context. Technology can provide rich learning environments using multimedia or increasing staff–student and student/student dialogue via electronic discussion. Feedback is an essential part of the learning process – computers can provide rapid and varied feedback via computer aided assessment, by e-mail or simple comments added to Word documents. Courses, curriculum, assessment, delivery, contact, ICT and communication must be reviewed as a whole. In this, technology is acting as a major driver of change.

Although future innovations in the computing industry cannot be predicted, it can reasonably be expected that change will happen. We, and our students, will have to adapt and learn to exploit these innovations in our lives, learning and teaching. Computers have increased communication, information, data analysis and retrieval to the extent that new rules of communication need to be learnt, for example: netiquette, to cope with large numbers of e-mails or the search and evaluation skills needed to use the web effectively.

National resources such as the discipline-specific internet tutorials provided by Resource Discovery Network (RDN) (www.rdn.ac.uk) can help us and our students gain these skills. Evaluation and synthesis are the higher order levels of learning that we aim to develop in our students.

Key questions

- How does your institution ensure that academics have the appropriate level of pedagogic understanding to use ICT effectively in teaching and learning?
- How well do staff use available resources, both internal and external?
- How do staff decide how to use ICT in their teaching?

Dissemination

Opportunities for staff to present and discuss their ICT developments with colleagues from across the university have been well received and it appears important to find ways of demonstrating examples of good practice to both enthusiasts and novices. Academics report that they find the opportunity to 'see what other people are doing' has given them ideas and the incentive to develop their own materials. Building a network of like-minded colleagues, itself a community of learning, provides an informal forum for experiences to be exchanged. These forums may operate virtually via discussion groups for staff using a similar piece of software, for example a VLE users group. This also provides a route for disseminating technical information and external references to the relevant staff. However, those choosing to come to these sessions are generally already convinced of the benefits of on-line learning; it is more difficult to attract staff busy with research and teaching commitments who still have to recognise the potential of learning technologies. Condron and Sutherland (2002) carried out a survey of learning environment support for HE and FE communities for the JISC and concluded that, while there is adequate support and dissemination of information for learning technologists and staff actively developing electronic learning materials, this does not necessarily permeate through to the majority of academic staff.

Key questions

- How are ICT developments in teaching and learning disseminated across your institution?
- What opportunities are there to develop communities of colleagues?
- Who gets to know about developments – how do we communicate beyond the committed enthusiasts?
- What impact has this dissemination had?

Institutional support

Introducing learning technologies into teaching requires front-loaded investment in infrastructure, facilities for staff and students, staff development and the production and evaluation of learning materials. Introducing learning technologies into an institution is a major strategic decision; the full costs both of implementing technical systems and promoting changes in learning and teaching must be recognised, supported by senior management and the process managed within an institution.

Introducing learning technologies into teaching is potentially a major change-agent that needs careful management.

Historically, many LT developments have resulted from individual 'enthusiasts' investing considerable time to pursue their innovation. The Higher Education Funding Council for England (HEFCE) and some institutional strategies provide opportunities for staff to bid for funding to support further innovation. Many institutions were initially attracted to e-learning by the expectation that ICT would reduce the per capita cost of teaching (Dutton, 1999). Although LT has considerable potential for improving the learning experience of students in large classes and may lead to economies of scale, it is neither cheap to produce nor provide. Many institutions do offer staff development and support via specialist units but fail to recognise the true potential of computers to improve both administration and teaching and the concomitant changes to working practice that are needed.

Few institutions recognise the time needed either for development or managing virtual learning within the allocation of contact hours for their academic staff. Although there is increasing recognition for quality teaching and support for innovative practice, promoting change, particularly with new media, e.g. multimedia software, involves risk taking. Anxiety over the ownership of materials created, in contrast to traditional lecture notes and handouts, the move towards a team approach to course development involves shared creation and use of materials. Indeed, increasingly there are national initiatives to promote sharing and reuse of resources, in particular the development of learning objects (e.g. Dolphin and Miller, 2002; JISC Distributed National Electronic Resource (DNER)). Materials are expensive to produce and maintain; it is becoming increasingly important that resources are shared and reused in an appropriate context. For many academics this change to shared resources and teamwork involves major changes in attitude.

Key questions

- What are the strategies and support mechanisms in place at your institution to promote and develop the use of ICT in the curriculum?
- What level of commitment underpins these mechanisms?
- Is the organisation seriously promoting team approaches?

Conclusion

Technology has a great deal to offer teachers and learners. It can provide a rich, stimulating learner-centred environment, feedback and the opportunity to develop communication between students and their teachers. Once staff overcome the barriers and appreciate the opportunities offered to enhance their teaching, and institutions recognise the investment in infrastructure, support and staff needed to develop these materials, the potential may be exploited fully.

References

Berners-Lee, T. (1989) *Weaving the Web*, San Francisco: Harper. Online. Available at: www.w3.org/People/Berners-Lee/ (accessed 10 December 2004).

Condron, F. and Sutherland, S. (2002) *Learning Environments Support in the UK Further and Higher Education Communities*, JISC Report. Online. Available at: www.jisc.ac.uk/index.cfm?name=mle_related_les (accessed 30 November 2004).

Dearing, R. (1997) *Higher Education in the Learning Society*, Report of the National Committee of Inquiry into Higher Education (Dearing Report) NCIHE.

Distributed National Electronic Resource (DNER). Online. Available at: www.dner.ac.uk (accessed 10 December 2004).

Dolphin, I. and Miller, P. (2002) Learning Objects and the Information Environment, *Ariadne*, 32. Online. Available at: www.ariadne.ac.uk/issue32/iconex/intro.html (accessed 30 November 2004).

Dutton, W. (1999) *Society on the Line: Information Politics in the Digital Age*, Oxford: Oxford University Press.

European Driving Licence. Online. Available at: www.ecdl.co.uk (accessed 30 November 2004).

Holley, D. and Haynes, R. (2002) *The 'INCOTERMS' Challenge – Students Avoid 'that Sinking Feeling?'*. Online. Available at: www.business.ltsn.ac.uk/events/BEST%20 2002/Original%20Abstracts/abs3html (accessed 30 Novemebr 2004).

Joint Information Systems Committee (JISC) Plagiarism Advisory Service. Online. Available at: http://online.northumbria.ac.uk/faculties/art/information_studies/Imri/ JISCPAS/site/jiscpas.asp (accessed 10 December 2004).

Keller, J.M. (1983) Motivational design of instruction. In Reigeluth, C. (ed.) *Instructional Design Theories and Models*, Hillside, NJ: Lawrence Erlbaum.

Laurillard, D. (1996) *Rethinking University Teaching, London*, London: Routledge.

Littlejohn, A. (2002) New lessons from past experiences: recommendations for improving continuing professional development in the use of ICT, *Journal of Computer Assisted Learning*, 8, 166–174. Online. Available at: www.strath.ac.uk/Departments/CAP/ allison/papers/jcal/newlessons.html (accessed 30 November 2004).

Littlejohn, A., Stefani, L. and Sclater, N. (1999) Promoting effective use of technology, the pedagogy and the practicalities: a case study, *Active Learning*, 11, 27–30. Online. Available at: www.strath.ac.uk/Departments/CAP/allison/papers/actlearn/act learn11.html (accessed 30 November 2004).

Mottley, J. (2003) Developing self-study materials with PowerPoint, *LTSN Bioscience Bulletin*, 9, 9. Online. Available at: ftp://www.bioscience.heacademy.ac.uk/ newsletters/ltsn9.pdf (accessed 10 December 2004).

Partington, P. (1999) Continuing professional development. In Fry, H., Ketteridge, S.W., and Marshall, S. (eds) *A Handbook of Learning and Teaching in Higher Education*, London: Kogan Page.

Perkins, D.N. (1985) The fingertip effect: how information-processing technology shapes thinking, *Educational Researcher*, 14, 7, 11–17.

Salmon, G. (2003) *E-tivities: The Key to Active Online Learning*, London: Kogan Page.

Seale, J.K. (ed.) (2003) *Learning Technology in Transition: From Individual Enthusiasm to Institutional Implementation*, Lisse: Swets and Zeitlinger.

Surry, D.W. and Land, S.M. (2000) Strategies for motivating higher education faculty to use technology, *Innovations in Education and Training International*, 37, 2, 145–153.

Thackwray, B. (1994) University staff: a worthwhile investment? In Knight, P.T. (ed.) *University-Wide Change, Staff and Curriculum Development*, Staff and Educational Development Association Paper 83, Birmingham: SEDA.

15

Online staff development: using the web to enhance teacher autonomy and student learning

Peter Mangan and Uma Patel

Introduction

This chapter examines the use of the web as a mechanism through which part-time university teaching staff, known as Visiting Lecturers (VLs) can access their entitlement to staff development. The identification of VLs' learning requirements results from self-assessment of their learning needs within the framework of an overall VL staff profile. An online staff development facility, AMBIENT, has been developed to address VLs' learning requirements. The chapter explores the issues that can act as barriers to VLs' online learning success and which expose as problematic the relationship between the availability of web-based staff development and evidence of successful learning. These issues include the predictable – access to the web and ICT skills; but also the unexpected – where working out professional identity in the context of the 'new managerialism' in higher education has assumed a new urgency. In conclusion, we reflect upon the paradoxes inherent within online staff development.

Staff profile and understanding requirements

The Certificate in Continuing Studies (CCS) Programme at City University, London, is delivered by over 150 part-time VLs, many of whom teach in other Continuing Education (CE) departments in the capital, as well as in the Further Education sector. In some cases the VLs are practitioners and teach in addition to their main work. The programme is a large, mainly open-access offering of adult learning through short, 10-week evening courses catering for the needs of over 4,000 students. The courses are organised into a very broad spread of subject groups spanning areas as disparate as archaeology, computing, novel writing, psychology, languages, cultural industries and art appreciation. Subject coordinators manage the subject groups. The coordinators, who are actively involved in management of the programme and quality assurance, also manage the VLs.

The VLs are the backbone of the programme. It is their academic commitment, subject expertise and enthusiasm that can be credited with the success of the programme. At the same time, part-time lecturers are workers who have been excluded from staff development available to full-time colleagues. To understand the requirements for staff development we had to establish some notion of a collective staff profile for VLs.

Building the profile could not be at the expense of asserting the strengths of the programme gained through its dedicated staff. However, to understand staff development needs, we had to develop a profile that identified common strengths, weaknesses and characteristics of the VLs. The information required to develop the profile was gathered from three sources: a sample of VL staff CVs was examined (care was taken to sample from across subjects and over a five-year period of recruitment and turnover); interviews were conducted with the VLs' line managers; and, finally, direct interviews were conducted with VLs themselves.

The raw data were analysed and the following key features identified as a generic staff profile for VLs:

- they teach across two or more institutions;
- they may have no sense of 'belonging to' one institution for the purposes of their part-time teaching work;
- they may have a 'full-time' commitment to paid work or study, or a number of other 'part-time' commitments;
- they may travel long distances to teach;
- they are unlikely to have had access to professional development for teaching;
- they are likely to view themselves as experts in their subject rather than as teachers;
- they share a common perception of isolation since they work alone and rarely meet colleagues who teach in the same subject area.

This staff profile is sufficiently different from the profile of a traditional HE lecturer to justify fuller investigation into the further staff development needs of this category of staff.

From the start it was possible to become locked into a deficit model, which solely concentrated on basic indicators of problems such as the number of complaints, staff turnover levels and student drop-out. However, it was clear that qualitative investigation would yield a richer picture so we turned instead to statements from feedback forms, and review and planning documents generated within the programme. These documents included comments from students, written statements from VLs documenting their perceptions of professional development needs, and observations of teaching by the subject coordinators and one of the researchers in a management role. This amounted to an accumulation of five years' of qualitative data from three perspectives: the students, the VLs and management responsible for quality assurance of teaching and learning. While this approach generated data that were genuine and grounded in the programme, they were not collected for the research purpose for which they were being mined. Apart from the care needed to look for patterns (not identifying individuals), we recognised that qualitative analysis of secondary sources is prone to multiple interpretations. We sought generality by refining our interpretation until the coordinators (who work directly with the VLs) could validate our analysis of staff development needs.

We found that beneath the basic indicators lay specific categories of issues around the teaching and learning experiences on the programme. The spread of these was comprehensive, covering, for example: the teacher's teaching style; assessment practices; lesson planning; the handling of questions; and, interestingly, issues around professionalism. There was evidence of: teachers getting the pace of the lesson wrong; teacher-talk dominating and closing off all class discussion; poor voice projection and little eye-contact; ignoring student questions; no use of positive reinforcement; and, talking to the whiteboard with back to the students. Many of these behaviours were predictable in instances where the staff had not been teacher trained but in the comments on professionalism there was also an indication of the accretion of poor practice. Evidence for this included lack of awareness of, for example, record keeping procedures, quality control, fire emergency evacuation arrangements, and a casual indifference to data protection issues.

Deciding on an approach that works *with* the features of the staff profile and addresses real rather than assumed 'needs', appeared to be a sensible way forward.

Staff development: workshop vs. online

Experience suggests that workshop-based conventional models of staff development are failing these staff. Our staff development provision, in common with many other HE institutions, is resourced on the basis that all teaching staff are full-time employees, and that staff actively work in a community of subject specialists sharing some physical space on campus. It is evident from the staff profile of VLs that this is inaccurate in every detail. VLs are part-time; they are isolated from colleagues who teach similar subjects; and they do not have a physical space on campus. At most, they share a 'hot-desk' and access to reprographic facilities. Understandably, there is little enthusiasm from VLs to make a long journey across London for a staff development activity that is arranged at a time of the day that conflicts with other work or study commitments.

The problems of workshop-based training are well known. Once set, the timing and location of the workshop always presents problems for full attendance. Aside from the venue and the facilitator's time, many VLs pull out as the date approaches or simply do not turn up. There is no opportunity for follow-up training, or to address the needs and concerns of individuals. This is not a problem that has an obvious solution: indeed, the problem is the time and space constraints of any face-to-face activity. From the management perspective it is difficult to make attendance a requirement without funding the same workshop to run on a reasonably large selection of alternative dates and developing time-consuming procedures for handling exceptions and dealing with non-compliance.

Given the particular difficulties VLs face in accessing face-to-face workshops it is tempting to think in terms of buying a ready made 'e-learning training solution'. Indeed, the benefits of e-learning are well documented (Rosenberg, 2000). It is not hard to present an attractive vision of a virtual community of practitioners, with online access to training and timely information. It is as well to remember that strong resistance to this kind of training has also been attested (Meggitt, 2002). On the other hand, the benefits of web-based staff development are known (Milligan, 1999). An important advantage in this case is captured in the multiple dimensions of flexibility. For example, online training has the potential to offer flexibility for:

- VLs to take the training at a time that suits their schedule;
- VLs to access the training from any location with internet access;
- VLs to work through the training at their own pace;
- VLs to select modules that suit their specific learning needs;
- the training content to be updated in response to feedback from the VLs;
- new training content to be added in response to emerging needs;
- incremental development of an ongoing programme of staff development linked to diagnoses of individual training needs.

In our investigation of 'learning needs' we adopted a Soft Systems Methodology (SSM) (Checkland, 1999) for structuring and analysing the requirements (Patel and Mangan, 2004). In theory, access to online staff development provides flexibility in terms of when and where training is undertaken. However, for those without internet access or ICT skills, online staff development simply presented different access problems to those engendered by face-to-face workshops. To address the real learning needs of many VLs it was necessary to incorporate the provision of physical access to the internet, and appropriate support for the development of the necessary ICT skills within the staff development package.

This has been realised in our online staff development facility – AMBIENT. The term AMBIENT is not an acronym. We chose the term because it signifies 'surrounding' and 'embedding', with the online product situated in a context (including people and processes) that surrounds teaching and learning. The design, development and initial evaluation of AMBIENT are dealt with elsewhere (Patel and Mangan, 2004). In this chapter, we are mainly concerned with the institutional contexts that frame the way AMBIENT is seen and used, and our own somewhat paradoxical and ambivalent position in relation to it.

Online staff development facility: AMBIENT

AMBIENT metaphorically 'surrounds' people and processes. In real terms this means that the different categories of workers involved with the CCS Programme are also users of AMBIENT. Users of AMBIENT include the VLs, subject coordinators and administrators, as well as the developer and content designer.

At present AMBIENT is hosted in a commercially available Virtual Learning Environment (VLE) – WebCT. This is a pragmatic option because it provides a unified customisable environment. In particular, WebCT is used to manage the registration and access process, to release learning content and enable communication (announcements, asynchronous discussion and email). However, we are very aware that some of the facilities like interactivity tools (e.g. quizzes), and tracking and reporting functions, are specific to management of student learning rather than staff development. Following the next phase of evaluation AMBIENT is likely to be moved to a more suitable environment.

The first time a new VL will hear about AMBIENT is when s/he accepts employment. At this stage the subject coordinator will ask the VL to complete a questionnaire to assess support requirements (e.g. access to the internet), and ensure that the new VL has the AMBIENT user guide. When the new VL is sent a contract the administrator will ensure that the user name and password are also included. A new VL is required to undertake an online induction programme and this is highlighted in the terms and conditions of employment. If the VL needs access to the internet or training in ICT skills, a drop-in tutorial is arranged.

When the VL logs on to AMBIENT they are presented with a 'homepage', which is the access point for all future online staff development activities. The 'Staff Induction Programme' is a sequence of units with a 'top' and 'tail'. The 'top' (the first activity) is an introduction to a virtual network of colleagues, and the tail (last activity) is a closure where the VL formally signs off the induction process and evaluates the experience. The system tracks the VL as s/he logs on to the Induction and accesses the units but this is a simple record of participation. All other activities including the interactive tests with feedback, and online interactions with colleagues are not logged. This is regarded as private to the individual and in this sense a safe trial-and-error learning environment.

Content in AMBIENT consists of self-contained units of 30 to 60 notional minutes of learning. For example, the new VLs' Induction programme consists of six units based on generic requirements deduced from the generic VL profile described earlier. The purpose of the training is explained to the VL in precise terms, as illustrated in this extract below.

It is intended that, on completion of this Induction process, you and we will be able to benefit in these four main ways:

● You will be able to identify key sources of information within the Department to help in your tutoring role
● You will understand the importance of accurate procedures to the smooth running of the Programme
● You will accept the necessity of timely and accurate return of information as required by the Department
● You will be capable of self-auditing your own teaching and administrative skills-base to inform the staff development process.

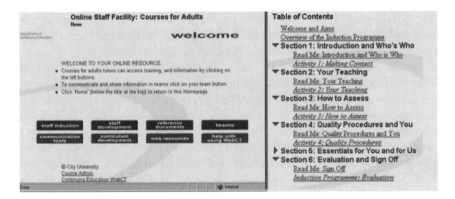

Figure 15.1 Staff Induction Programme – start-up screen

Each of the units that follows the Introduction, targets a different category of need common to new recruits. For example, the section on 'Who's Who', goes beyond information in the staff handbook and enables the VL to make contact with other colleagues in the same subject area with similar interests. The section on teaching (called 'Your Teaching') includes sample case studies of students on the programme, as well as sections on preparing to teach, teaching styles and day-to-day procedures like record-keeping. There are also sections on assessment and quality procedure, health and safety, professionalism and continuing professional development. The Induction ends with an evaluation and sign-off. As part of the evaluation the VL is invited to discuss how the institution can support their teaching, and what training they would like to see on offer.

For the sake of consistency all the units are presented in two parts – a section of presented material followed by an activity section. Examples of presentation material are case studies, links to multimedia, and printable reading materials carefully structured into discrete A4 sections. Through the presentation materials the learner is encouraged to think actively about the material with frequent reflection and recording tasks linked to practice. Within the Activity section, tasks include: using the asynchronous communication tools in WebCT (conferencing facility) to collaborate with subject specialists; using email to communicate with subject coordinators; engaging in problem solving; and responding to multiple-choice questions with rich feedback and checklists of action points.

Some of the units need frequent updating – for example, the introduction to 'Who's Who' – while others are generic – for example, 'Observing Yourself and the Learner', and 'Practical Board Work'. Units can be combined to form a learning sequence (the Induction is an example of a learning sequence for new recruits). This incremental approach to developing content goes beyond transferring standard workshop-based training to the web.

The idea of short, self-contained units of learning combined to form a sequence is technically simple. The innovation is that the professional development is embedded into the programme management process and annual review of teaching and learning. After the Induction subsequent training takes into account interests, performance and needs of the individual tutors. The targeting of future training is embedded in the quality assurance cycle when the tracking and feedback data are collated from the Induction programme. This information is essentially the VLs' views on their own performance and their professional development needs. Teaching observations and annual reviews are informed by these data. Observations of teaching, and information from the VLs' evaluation during the 'Induction', are then used to negotiate and agree reasonable performance and training targets to balance the needs of the individual and the institution. The line manager and the VL agree an annual learning sequence from the online units on offer. In this way staff development is transformed from 'cycle time' where it has a fixed position in the annual academic calendar to 'just-in-time' where it is available at anytime of year as an ongoing process of short, situated learning, at a time, place and pace that suits the VL.

In the past two years, all new staff have completed the online Induction within the first six weeks of employment. We adopted an economical approach to evaluation because we wanted the VLs to focus on articulating their future training needs. Our preliminary, post-Induction evaluation consisted of six questions and the VLs were asked to respond on a 5-point satisfaction scale. Although this type of evaluation is a blunt instrument, responses of 'satisfactory', scoring 3 and above, (shown next to the question) can be revealing:

- How relevant was the information to your role as tutor? 68%
- How useful did you find this programme? 71%
- How easy to use did you find the programme? 65%
- How good was the presentation of materials (graphics, layout, etc.)? 55%
- How well was the activity pitched? 64%
- Overall, how effective do you think the programme was? 69%

The responses show a surprising acceptance of this approach to staff induction. It is possible that the staff development utility has a role in retaining VLs, although it would be difficult to show this conclusively. There is some anecdotal evidence that the VLs valued the attention and being part of a new initiative in which they 'feel' they have a voice. The real challenge, however, is to embed AMBIENT into all aspects of staff development (e.g. appraisal, peer review, self assessment, target setting, and monitoring, as well as induction of new staff). This means going beyond compulsion to reinforce teacher autonomy and expertise – so that AMBIENT drives a developmental culture.

The impact of increased entitlement to staff development

AMBIENT was the response to the pressing need for staff training as part of assuring the quality of teaching and learning on the CCS Programme. This activity coincided with the advent of UK legislation on the employment rights of part-time staff whereby the fixed term employee cannot be treated less favourably than similar, permanent employees. The use of successive fixed term contracts is, also, now greatly limited by law (Department of Trade and Industry, 2002). As a result, the relationship between the institution and the employee has altered in law and new contracts reflecting the change have been issued to the VLs. A key outcome resulting from the changes has been the requirement for institutions to provide greater opportunities for the VL to access training. The assumption is that the more explicit the entitlement, the greater the take-up, though for reasons outlined above, this effect cannot be taken for granted. In building VLs' capacity to engage with their own development using the web, four broad areas needed to be examined.

Professionalism

The opportunity to work on self-development with the aid of an online programme should reinforce the VL's sense of identity as an autonomously functioning 'professional'. In the context of developing and training these part-time staff, there may be an advantage in having recourse to a traditional conception of the professional as subject expert, supplementing that expertise through training to enhance teaching performance. The online product must, of course, be sufficiently broad in scope to reinforce the individual's notion of professionalism. Properly constructed, this enables the VL to gain a greater understanding of their working environment as characterised as one beset with accountability measures, 'to promote the potentially conflicting aims of efficiency, effectiveness, economy, responsiveness and quality' (Eraut, 1994: 5).

The emphasis on professionalism within the product is an attempt to build in a common strand around which staff can cohere. It binds together VLs who teach subjects spanning 13 subject benchmark areas within the Quality Assurance Agency for Higher Education scheme (QAA, 2002) to which the programme must adhere for audit purposes. In addition, it grounds the change in practice which the product will instil firmly within the delivery of the academic subject, thereby making the context of use much less remote from the training activity. To summarise: the exploration of the concept of professionalism in its broader sense is undertaken in order to orientate VLs and to enable them to engage in discipline-based development of their teaching.

Motivation

On one level the concept of 'teacher autonomy', is about motivating VLs to take responsibility for their own learning about student learning. Tharenou's version of Expectancy Theory in cognitive psychology (2001), suggests that three factors influence motivation:

- Expectancy (if I try can I succeed in finishing this?).
- Instrumentality (what are the chances that I will be rewarded if I do this?).
- Valence (how much do I value the rewards?).

Of these, instrumentality is the most influential. Making the connection between quality of teaching and 'rewards' is therefore highly desirable.

Whether a course runs or not depends on recruitment, and whether a course continues to be offered, or not, depends on both recruitment and retention. The exact viability point is clearly debatable. Nevertheless, what is highly visible is the relationship between *demand* (for learning) and work (number of hours that VLs are employed). The exact causes of fluctuations in *demand* (for learning) are complex. Nevertheless, what is visible is the relationship between *student satisfaction* (feedback from students on their learning experience), and *demand* (number of students retained, returning and recommending).

A simplistic correlation between the student's experience of learning and level of demand is not claimed. There are others factors that cannot be ignored, such as the quality of the supporting services and, indeed, market trends. It should be noted that VLs, in common with HE teachers everywhere are feeling the tremors and earthquakes of a shifting landscape. Higher student expectations, increased competition, increased accountability, larger groups, base entry level, and cultural and language diversity are all significant challenges. On the other hand, if we want to engage VLs in training and development, a powerful driver is the perceived connection between student experience, demand for learning, and their employment.

Just-in-time learning

The product has been created mindful of the claims that may be made on its behalf should it be categorised as a 'work-based learning' initiative. It cannot be assumed that the VLs will enter into this learning voluntarily and positively on the basis that 'no one can force another person to learn' (Major, 2002). If in some sense autonomy is incorporated into their identity as professionals, the approach in persuading staff to engage with this learning must rest on the attractiveness of the product in terms of its ability to deliver results rapidly. This is not just a 'selling point' for busy professionals coaxed to go online but is based on the pragmatics of having them *stay* online, once they have entered the site. We cannot assume that what is learned in one context (online) will easily transfer to another one (the teaching space). The product design accepts that neither knowledge nor skill 'transfer without being resituated in the new context, which will require significant further learning' (Eraut *et al.*, 2000: 259). As a result, the product has breadth to cover the span of user-types and its focus is on practical staff development solutions that can be implemented immediately. For example, a VL could check a procedure online minutes before starting to teach and could evaluate an approach taken, minutes after teaching ended.

The political context for online staff development

This UK web-based initiative takes place against a background of government policy to expand the numbers within higher education and a consequent pressure on resources. Part of that policy development has seen the post-compulsory sector become 'thoroughly embedded within the dynamics of a quasi-market and infused with the values of commerce and business' (Ball *et al.*, 2000). In turn, there has been the growth of the idea that the knowledge seeker has become a consumer whose learning has to become 'self-directed'. If this was the reality into which the product was to be pitched and if the VL was to be configured as an isolated toiler within the online space, then these tensions needed to be admitted in creating a product that could survive and thrive despite them. Perhaps the greatest of these tensions is to be found in the daily reality now within higher education of a burgeoning managerialist culture. This reveals itself in the current discourse of higher education associated with finance and commerce, delivery of learning outcomes, franchising of courses, audit of skills, customer focus and so on (Trowler and Cooper, 2002). Clearly, there are reasons to be careful.

It is important to assert that the values that informed our approach to product design and implementation are based on our experience of what was likely to work with this group of staff. Anticipated criticism of recalcitrant VLs, whereby any 'resistance' could be construed as ideologically opposed to a managerialist ethos (which is, itself, ideologically determined), is neither here nor there: what counts is what works. What will *not* work is 'too forceful a superimposition of the extrinsic values of accountability and relevance which can only lead to intellectual subservience, and thence to academic sterility' (Becher and Trowler, 2001). In avoiding this we would also wish to avoid the product becoming yet another blunt instrument in the bureaucratic armoury of institutions, used to herd staff towards what Martin (2001) has called the absurdity of 'directed self-directed learning'.

Conclusion: one challenging paradox

In seeking to improve the uptake of online staff development for VLs post-induction, we emphasise the importance of developing a more explicit understanding of professionalism and of ensuring online staff development packages are developed that are in tune with factors known to motivate VLs. AMBIENT can be presented as empowering the worker by enhancing teacher autonomy and the quality of teaching and learning. This is a system developer's point of view because the technology is being offered as the solution to rapid changes in requirements for staff development. On the other hand, it is necessary to conclude that AMBIENT may also be perceived as a management tool deployed to increase teacher accountability. This could well be the VLs' perspective, as they may question what personal rewards result from coping better with larger classes, increased administration and checks on 'traditional' academic freedoms.

References

Ball, S., Maguire, M. and Macrae, S. (2000) Worlds apart – education markets in the post-16 sector of one urban locale 1995–98, in Coffield, F. (ed.) *Differing Visions of a Learning Society Vol. 1*, Bristol: The Polity Press.

Becher, T. and Trowler, P. (2001) *Academic Tribes and Territories: Intellectual Enquiry and the Culture of Disciplines*, 2nd edn, Buckingham: SRHE/Open University Press.

Checkland, P. (1999) *Soft Systems Methodology in Action*, Chichester: John Wiley.

DTI (Department of Trade and Industry) (2002) Employment Relations, online, available at: www.dti.gov.uk/er/fixed (accessed 27 November 2004).

Eraut, M. (1994) *Developing Professional Knowledge and Competence*, London: Falmer Press.

Eraut, M., Alderton, J., Cole, G. and Senker, P. (2000) Development of knowledge and skills at work, in Coffield, F. (ed.) *Differing Visions of a Learning Society Vol. 1*, Bristol: The Polity Press.

Major, D. (2002) A more holistic form of higher education: the real potential of work-based learning, *Journal of The Institute for Access Studies*, 4, 3, 26–34.

Martin, I. (2001) A note of unfashionable dissent: rediscovering the vocation of adult education in the morass of lifelong learning, *Proceedings of the 31st Annual Conference of SCUTREA*, Boston, Lincolnshire: SCUTREA.

Meggitt, J. (2002) VLEs and exclusion, *Journal for Continuing Liberal Adult Education*, 22, June.

Milligan, C. (1999) *The Role of Virtual Learning Environments in the Online Delivery of Staff Development*, online, available at: www.jisc.ac.uk/uploaded_documents/573r1 full.pdf (accessed 27 November 2004).

Patel, U. and Mangan, P. (2004) Online support for part-time teachers' staff development, in Groccia, J. and Miller, J. (eds) *Enhancing Productivity in Higher Education*, Bolton, MA: Anker Publications.

QAA (Quality Assurance Agency for Higher Education) (2002) online, available at: www.qaa.ac.uk (accessed 17 December 2004).

Rosenberg, M. J. (2000) *E-learning: Strategies for Delivering Knowledge in the Digital Age*, London: McGraw-Hill Education.

Tharenou, P. (2001) The relationship of training motivation to participation in training and development, *Journal of Occupational and Organisational Psychology*, 74, 599–621.

Trowler, P. and Cooper, A. (2002) Teaching and Learning Regimes: implicit theories and current practices in the enhancement of teaching and learning through educational development programmes, *Higher Education Research and Development*, 21, 3, 221–240.

16

Inclusive learning in higher education: the impact of policy changes

Alan Hurst

Introduction

Imagine the following scenario. A tutor is responsible for lecturing to the whole of a particular year group on a popular course. There are three hundred students in his class. Of these, twenty have declared that they have a disability. This could result in the tutor having to make as many as twenty individual adaptations. Clearly, this would be very time-consuming and a significant additional burden for somebody already working at full stretch and in a context where other activities have higher priority. However, assume that adaptations are made and are successful for all students – except one who then chooses to take out a case for discrimination on the grounds that his needs arising from his disability were not met. Apart from being more time-consuming and potentially expensive in terms of legal fees, and risking the award of costs and damages if the judgment is found in favour of the student, for the tutor there is personal embarrassment and for the institution, unwelcome negative publicity. Legislation in the UK (in force from September 2002) means that changes to methods of learning and teaching have to be made.

With forethought and advance planning it is possible to avoid making lots of adaptations. Usually in lectures, students listen and make notes. Yet, within the group there might be students who rely on lip-reading to acquire information. While watching the tutor all the time, it is difficult to look down and make notes. The tutor also needs to remember always to face the class, to avoid moving around while speaking, to avoid standing in a position where bright light means that only a silhouette is visible, and to avoid talking while writing on the board. Another student is deaf and uses sign language interpreters who the student will need to watch all the time if communication is to be effective. Again, making notes might be a problem although a volunteer or paid note-taker could be used. A third student is visually impaired and encounters difficulties if overhead transparencies are used, especially if copying is required. A fourth student has manual dexterity difficulties, which make writing impossible. Finally, there are a number of students with dyslexia who find it hard to make coherent notes. The needs of all these students can be met with one simple action on the part of the tutor – the provision of lecture notes and their availability in different formats.

This example shows how tutors can make courses accessible, and learning and teaching inclusive – and in ways that benefit all students. Strategies such as this help both students and tutors. The purpose of this chapter is to explain the need for change and to show how we can adopt strategies that can help all our students.

Developing policy and provision for students with disabilities in the United Kingdom since 1990

For many years, there has been concern about the under-representation of particular social groups in higher education. In the main, this was linked to social class, gender and minority ethnic communities. Around 1990, the major focus of attention began to shift towards ensuring that people with disabilities had full access to institutions and their courses. While this challenge remains, progress has been made on several fronts. From the perspective of students, improved financial support through the Disabled Students Awards (DSA) became available from 1990; this has been extended gradually to embrace some of those originally excluded because of the means test on parental income or their part-time and/or postgraduate status. Higher education institutions in the UK have benefited from several strategies and innovations introduced by the national funding councils, most recently the additional premium attached to students with disabilities. Following this, attention has switched to considering the quality of the experience. This has been given significant impetus by the Quality Assurance Agency's Code of Practice Section 3 'Students with Disabilities' (QAA, 1999) and by new anti-discrimination legislation, SENDA (the Special Educational Needs and Disability Act 2001) and its associated Code of Practice (DRC, 2002).

The Special Educational Needs and Disability Act 2001

In the UK, legislation against discrimination on grounds of gender and ethnicity has a longer history than that on grounds of disability. The Disability Discrimination Act 1995 (DDA) was the first serious attempt to redress the situation. Having defined 'disability' ('a physical or mental impairment that is substantial and has adverse long term effects on the person's ability to carry out normal day-to-day activities'), the law focused on access to employment and to goods and services. Education was omitted from the DDA. The Special Educational Needs and Disability Act 2001 (SENDA) alters this and covers all sectors of education. The first stage of implementation began in September 2002, auxiliary aids and services being covered from September 2003, and the physical environment from September 2005. It uses the same definition of 'disability' and the same definition of 'discrimination' and associated concepts. Discrimination occurs if someone is treated less favourably for a reason that is disability-related and there is no justification for the action. Discrimination might occur if 'reasonable adjustments' are not made. If discrimination is alleged, first there is an attempt to reconcile the disputing parties through the Disability Rights Commission (DRC) but if that fails the next stage is the county court, which might then award financial compensation and issue injunctions. Within higher education, all services are covered by the law including learning, teaching and assessment, distance and e-learning, and partnership and overseas provision. The rest of this chapter considers how discrimination can be avoided by making 'reasonable adjustments' and also by complying with the anticipatory requirement of the SENDA. Changes should not be made as a direct result of enrolling a student with a disability; rather, those responsible for the course should have planned in advance for what they need to do to make the course accessible and inclusive. There is a key role here for staff training and the development of high levels of disability awareness, since the provision of such training could be central to any defence if discrimination is alleged.

Within the law it remains possible to refuse entry to a student with a disability on a number of grounds. First, the decision might be based on the need to maintain academic standards. However, in order not to put themselves at risk, course teams and admissions tutors need to be clear about criteria used to select students. Second, the decision might stem from there being parts of courses that are a basic requirement but which some students with disabilities might be unable to complete and where 'reasonable adjustments' cannot be made. This is often linked to the involvement of external professional and regulatory bodies whose own position is altered as a result of changes to the employment section of the DDA (September 2004). Third, the decision might be taken where, if 'reasonable adjustments' are made, they are 'material' and 'substantial', perhaps involving high costs within a very restricted budget. It is too soon after the introduction of the new law to comment further on its interpretation.

If discrimination is alleged to have taken place, there are key questions to consider. First, the individual needs to have a disability as defined by the law. Second, does the law cover those services? Third, has there been either less favourable treatment or lack of 'reasonable adjustment'? Fourth, has the student disclosed a disability? If the institution can prove that the individual did not disclose, it is unlikely that the allegation can be proved. However, there is a responsibility on institutions to have taken steps to ensure that students have several opportunities to disclose information about their disability. In itself this raises further questions, since there are issues about who the information is disclosed to and also whether the individual asks that the information remains confidential since confidentiality requests are seen as 'reasonable adjustments'. Specific guidance on matters relating to disclosure and confidentiality has been issued (DfES, 2002a and 2002b; LSC, 2003) and there is also some useful general information (Skill, 2002).

Underpinning the law is a philosophy based on a social model of disability (Oliver, 1990). This concept emerged in contrast to the individual/medical/deficit model. The latter focuses on individuals and views them as being sick in some way. They have to engage in social life as best they can. The social model sees the challenges they face from a different perspective. Any difficulties encountered result from the ways in which society has been devised. Instead of trying to change individuals to fit society, changes are made to society to ensure that individuals can participate. This is the basis of inclusive learning and was demonstrated clearly in the Tomlinson report on further education (FEFC, 1996).

Adjustments and strategies

In the light of these legal duties and responsibilities, a range of reasonable adjustments and anticipatory strategies are outlined in relation to four aspects of learning and teaching: the provision of information, the design of courses, the delivery of the curriculum and the assessment of learning.

Provision of information

There are two stages when students are provided with information – the admissions stage and at entry. Taking the former first, it is important to look at what is said about programmes/courses/modules in published information. The information must be honest and not misleading in any way. For instance, courses in visual arts might present significant barriers for people with visual impairments. In describing module A206 'The Enlightenment' the Open University says:

> printed course materials are available on audio-cassette and in comb-binding, and there are transcripts of audio-visual materials. Four weeks of the course are devoted to music and three weeks to art history. Alternative questions are provided when assignments depend on visual or aural material.

This is much more encouraging than blocking entry to some potential students and risking a legal challenge. Sometimes flexibility might be limited by the close involvement of professional bodies who prescribe certain kinds of learning experience, which those with particular impairments might find impossible to complete. Often these are associated with professional courses and are linked to a licence to practice. Much will depend on what is defined as core to the course and so it is important to make this clear at the earliest opportunity.

Information aimed at capturing the initial attention of prospective students should also be sensitive to the use of language and terminology. It is important to avoid using words that might give offence. It is also important to remember that those whose first language is British Sign Language might have difficulties accessing information unless it has been moderated by someone familiar with BSL since English and BSL do differ. Attention needs to be given to the tenor of the information especially if what is conveyed is excessively negative. There are also the visual images that are used. Apart from being inaccessible to those with visual impairments, many of those responsible for publicity make use of traditional images of people with disabilities and so contribute towards the perpetuation of stereotypes. Not all students with disabilities use wheelchairs, not all students who are blind have guide dogs to aid their mobility. It is not easy to present visual images of those with hidden impairments. One solution is to use only images of head and shoulders if students do feature in publicity.

Increasingly, prospective students are gathering information using electronic means. Hence, it is necessary to ensure that institutions' websites comply with basic accessibility criteria. It might be necessary to sacrifice some originality and visual appeal to ensure all potential users can obtain information easily. For example, a website that asks the user to use a mouse to click on a moving image could create unnecessary problems not only for those with visual impairments but also for those with limited dexterity.

The second point at which information is provided is at entry. For example, students are given details about how courses will be taught and assessed. For disabled students there might be a need to provide additional information. For example, it would be helpful to students who are hard-of-hearing to say that the policy of the Department is that all tutors will wear radio microphones or have their sessions recorded on to cassette tapes. Another example, which would benefit students with a range of impairments, is that lecture notes and other teaching materials are available on the intranet. Booklists could have essential texts marked since some students find browsing in libraries difficult because of their impairments. Note the other benefits of these approaches. First, they avoid disabled students having to make extra effort to find and negotiate with individual tutors. Second, they avoid inconsistent practices. Third, they might obviate the need to declare their disability, a sensitive issue discussed earlier. Finally, they could prevent claims of less favourable treatment and putting disabled students at substantial disadvantage

Curriculum design

To fulfil the requirement to anticipate the needs of students with a range of impairments, it would be helpful if questions about this could become part of routine procedures when new courses are validated and when existing courses are reviewed. Part of this might be to ask course teams to identify the core requirements of their courses. If students are unable to meet these, then it might be possible to refuse the offer of a place at application stage. The sector has been assisted in identifying course requirements by the introduction of sub-ject benchmarks and use of programme specifications. However, care is needed when drawing up core requirements. For example, a course in marine biology might require students to analyse specimens – but does this imply that students have to collect their own? This could present barriers for wheelchair users. A second example is a course in sports science in which the requirement is to demonstrate lower body movements. Is the impli-cation that this will be done using one's own body or can it be demonstrated using models or other people? If not, students with paralysis will encounter barriers. In considering the law, a 'reasonable adjustment' might be made in these two examples.

A number of questions centre upon attendance requirements. Some impairments impact upon students intermittently, for example students with M.E. (myalgic encephalitis) or those who are mental health service users. Some days their impairment makes it diffi-cult for them to be present in class. Perhaps, on some courses, classes are time-tabled on an intensive basis. A 'reasonable adjustment' to check at validation might be to ensure that access to course content is available online.

Some courses require visits and placements. The law makes it clear that institutions are responsible for these activities. It is important to check with course teams whether they have procedures in place to undertake risk assessments. To offer additional insights into the experience of fieldwork, as a 'reasonable adjustment' and demonstrating anticipatory duty, one institution has produced video films so that, for example, students with impaired mobility can anticipate what the challenges might be at an early stage. If the video is also signed, captioned and has a voiceover it makes it accessible also to students with visual and auditory impairments. To participate in visits, field work and work placements, addi-tional costs might be incurred – for example for transport and accommodation that is acces-sible and adapted – and this could be checked at the validation stage so that if students with disabilities do participate, strategies are in place to deal with any questions of finance.

Many courses involve students working in laboratories and other specialist areas. These are intended to allow students to acquire a range of practical skills. At validation, questions could be asked about how risk assessment might be undertaken. In this instance there is also the need to comply with heath and safety regulations. Further questions could cover the extent to which rooms and equipment might be adapted. Developments in technology allow for simulations and for 'virtual realities' that might constitute 'reasonable adjustments'. It is possible to install workbenches that have adjustable height so that wheelchair users can carry out tasks safely and effectively. When specialist facilities are being refurbished, adaptations such as this demonstrate that an institution is taking seriously its anticipatory duties. Many of the barriers to inclusive learning can be overcome using simple solutions. The work of Hopkins and Jones demonstrates ways in which students with disabilities can participate fully in laboratory-based learning without endangering health and safety (Hopkins and Jones, 1998).

Following the SENDA, a number of very useful audit documents have been published that offer additional information (SWANDS, 2002; RNID, 2002).

Learning and teaching

In suggesting ways in which tutors can comply with legislation, much of what follows has drawn upon the 'Teachability' project sponsored by the Scottish Higher Education Funding Council. The Teachability booklet, which is designed to be used by individuals and departments, provides a structured framework for looking at current classroom practices. There are two basic premises: that what is good practice for students with disabilities is good practice for all students and that academic staff are in the best position to develop inclusive learning since they are responsible for designing and delivering courses (SHEFC, 2000). The approach to prioritising anticipatory reasonable adjustments, advocated by Teachability, is for departments to develop clarity about what is core to a course. If there are some things that a student must be able to do, then it is sensible to start there in looking for anticipatory reasonable adjustments. The determining of core requirements, with justification, also offers a standard against which applicants can be considered. If a particular disabled applicant cannot, with reasonable adjustments made, do these things, then there may be grounds for not accepting the student onto the course.

The identification of core requirements might indicate that there are some barriers that are intrinsic to the subject and make it impossible for students with some impairments to participate. Often this relates to competence to practise professionally. For example, a course in dentistry will involve students in practical activities such as tooth extraction. The nature of some impairments means that this rules out some potential students because of their particular impairment. Some barriers to inclusive learning result from a chosen method of delivery. Using videos that lack captions or voiceover could present difficulties to blind and deaf students. Tutors might have to consider ways of ensuring that learning takes place using alternative strategies, perhaps by providing a transcript and commentary on the video and the purposes of showing it. Some barriers to learning arise inadvertently because tutors lose their sense of heightened awareness. It is easy to forget that dimming lights when using video and films can impair communication for those using lip-reading to follow what is happening.

Some of the considerations when learning takes place in large groups were outlined in the scenario described at the start of this chapter. Additional considerations include the physical accessibility of the room. In some places, students who use wheelchairs have to enter and leave rooms by routes different to those used by the rest of the class. They might have to sit in a position that isolates them from their peers. This has the strange effect of drawing attention to both their presence and absence from class. Using maps and diagrams with large learning groups might create problems if these are displayed on an overhead projector. If there are students working with BSL interpreters, tutors need to recognise the value of having short breaks to allow some respite from the intense concentration necessary for both student and interpreter. Deaf students using interpreters might also encounter some difficulties when they want to ask a question. The translation and transmission of information from tutor to interpreter to student and the thinking processes that might stimulate a question take time and it could be that some minutes have passed before it is possible to relay this to the tutor. This should not be defined as slow thinking on the part of the student.

There are a number of ways in which learning might be made more effective when students with disabilities are in small groups. At the start of each meeting, it is helpful if everyone present introduces himself or herself so that a student who is blind knows who is present. Names should also be used when making contributions to group discussion. Where there are deaf and hard-of-hearing students in the group it is useful to establish some ground rules such as those speaking indicate that they are doing so by raising their hand and that only one person should speak at once. Other students in the group should also be prepared to be patient and understanding if someone has a speech impairment. Understanding is also required in recognising that some impairments are not obvious and that some students might have conditions that affect their attendance and participation. A good example of the latter are students with Asperger's syndrome who might find it difficult to relate to their peers. Tutors might need to explore ways of facilitating participation, for example by using pairs, trios, etc. within the small group itself.

Finally, it is important that whatever 'reasonable adjustments' have been made there are mechanisms to allow students with disabilities to provide feedback and evaluation so tutors can monitor their effectiveness. Many institutions ask students to complete evaluation forms at the end of each module or course. To formalise the feedback from students with disabilities, it might be possible to amend the form so that students can comment on how their support needs were addressed. If such a system is implemented, care must be taken to ensure that confidentiality is not put at risk. However, by formalising the process, institutions show that they are carrying out their legal responsibilities in a professional way.

Academic assessment

Arguably it is within the area of assessment that it becomes clearest how those practices that help students with disabilities are also those that help all students. Arguably, too, the area is one in which potential challenges to the law are more likely to occur. To begin with, all students benefit from early and clear information about how they are to be assessed during their courses. This includes basic points such as whether there is oral assessment and written assessment; group assessment and individual assessment; a balance between course work and end-of-programme unseen examinations, etc. Following from this, all students benefit from having clear criteria against which their work will be judged. For example, with written assignments, the criteria could be for quality of opening and closing sections, use of supporting sources, references to relevant concepts and theories, and overall presentation. Ideally this should be accompanied by clear information about how the overall mark/grade will be computed. For example, is presentation awarded the same maximum as the quality of the opening and closing sections? The move to link learning outcomes with assessment strategies aids progress with this aspect.

For students with disabilities there are additional considerations. If the course is assessed using some kind of traditional examination, there are aspects of the physical environment to address. Apart from the obvious point about access to buildings and rooms for those with impaired mobility, it is important to consider whether nearby facilities are also accessible. Sometimes students with disabilities might have to use lavatories and rest rooms so their availability and location must be checked. Students who are visually impaired might have to use special equipment when answering exam questions. This might be noisy and distract other students. One solution is to use a separate room and an additional invigilator. Some disabled students dislike the separation and the feelings of loneliness and isolation this creates, and at a time when they need to demonstrate their attainment. Deaf students on courses that are assessed by formal unseen examinations could be disadvantaged if the carrier language has not been checked by an experienced BSL user. Students with specific learning difficulties are often offered additional time to complete their answers. If the examination uses the same room as other students, there will be some disruption when the exam ends and other students leave the room. One 'reasonable adjustment' to address this might be to consider whether attainment can be measured if students with specific learning difficulties complete fewer questions in the same overall time as other students. Some authors have questioned the effectiveness of additional time (Williams and Ceci, 1999; Ofeish and Hughes, 2002).

A key issue in relation to making 'reasonable adjustments' is the scope for negotiation and flexibility. Where students are pursuing programmes of study for which the institution has total responsibility, the possibilities for implementing different strategies are greater than in those programmes that have very close links to professional bodies. Where there is flexibility, it is possible to distinguish between assessment that is modified, and assessment that is a genuine alternative. Allowing students with specific learning difficulties to complete fewer questions but within the same time period as described above is an example of a modified assessment. Alternative assessment is illustrated by allowing a student who is a sign language user to sign answers to a video camera instead of writing them down.

Formal assessment might involve other strategies, for example practical activities in laboratories and workshops. When assessment uses coursework only, other points emerge. For example, if written assignments test individual initiative and research skills, what reasonable adjustments can be made to include students whose access to libraries and print sources is limited? Other issues concerning assessment and students with disabilities have been explored elsewhere (McCarthy and Hurst, 2001).

Closing comments

The implementation of the Special Educational Needs and Disability Act 2001 offered new opportunities to review our current policies and practices on learning, teaching and assessment. It marked a change in roles and responsibilities within institutions. No longer is it possible to assume that students with disabilities 'belong' to colleagues working in student support services where the work they do might be seen as an optional extra. There is a major shift. Making policy and provision for students with disabilities has become an important part of core business and involves *everyone*.

The move to ensuring that pedagogy is inclusive will benefit all and lead to an experience of higher education of the best quality. To move towards this we must use the four As: awareness of disabilities; audit current practices; anticipate future needs; and act to implement inclusive learning.

References

DfES (Department for Education and Skills) (2002a) *Finding Out About People's Disabilities: A Good Practice Guide*, London: DfES.

DfES (2002b) *Providing Work Placements for Disabled Students: A Good Practice Guide for Further and Higher Education Institutions*, London: DfES.

DRC (Disability Rights Commission) (2002) *Code of Practice: Post-16*, London: DRC.

FEFC (Further Education Funding Council) (1996) *Inclusive Learning: The Report of the Tomlinson Committee*, London: HMSO.

Hopkins, C. and Jones, A.V. (1998) *Able Scientist Technologist: Disabled Person*, published privately – contact the authors via the University of Loughborough.

LSC (Learning and Skills Council) (2003) *Disclosure, Confidentiality, and Passing on Information*, Coventry: LSC.

McCarthy, D. and Hurst, A. (2001) *A Briefing on Assessing Disabled Students*, Briefing 8 in the LTSN Generic Centre Assessment series, York: Learning and Teaching Subject Network Generic Centre (LTSN).

Ofeish, N.S. and Hughes, C.A. (2002) How much time? A review of literature on extended test time for post-secondary students with learning disabilities, *Journal on Post-Secondary Education and Disability*, 16, 1, 2–16.

Oliver, M. (1990) *The Politics of Disablement*, London: Macmillan.

QAA (Quality Assurance Agency for Higher Education) (1999) *Code of Practice Section 3: Students with Disabilities*, Gloucester: QAA.

RNID (Royal National Institute for Deaf People) (2002) *Deaf Students in Higher Education: How Inclusive Are You?*, London: RNID.

SHEFC (Scottish Higher Education Funding Council) (2000) *Teachability: Creating an Accessible Curriculum for Students with Disabilities*, Edinburgh: SHEFC.

Skill: National Bureau for Students with Disabilities (2001) *A Guide to the Special Educational Needs and Disability Act 2001*, London: Skill.

SWANDS (South-West Academic Network for Disability Support) (2002) *SENDA Compliance in Higher Education: An Audit and Guidance Tool for Accessible Practice within the Framework of Teaching and Learning*, Plymouth: University of Plymouth.

Williams, W. and Ceci, S.J. (1999) Accommodating learning disabilities can bestow unfair advantages, *Colloquy: The Chronicle of Higher Education*, online, available to subscribers at: www.chronicle.com (accessed 27 November 2004).

17

Reframing equality of opportunity training

Glynis Cousin

Introduction

In this chapter I want to suggest that some of the values underpinning equal opportunity training in organisations are outdated. In the light of this, I argue that equal opportunity (or managing diversity) trainers could profit from an engagement with contemporary theoretical insights about the nature of identity formation and the problems that attend classifying humanity. In exploring these insights, my aim is to soften the trainer/trainee division implicit in conventional staff development approaches in order to strengthen the learning on both sides of this divide.

Representating oppression

However problematic the visibility of hitherto excluded groups in public life, arguably increasing numbers of people can envision wider personal horizons for themselves. As Scott puts it, 'as traditional class, gender and other distinctions fall away, individuals are freer to write their biographies' (Scott, 1997: 44). Although this is good news for champions of equal opportunities, it both undermines their basic premise that the victims of inequality can be easily identified by their socially ascribed status (e.g. black, women) and the stability of the binary classifications associated with these ascriptions (e.g. black/white and women/men). While important changes have come from naming and targeting specific social groups in equality of opportunity campaigns, it is probably time to review the way we view the social classifications they have generated.

The limits of classification

An important challenge for those involved in equality and diversity politics is to avoid a reliance – conscious or not – on the dualisms of good and bad, innocent and culpable,

oppressor and victim, etc. with an appreciation of paradox and of the limits of classifying humans for whatever purpose. Such an appreciation requires that a tension between
classifying and understanding is managed. On the one hand, once you start putting people
in boxes, even for the laudable reasons of socially engineering more equality among
groups, the boxes are inevitably placed in a hierarchy that is incapable of holding
uncertainty. King refers to the building of such hierarchies as 'antinomy mongering':

> The counterpoised abstractions of black and white, conservative and radical, slave names
> and 'free' names, Christianity/Islam, male/female, always have some basis in fact, but
> rather more in fancy. Their falsity is startling in its implications. What is useful in them
> is not the reality, but the esprit simplificateur which they unleash. These simplistic
> antinomies become the essential means by which humans, in an alienated, overcrowded
> and hierarchical world, presumptively invent, order and subjugate themselves and others.
>
> (King, 1991: 499)

Similarly, Bauman argues that the impulse to classify concerns a desire to repress
uncertainty and ambivalence. Classification, writes Bauman (1991) has no tolerance for
ambivalence. For Bauman, the drive to classify is an anxious urge to avoid chaos, a
modern neurotic endeavour to have a place for everything and everything for a place:
Muslims here, Jews there. In classificatory systems nothing can be left murky, ambivalent,
in the middle, shifting and chaotic:

> The ideal that the naming/classifying function strives to achieve is a sort of commodious
> filing cabinet that contains all the files that contain all the items that the world contains
> – but confines each file and each item within a separate place of its own (with remaining
> doubts solved by a cross-reference index). It is the non-viability of such a filing cabinet
> that makes ambivalence unavoidable.
>
> (Bauman, 1991: 2)

The more you try to classify, the more divisions and diversity you create in an unstop-
pable effort to stop ambivalence. This problem is exemplified in ethnic monitoring
systems. There are debates in this policy field about what categories to use and what
they signify (Anwar, 1990; Modood, 1992) because whatever new categories of 'race',
colour or ethnicity are developed and revised, there are always those who resist placing
themselves in them. For instance, in a recent HESA (1999) report of higher education
participation, out of a total of 16,150 students only 11,650 gave returns on ethnic classification. Similarly, in Bird's (1996) research significant numbers of students are refusing
to co-operate with ethnic monitoring policies because its categories do not explain their
lives, as the following two students said to him:

> I didn't know which box to tick . . . in the end I ticked both the white and the black
> box. I am British and black . . . I don't know why I am being asked if I am Afro-
> Caribbean. (Maria)

As I have discussed elsewhere (Cousin, 2002) these testimonies illustrate the difficulty ethnic monitoring has in keeping pace with hybrid identities (Hall, 1992; Bird,
1996; Gilroy, 2000). Identity is more about becoming than being (Sarup, 1996) and if

this is increasingly so, monitoring categories will lose their explanatory power accordingly. Another point to remember is that we 'become' through our relations with others. Appreciating the relational in identity formation is an important way of avoiding assigning an essence to people as if there really is something about being, for instance, 'black' or 'Japanese' that can be captured in all black and Japanese people.

I should stress that classifications have their place. Equal opportunity activists have done much to introduce enlightening definitions to contest conservative ones or to break oppressive silences. If we cannot make predictions about life chances based on naming real social trends, we are left with a runaway pluralism that has no starting point for the development of a more just world. The key is to avoid entrapment in reductive identities without denying such trends. For instance, anyone claiming to speak as 'a woman' or a 'gay man' may well be referring to collective experiences of blocked opportunities but the reference cannot exhaust explanation. As Gorz (1989) reminds us, social identity is a very rough and ready construct: 'Each individual is also for himself a reality which exceeds what society gives him the means to say and do and that no one actually coincides with what the sociologists call their social "identity"' (Gorz, 1989: 179).

Paradox and identity

Another question concerns the paradoxical nature of our relations with others. For Rose (1993) a thoughtful engagement with social categories involves a discovery of yourself in the Other so that she/he is never 'unequivocally Other'. Such a perspective will enable an understanding of *his* reflexive self as well as your own for 'the "Other" is equally the distraught subject searching for its substance, its ethical life' (Rose, 1993: 8). I am not sure about the 'distraught' bit but Rose's general point is that humans are paradoxically related to others. In the context of understanding human society, the claim that A can never be not-A is a denial of the interplay between sameness and difference that characterises the encounter of any human with any other human. Webb (1996), drawing on Gademer's view that learning comes from human connectivity, argues in parallel to this issue that developers who position themselves as the 'knowing other' of the developee will never really see or hear the people they want to influence. This is vividly the case in models of awareness training where the trainer's role is to pull the trainees up to his/her 'level' of knowledge and moral altitude, often from a position of claimed experiential privilege (e.g. a woman facilitating awareness training about sexism). Webb quotes Morss in drawing out his point:

> Development . . . is a technique for setting a . . . distance between oneself and another, that is of categorising the other as a less mature version of oneself. It says to the other that here is a path which we share and on which I am ahead: 'I am your future . . . you will become (like) me'.
>
> (Webb, 1996: 33)

Webb suggests that the best way to overcome this hierarchy between developer and developee is for staff developers to position themselves as learners with those they are training. Operationally, this is about building relationships based on conversational exchanges in which each party to the exchange is changed. This is a challenging notion for awareness trainers for whom Webb poses the question: 'If you are a staff developer, try thinking about your dealings with the people you "develop". How "equal" is this relationship and how do you attempt to privilege your own view of the world?' (Webb, 1996: 33).

A democratic disposition for trainers would need to embrace the paradox that any human encounter is one of sameness *and* difference. As Rose has suggested, an ethical meeting with the other would make the assertion: I am like you *and* I am not like you. This identity position both avoids a simplistic humanism and keeps 'demonisation' at bay because the other is never wholly 'over there'. The more people are able to think paradoxically about difference, the more they will avoid restrictive formulations of it. A paradoxical reading of difference also avoids the kind of cultural relativism that offers, at best, only fragile solidarities between humans. This is because it insists that no social group can occupy the shoes of another and that cultural/national groups exhibit fixed, definable and predictable traits (see, for instance, McSweeney's (2002) critique of Hofstede's much cited models of cultural difference).

Unfortunately, paradoxical thinking has not always been clear in equal opportunity practices or awareness training where evidence of what Foucault (1991) called 'reverse discourse' is sometimes apparent. In this case, old prejudices underpinning binaries like male/female, white/black are reversed for new moralist readings and the antinomy mongering of which King speaks. Equality of opportunity policy statements are caught in a predicament here. On the one hand, they must offer statements like the following from a public institution:

The ILT aims to ensure that no one is treated less favourably than another, for example on the grounds of ethnic origin, nationality, disability, age, sex, religion, marital status, family responsibility or sexual orientation, in any matter relating to employment.

(Institution of Learning and Teaching)

On the other hand, naming categories of people like this tends to set them up as victims with awareness training framed as being 'about them'. Take for instance, the following Code of Practice randomly selected from a university web page:

Staff responsible for short-listing, interviewing and selecting candidates should also be clearly informed of selection criteria and of the need for their consistent application. They should be given training on recognition of stereotypical views and the effects which generalised assumptions and prejudices about race, colour, nationality, ethnic or national origins, sex, marital status, sexual orientation, parental status, socio-economic background, age, disability, religion or political belief might have on selection decisions. Existing training and staff development programmes must, where appropriate, include equal opportunities issues.

This extract, much the same as many enshrined in similar policy documents, contains two 'shoulds' and one 'must'; it presents fourteen categories of potential discrimination and asserts the compulsory nature of the training to gain 'recognition of stereotypical views'.

The moral force of statements like this is towards a blame culture that is unattractive for the blamed (the chief culprits usually being white, heterosexual, middle-class men) and a 'victimology' that contracts the space for a dialectic between social determination and choice.

The reflexive self

Arguably, we would win more support for equality causes if the default position were that people are ethical, reflective subjects rather than the power invested/divested ones implied by their social position. There is evidence, for instance, that men and women are reflecting on their gendered identity in unprecedented ways. The important issue here is not whether these reflections are 'right' or derive from 'protest masculinity' or a conservative post-feminism but that they are taking place. As Giddens (1991, 1992) has pointed out, increasing numbers of people are engaged in a general quest to shape themselves and their relationships with the support of a self-development genre of books and television programmes. People are developing more mature ways of thinking about 'otherness' in the process. Emotional literacy is growing and this implies, among other things, that the very term 'awareness training' is problematic because it suggests a journey from unawareness to awareness.

I do not want to overstate the extent of emotional literacy about equality or to suggest that battles against sexism, racism and so forth have been wholly won. But I do want to suggest that we have made gains that need to be honoured, and that trainers must attribute to others the capability for self-reflexivity that they attribute to themselves. If we are to achieve a paradigm shift towards a more dialogic approach to equality of opportunity politics (or its sibling diversity politics), we will need to move towards more appreciative forms of conversation, appreciative of people's emotional literacy, their ethical sensibilities and their own resistances to classification.

References

Anwar, M. (1990) Ethnic classifications, ethnic monitoring and the 1991 Census, *New Community*, 16, 4, July.

Bauman, Z. (1991) *Modernity and Ambivalence*, Cambridge: Polity.

Bird, J. (1996) *Black Students and Higher Education: Rhetorics and Realities*, Buckingham: SRHE/Open University.

Cousin, G. (2002) Counting diversity, *Journal of Further and Higher Education*, 26, 1, February.

Foucault, M. (1991) *Discipline and Punish: the Birth of the Prison*, Harmondsworth: Penguin.

Giddens, A. (1991) *Modernity and Self-Identity: Self and Society in the Late Modern Age*, Cambridge: Polity.

Giddens, A. (1992) *The Transformation of Intimacy: Sexuality, Love and Eroticism in Modern Society*, Cambridge: Polity.

Gilroy, P. (2000) *Between Camps: Nations, Culture and the Allure of Race*, London: Routledge.

Gorz, A. (1989) *A Critique of Economic Reason*, London: Verso.

Hall, S. (1992) New ethnicities, in J. Donald and A. Rattansi (ed.) *'Race', Culture and Difference*, London: Sage.

HESA report (1999) *Times Higher Education Supplement*, 16 July.

King, P. (1991) Modernity: All 'niggers' now? Or new slaves for old?, in *New Community*.

McSweeney, B. (2002) Hofstede's model of national cultural differences and their consequences: A triumph of faith – a failure of analysis, *Human Relations*, 55, 91, 89–118.

Modood, T. (1992) *Not Easy Being British: Colour, Culture and Citizenship*, Stoke-on-Trent: Runnymede Trust and Trentham Books.

Rose, G. (1993) *Judaism and Modernity: Philosophical Essays*, Oxford: Blackwell.

Sarup, M. (1996) *Identity, Culture and the Postmodern World*, Edinburgh: Edinburgh University Press.

Scott, P. (1997) The postmodern university? Contested visions of higher education in society, in A. Smith and F. Webster (eds) *The Postmodern University?*, Buckingham: Open University Press.

Webb, G. (1996) *Understanding Staff Development*, Milton Keynes: SRHE/Open University Press.

Index